Developing Ethical Principles for School Leadership

Co-published with UCEA, this new textbook tackles Standard #2 of the Professional Standards for Educational Leaders (PSEL)—Ethics and Professional Norms. This volume includes specific strategies for school leaders to develop knowledge and skills in supporting the learning and development of all students, as well as understanding the dynamics and importance of ethics in leadership practice. By presenting problem-posing cases, theoretical grounding, relevant research, implications for practice, and learning activities, this book provides aspiring leaders with the background, learning experiences, and analytical tools to successfully promote ethical leadership and student success in their contexts.

Special features include:

- Case Studies—provide an opportunity to practice ethical reasoning and engage in the discussion of complexities and debates within each case.
- Learning Activites—a range of exercises help readers make connections to the PSEL standard.
- Important Resources—includes resources that support and encourage students to explore each of the chapter's elements.

Lisa Bass is Assistant Professor of Education at North Carolina State University, USA.

William C. Frick is the Rainbolt Family Endowed Presidential Professor of Educational Leadership and Policy Studies at the University of Oklahoma, USA.

Michelle D. Young is the Executive Director of the University Council for Educational Administration (UCEA) and Professor of Educational Leadership and Policy at the University of Virginia, USA.

PSEL/NELP LEADERSHIP PREPARATION SERIES

Series Editors: Michelle D. Young, Margaret Terry Orr

The New Instructional Leadership
ISLLC Standard Two
Edited by Rose M. Ylimaki

Political Contexts of Educational Leadership
ISLLC Standard Six
Edited by Jane Clark Lindle

Developing Ethical Principles for School Leadership
PSEL Standard Two
Edited by Lisa Bass, William C. Frick, and Michelle D. Young

Developing Ethical Principles for School Leadership

PSEL Standard Two

Edited by
Lisa Bass, William C. Frick,
and Michelle D. Young

Routledge
Taylor & Francis Group

NEW YORK AND LONDON

First published 2018
by Routledge
711 Third Avenue, New York, NY 10017

and by Routledge
2 Park Square, Milton Park, Abingdon, Oxon, OX14 4RN

Routledge is an imprint of the Taylor & Francis Group, an informa business

Library of Congress Cataloging-in-Publication Data
A catalog record for this book has been requested

ISBN: 978-1-138-91884-9 (hbk)
ISBN: 978-1-138-91885-6 (pbk)
ISBN: 978-1-315-68823-7 (ebk)

Typeset in Aldine 401 and Helvetica Neue
by Florence Production Ltd, Stoodleigh, Devon, UK.

A co-publication of Routledge and the University Council for Educational Administration—UCEA

Contents

Series Foreword

The University Council for Educational Administration (UCEA) formed in the mid-1950s to address leadership preparation quality and to promote research-based studies of leadership in educational institutions. The 1950s represented a critical time in the development of educational administration from a theory movement (e.g. organizational theory and scientific management) to an emphasis on empiricism and leadership preparation. Issues surrounding school leadership preparation revolved around developing master pedagogues into effective managers of educational operations. UCEA leaders attempted to fill some voids in principal and superintendent preparation, including effective mentoring, syllabus development, monographs about innovation in leadership preparation, and effective preparation pedagogy. Not surprisingly, some of the resulting university programs took perspectives from similar fields such as operations and management, industrial psychology, and business schools. Thus, in the early years, a functional curriculum emerged for graduate-level leadership development.

By the late 1980s, the next generation of university professors and leaders observed a gap produced by the curricular traditions of instrumentalism and organizational management. Among courses on law, finance, community relations, supervision, governance, and, of course, theories of administration, this generation of leadership educators noted a glaring oversight on the core technology of schooling: learning and instruction. Questions regarding the relationship between instruction, learning, and leadership were supported by a growing body of empirical literature with answers ranging from research findings about instructional leadership (e.g. Edmonds, 1979; Hallinger & Murphy, 1985), changes from hierarchical leadership to more collaborative teams (e.g. Lieberman, 1986), as well as specific understandings of how to transform contextual influences on schooling into funds of knowledge for learning (Moll, Amanti, Neff, & Gonzalez, 1992). The broader policy context influenced the focus of the UCEA work on leadership preparation over time, including particularly the educational accountability and standards movements in states focused on school reform, school improvement, effective instructional supervision, and student learning. These policy trends led to a galvanizing focus on standards for school leaders aimed at improved teaching and learning in all schools.

Under the leadership of Joseph F. Murphy, Michelle Young, and others, the UCEA has played a major mediational role in the leadership standards movement, working along with the Council of Chief State School Officers (CCSSO) and some members of the Education Testing Service (ETS) to develop the Interstate Leadership Licensure Consortium (ISLLC), representing a consensus on standards for school leaders' policy and practice. In 1996, the initial version of these standards, known as ISLLC *Standards for School Leaders*, rolled out for whole or partial adoption by the various United States for purposes of certification and evaluation of principals and superintendents. A parallel form of standards for leadership preparation accreditation emerged in 2001 as the Educational Leadership Licensure Consortium (ELLC) associated with the National Council for the Accreditation of Teacher Education (NCATE). ELLC standards differentiated from ISLLC primarily with a focus on field experiences along with a continuous program improvement system for evaluation of programs preparing principals, superintendents, and emerging programs for teacher leadership and instructional coaches. Murphy and the UCEA led a revision of the ISLLC standards in 2008 and ELCC responded with revisions to its preparation program standards in 2011. By 2015, the National Policy Board for Educational Administration (NPBEA) and the CCSSO reacted to the changing contexts of leadership preparation, the pace of knowledge production and digital innovations and produced another version of the standards known as the Practice Standards for Educational Leadership (PSEL), clearly establishing this form of standards as primarily policy guidance for states' laws and regulations about practicing school leaders. The NPBEA turned to the work of preparation standards based on PSEL, but focused on aspiring leaders' learning experiences, practices, and competencies in their programs. These program standards are known as the National Educational Leadership Preparation (NELP) Standards and NCATE's replacement organization, the Council for the Accreditation of Educator Preparation (CAEP) intends these as accreditation and national recognition requirements for university-based advanced preparation programs. In all of these leadership standards iterations, UCEA has provided research-based expertise to various policy organizations regarding effective leadership preparation and practice (Young, Anderson, & Nash, 2017).

Policy trends also reflect an increasingly complex reality for education, schooling, and leadership thereof (Lindle, 2014). We can observe a pattern of changes, including shifts toward centralized curricula (state standards, Common Core State Standards Initiative) and new public governance as well as an increasing plurality of students due to internal demographic shifts and population migrations (Uljens & Ylimaki, 2017). The various versions of the Standards from ISLLC to NELP maintain a steady focus on the key obligation of schooling and school leaders, that of ensuring student success. In fact, the revisions cycles display UCEA's and partners' awareness and responsiveness to ongoing school and community dynamics and external influences that can either support or block student success. Such complexity demands a new education theory movement as well as empirically informed leadership preparation programs, which in turn, clarify a high standard and vision of student success in the face of rapid and complex shifts in external influences (Ylimaki & Uljens, 2017). This series of books, *PSEL/NELP Leadership Preparation Series,* reflects those ongoing rapid changes. The UCEA and Routledge's partnership offers instructors and aspiring leaders insights into the dynamic challenges that school leaders must confront to maintain a steady focus on their primary responsibility to ensure that all students learn.

Jane Clark Lindle
Clemson University

Rose M. Ylimaki
University of South Carolina

Michelle D. Young
University of Virginia

REFERENCES

Edmonds, R. (1979). Effective schools for the urban poor. *Educational Leadership, 37*(1), 15–24.

Hallinger, P., & Murphy, J. (1985). Assessing the instructional management behavior of principals. *The Elementary School Journal, 86*(2), 217–247.

Lieberman, A. (1986). Collaborative research: Working with, not working on. *Educational Leadership, 43*(5), 28–32.

Lindle, J. (Ed.). (2014). *Political contexts of educational leadership: ISLLC standard six.* New York: Routledge.

Moll, L. C., Amanti, C., Neff, D., & Gonzalez, N. (1992). Funds of knowledge for teaching: Using a qualitative approach to connect homes and classrooms. *Theory Into Practice, 31*(2), 132–141.

Uljens, M., & Ylimaki, R. M. (2017). Non-affirmative theory of education as a foundation for curriculum studies, didaktik and educational leadership. In *Bridging educational leadership, curriculum theory and didaktik* (pp. 3–145). Cham, Switzerland: Springer.

Ylimaki, R. M., & Uljens, M. (2017). Theorizing educational leadership studies, curriculum, and *Didaktik*: NonAffirmative education theory in bridging disparate fields. *Leadership and Policy in Schools, 16*(2), 157–227.

Young, M. D., Anderson, E., & Nash, A. M. (2017). Preparing school leaders: Standards-based curriculum in the United States. *Leadership and Policy in Schools, 16*(2), 228–271.

Foreword

Joan Poliner Shapiro
Temple University, College of Education

In January 2017, there was an attempt to close the Office of Government Ethics in Washington, D.C. It turns out that citizens throughout the country heard of this plan and responded immediately, in tweets, emails, and phone calls, by indicating their displeasure at the idea. That overwhelming response forced the new president to put a stop to that plan and ask those in his party to move on to other issues.

What does this tell us? It says that *ethics matters*. And surely it does not matter just for our government officials but for all professionals in all areas, including educational leaders. A good example of the importance of ethics to educational leaders was displayed when it came to the Professional Standards for Educational Leaders. Similar to the desire to end the Office of Government Ethics, it was hard to keep the ethics standard alive. Some educators said it should simply be incorporated into all of the standards. Others felt it was so self-evident that it should not even be mentioned. But a group of educators believed it was so important that it deserved to be one of the main pillars of Educational Leadership. They worked hard to make it Standard 2 of the Professional Standards of Educational Leaders (PSEL) of 2015. In so doing, they moved ethics up from Standard 5 in the Interstate School Leaders Licensure Consortium (ISLLC) Standards of 2008. Through their efforts and through its placement as the 2nd standard, it should be clear that novice district and school administrators as well as experienced educational leaders need to take ethics very, very seriously.

In an era of diverse, sometimes overlapping and emerging standards, this book is intended to help the reader negotiate what is expected of ethical educational leaders today. It will assist in making the transition from the Interstate School Leaders Licensure Consortium (ISLLC) Standards of 2008 to the Professional Standards of Educational Leaders (PSEL) of 2015. It will contribute to an understanding of the alignment of the 2015 national standards of the profession with the National Educational Leadership (NELP) Standards. In particular, it will unpack the varied meanings of the elements in Standard 2 (PSEL). It will also assist in moving from the aspirations inherent in all of those elements to praxis. Additionally, it should resonate with the novice and the experienced school and district administrator. Above all, it should inspire educational leaders to move towards transformative leadership and away from the transactional management of schools.

What does it mean to be a transformative educational leader rather than a transactional one? In the New DEEL (Democratic Ethical Educational Leadership), the difference between a transformative and a transactional leader is described. The New DEEL is a movement that began in 2004 and has grown over time in the U.S. and beyond. As defined in New DEEL writings, a transformative educational leader should have ethical beliefs that include being guided by an inner sense of responsibility; leads from an expansive community-building perspective; integrates the concept of democracy; includes social justice and school reform through scholarship, dialogue and action; operates from a deep understanding of ethical decision making; and considers one's career as a calling. The New DEEL vision centers on democracy and ethics going hand-in-hand and that these concepts should be at the center of the educational leader's beliefs and agenda.

In this book, Standard 2 contains many of the attributes of a New DEEL leader. It calls for upholding the values of democracy, equity, social justice and many other important concepts. The book's editors, Lisa Bass, William Frick and Michelle Young, with the help of chapter authors, have designed a work that not only unpacks the diverse elements in the 2015 PSEL ethics standard, but also provides resources and offers opportunities for practice. In this way, the ethics standard and its elements become meaningful and useful. In particular, the suggested resources often link a community of supportive social justice leaders who can advise each other about activities that are of value. This includes not only application of learning about the standard, but also offers ways to highlight standard-based formative assessment.

This volume will be a valuable contribution to the novice and experienced educational leader as well as to an educational leadership faculty member who wishes to understand in more detail and depth how the ethics standard can contribute to a student's learning and to the field. This work offers strategies and activities to encourage and foster ethical educational leaders. It discusses in detail the elements that make up this standard. It also provides the knowledge to move from the transactional manager to the transformative educational leader that is so desperately needed in this challenging, unstable era. Finally, it is hoped that, after reading this book, an educator will understand the importance of Standard 2 and will come to the conclusion that indeed *ethics matters*.

Preface

William C. Frick, Lisa Bass,
and Michelle D. Young

It has never been more important to have well-prepared educators leading our schools. Over the last 25 years, the field of education has changed significantly as educational leaders and policy makers face challenges that make the work of educating students increasingly difficult. Education policy has changed, state and national standards have changed, teacher practices have changed, and the students that schools serve have changed. For example, the 2010 United States Census revealed a significant shift in the nation's racial make-up, a shift that has been reshaping public schools for years. According to the census, 14 states have been "majority-minority" states for several years (Frey, 2013). As these states and their public schools have become increasingly diverse, the racial achievement gap in schools has increased (Hemphill, Vanneman & Rahman, 2011; Vanneman et al., 2009).

INTENDED AUDIENCE

Both scholars and laypersons interested in ethics and education can benefit from the contents of this book; however, the intended audience are professors and students of educational leadership. Professors can use this text to guide students of educational leadership through substantive discussions of the ethical standards of PSEL and NELP. Given the essential role that educational leaders play in fostering positive school culture, supporting teacher effectiveness and supporting student learning, addressing the achievement gap has become a chief concern of educational leaders, competing for leader's time and attention with other significant concerns and responsibilities, including creating broad opportunities that address gaps in student performance. Eliminating the achievement gap through effective and thoughtful ways to support opportunity through ensuring high-quality education for all students depends not only upon leaders' knowledge and skills concerning student learning, teacher development, resource allocation, etc., but it also requires a deep understanding of ethics and the ability to consider ethical dilemmas, moral and legal consequences, and potential conflicts between individual and group rights in their decision-making processes. The wide variance in beliefs concerning what is ethical and what is considered unethical serves as a barrier to furthering discussions on ethics, especially when the discussions end in debate. These misunderstandings and debates concerning the nature of ethics are unfortunate, as now is the time we need to invoke ethical understanding in schools and society.

OUR PURPOSE AND HISTORICAL BACKGROUND OF STANDARD DEVELOPMENT

The purpose of this book is to juxtapose PSEL and NELP standards with pedagogy and epistemology with respect to ethical frameworks as applied to educational leadership. In other words, we analyze the standards, which are informed by ethical theory, with the end goal of impacting leadership practice. In this book, we focus specifically on the development of ethical educational leaders, work that depends upon the study of ethics in educational leadership. As noted in the paragraphs below, the field has continued to highlight the focus of ethics in its national standards; we encourage scholars of leadership and ethics to work together to build a base of scholarship that supports ethical leadership preparation and practice. This practical standards-based text serves to move the field in that direction.

During the last twenty years, a good deal of energy has been invested in the question of what key values and responsibilities should shape school and school system leadership. In the US, this has been facilitated primarily through the development of a set of national educational leadership standards (the Interstate School Leaders Licensure Consortium [ISLLC] Standards, 1996, 2008), which are used to develop, support and evaluate leaders at all levels of the US education system. Since the early 2000s, the Educational Leadership Constituent Council (ELCC) standards, which were aligned to ISSLC, informed the work of educational leadership preparation, playing an important role in setting commonly agreed-upon expectations for effective leadership and providing a conceptual framework that guides preparation and certification (Young & Mawhinney, 2012). Recognizing the fact that expectations for educational leaders continue to increase and that school leaders need to be prepared and supported in order to meet changing expectations, stakeholders in the US have revised the 2008 ISLLC standards and subsequently the ELCC standards (Young & Perrone, 2016). The revised ISLLC standards, now known as the Professional Standards for Educational Leaders (PSEL), maintain that effective educational leaders have expertise in the following ten domains:

1. Mission, Vision, and Core Values;
2. Ethics and Professional Norms;
3. Equity and Cultural Responsiveness;
4. Curriculum, Instruction, and Assessment;

 5. Community of Care and Support for Students;
 6. Professional Capacity of School Personnel;
 7. Professional Community for Teachers and Staff;
 8. Meaningful Engagement of Families and Community;
 9. Operations and Management; and
10. School Improvement.

(NPBEA, 2015)

Significantly, the effort to revise the standards did not occur without controversy as those revisions pertain to ethics and moral practice (Superville, 2015).

THE ROLE OF THE STANDARDS IN SHAPING LEADERSHIP PRAXIS

The revised standards, Professional Standards for Educational Leaders (PSEL), and National Educational Leadership Preparation (NELP), serve to address the ever-expanding role of educational leaders, as student bodies become more diverse and accountability for student outcomes is at an all-time high. As such, these standards address key changes in the educational leadership field and respond to input from practitioners and policy makers. The PSEL standards define educational leadership broadly, so as to frame the role of educational leadership in a general sense. In contrast, the NELP standards, which are aligned to the PSEL standards, provide greater specificity around performance expectations for beginning-level building and district leaders. Like the ELCC that preceded them, the NELP standards will be used by the Council for the Accreditation of Educator Preparation and states to review educational leadership preparation programs. Therefore, NELP standards will be used to guide program design, accreditation review, and state program approval (Young, 2016). This important text was conceptualized at the nexus of these different sets of standards—the ISLLC standards, the new PSEL standards, the ELCC standards and forthcoming NELP standards. However, as the chapters are looking to the future of educational leadership preparation and practice, the authors refer to the PSEL and NELP standards in their discussions of preparing and developing ethical educational leaders.

Importantly, the role of ethical leadership continues to hold a prominent place within these various sets of standards. This recurring role serves as an historical acknowledgment of the importance of an ethical approach to educational leadership and as an anchor for the daily practice of administrators as they work collectively to develop a common vision, support quality instruction, foster school improvement, and build a strong community of engagement committed to student learning. The implications of new model PSEL and NELP Standards for the practice and development of current and future school and school system leaders are far reaching. Emphasizing the centrality of ethics in the work of educational leaders as they promote the success of all students is paramount for the field. This is especially pertinent since few challenges are as persistent and complex in educational administration as the self-reflective assumption of moral commitments and on-the-ground ethical decision making, especially in today's dynamic, multicultural, and high-stakes environment of schooling (Strike, Haller, & Soltis, 2005; Young, 2016; Young & Perrone, 2016).

The practical significance of professional standards for preparation and practice is a given, but educational leadership as transformative practice is arguably far more than a set of standards and codes to be applied passively to practice bereft of informed independent judgment with respect to setting and context (Young, 2016; Young & Perrone, 2016). More appropriately, standards can serve as guideposts toward activating moral motivations that ultimately solidify professional identity (Frick & Covaleskie, 2014). Today's 21st-century requirements for educational leadership recognize the necessity to adopt personal, professional, organizational and civic agendas for ensuring every student's success (NPBEA, 2015). This is no small matter, and such an orientation is imbued with significant trial, risk, and thought criminality (English, 2016), in addition to advocacy, truth-telling, and counter-conduct (Niesche & Keddie, 2016).

Leadership matters, but not just any kind of leadership, especially when we aim to articulate a special form of leadership specific to schooling, equity and democracy. Most, if not all, of this book will argue for educational leadership as philosophy. This might be a strange statement to some, but that is in essence what exemplar leadership for schooling must be, practical philosophy in action—*praxis* (Young, 2016; Young & Perrone, 2016). This aim contrasts with much of what we know about leadership from other disciplines and learned professions that focus mainly on corporatist (Burns, 2015) and/or strong culturally defined conceptions of positional occupancy of organizational or governmental office (Abowitz, 2013). Educational leadership for the public purposes of schooling is qualitatively different, and what is essentially unique to the profession is the centrality of expansive ethical decision making, reflexivity in practice, and moral action. The work is about "human completion" (Freire, 1970/2003, p. 47) achieved through inquiring relational practice that embraces equitable goals, public organizing actions, and deliberative democratic methods through community (Strike, 2007), while simultaneously seeking out and responding in ways that support the best interests of students (Shapiro & Stefkovich, 2016).

ORGANIZATION OF THE TEXT

Given the above imperatives, this book provides: 1) content elaboration of the "ethics" Standards; 2) foundational explanation of that content; 3) exercised internalization of ethical reference points and values of subjective struggle to understand ourselves and the world; 4) application of ethical reasoning in practice, case study; 5) engendering of moral imagination, and 6) informed, reasoned guidance for moral leadership in schooling. Although highly informed and thoughtful preparation and development work is being done (e.g. Buskey & Pitts, 2009; Jenlink, 2014; Strike, Haller, & Soltis, 2005; Frick & Covaleskie, 2014), we can and must do better. This text acknowledges the important tenets of social justice and equity, while serving to further stimulate and expand the ethical dimensions of professional preparation for novice aspirants as well as incumbent leaders.

The book is presented in seven chapters. This Preface provides the reader with insight into the importance of ethics in educational leadership preparation and practice, and discusses the significance of organizing the text around the NELP and PSEL standards. Just as standards overlap, there is some overlap in the discussion of standards. Each chapter contains explanatory text surrounding a standard, questions and/or learning exercises throughout the chapter, text boxes that contain key words and concepts, a case study, and concludes with suggestions for further exercises. Theoretical discussions are supported by pedagogical tools, such as definition boxes. This organization allows the text to be a standalone text in the instruction of ethics. Chapters adequately cover a discussion of the standards, pedagogical learning tools, a case study for discussion, and other resources and activities. This wrap-around text is useful because it is comprehensive and follows best practices for a variety of adult learning styles.

Chapter 1, Being an Ethical Leader Means Taking Responsibility for Students' Academic and Social Success, by William Frick, Steven Gross, and Alison Wilson, provides varying definitions of ethical leadership and subsequently brings to the fore the important balance of caring for school children's academic and social well-being, while adhering to professional ethical standards. As Chapter 1 notes, leaders in educational settings at all levels face complex ethical dilemmas that are best resolved through deep reflection and understanding of ethical principles. In order to respond effectively to such problems, leaders must have an expanded understanding of ethical reference points. This means being able to reason and act using Multiple Ethical Paradigms (MEP), including the ethics of justice, care, critique, community, virtue and the profession. Further, students of educational leadership must see the ethical dilemmas they face in the context of varying degrees of turbulence, ranging from light, moderate, severe, and extreme as well as the underlying forces of stability, cascading, and positionality that raise or lower the level of turbulence in a given situation.

Chapter 2, Modeling Ethical Leadership, by Marla Susman Israel and Lisa Bass, discusses the importance of the school leader's role in promoting ethical leadership through their leadership style, and in their actions. The ethical leader strives to lead by example, and this chapter illuminates the qualities such leaders exude in their practice. Aspiring leaders who wish to model these qualities need to see themselves as educational thinkers who understand the traditions they follow. Equally, they need to see how rich perspectives of ethical reasoning can be used to enhance their practice, especially under turbulent conditions. Underlying our ideas about educational leadership is our own way of seeing the world, specifically, one's philosophy of education.

Chapter 3, Supporting Democratic and Ethical Schools, by Susan Faircloth, discusses the importance of democratic leadership, as well as the intersection of democracy and the principle of equity. In this chapter the author delineates the ethics of democracy and equity in leading schools in students' best interest. Faircloth makes clear that without equitable and democratic structures, it will be impossible to witness equality of opportunity or equal outcomes in schools.

Chapter 4, Safeguarding the Values of Diversity and Equity, by Lisa Bass and Karen Stansberry Beard, provides a framework for school leaders who strive to effectively promote diversity in the school setting. The authors discuss the importance of acknowledging diversity while taking current and future student diversity into consideration in leadership, planning, and decision-making. This chapter describes and outlines the characteristics of school leaders who are conscious of the need to acknowledge diversity in their schools, and supports school leaders who desire to invest in expanding their knowledge of all forms of diversity (i.e. gender, differently abled students, racial and ethnic diversity, sexual orientation, age, socio-economic class, family composition, religious identity, native language, etc.).

Chapter 5, The Moral and Legal Dimensions of Decision Making, by Susan Bon, discusses the role of educational leaders as moral and ethical agents. This chapter highlights the significance of law and ethics as it pertains to educational leaders. The author also discusses how law and ethics serve as both a compass and foundation toward honoring professional ethics in the school setting.

Chapter 6, Supporting Socially Just, Equitable and Inclusive Schools, by Barbara Pazey and Carl Lashley, explores the connections and intersections between socially just leadership and ethical leadership. The authors discuss ways of supporting teachers and school workers in establishing schools that are safe, welcoming, and effective for all students.

Chapter 7, Future Directions in the Development of Ethical Leadership, the conclusion of the book, draws connections between the various ethical challenges that educational leaders face, policy and practice trends, and potential future conditions. Lisa Bass, William Frick and Michelle Young identify key areas in which leadership development will be important, and provide suggestions for educational leadership faculty and leadership candidates for continuing their growth in these areas.

Although the purpose and topic of each chapter in the text is different, they are structured to provide common resources across the book. For example, each chapter is organized to include a theoretical basis, orientation to the standards, a case study, or reference to appropriate case studies, opportunities for practice or learning activities, and resources that support and encourage students to study further each of the chapter's elements. Readers will also find triangulation with respect to content and references. The overlap is due to the overlap present in the standards and the comprehensive nature of the seminal ethical literature consulted for this work.

This general orientation to the importance of ethics in education, and the essence of the standards as guideposts toward our individual and collective formation as leaders within the profession, reaffirms our commitment to actively work against demoralization (Santoro, 2011) and assert ourselves as moral subversives (Buskey & Pitts, 2009) within the complex amalgam of aims, goals and purposes cast upon schools. According to recent empirical research by Greer, Searby, and Thoma (2015) we have work to do with preparing educational leadership students and developing practicing incumbents. Our goal is to prepare them to move from "conventional, hierarchal, by-the-book decision making—as a default mode" with preferences oriented toward moral certainty, uniform application of policy, and a sense of fulfilling duty (Rest et al., 1999), to an adoption of post-conventional schema that

> prioritizes moral ideals and relies on theoretical frameworks for resolving complex moral issues (Bebeau & Thoma, 2003; Rest et al., 1999; Thoma, 2006). Postconventional thinkers respect social norms but place a primacy on moral criteria, in contrast with more pragmatic claims; they draw on shared ideals that are fully reciprocal, not hierarchal, and hence not bound by status or class. They are given to self-reflection, making decisions that are open to scrutiny, based on logical criticism or the collective experience of the community.
>
> (Thoma, 2006, p. 527)

REFERENCES

Abowitz, K. K. (2013). *Publics for public schools: Legitimacy, democracy, and leadership.* Boulder, CO: Paradigm.

Bebeau, M. J., & Thoma, S. J. (2003). Guide for DIT-2. Minneapolis, MN: University of Minnesota, Center for the Study of Ethical Development. Retrieved from: www.ethical development.ua.edu/

Burns, J. (2015). The moral bankruptcy of corporate education. Teachers College Record. Retrieved September 11, 2015 from: www.tcrecord.org ID Number: 18091

Buskey, F. C., & Pitts, E. M. (2009). Training subversives: The ethics of leadership preparation. *Kappan, 91*(3), 57–61.

English, F. W. (2016). The transformational leader as thought criminal. In S. J. Gross & J. P. Shapiro (Eds.), *Democratic ethical educational leadership: Reclaiming school reform.* New York: Routledge.

Freire, P. (1970/2003). *Pedagogy of the oppressed.* New York: Continuum.

Frey, W. H. (2013, June 19). Shift to majority-minority population in the U.S. happening faster than expected. Brookings Up Front. Retrieved from: www.brookings.edu/blogs/up-front/posts/2013/06/19-us-majority-minority-population-census-frey

Frick, W. C., & Covaleskie, J. F. (2014). Preparation of integrity. In C. M. Branson & S. J. Gross (Eds.), *Handbook of ethical educational leadership* (pp. 386–404). New York: Routledge.

Greer, J. L., Searby, L. J., & Thoma, S. J. (2015). Arrested development? Comparing educational leadership students with national norms on moral reasoning. *Educational Administration Quarterly, 51*(4), 511–542.

Hemphill, F. C., Vanneman, A., & Rahman, T. (2011). Achievement gaps: How Hispanic and White students in public schools perform in mathematics and reading on the National Assessment of Educational Progress. Washington, DC: National Center for Education Statistics, Institute of Education Sciences, US Department of Education.

Interstate School Leaders Licensure Consortium (ISLLC). (1996). Standards for school leaders. Washington, DC: Council of Chief State School Officers.

Interstate School Leaders Licensure Consortium. (2008). Educational leadership policy standards. Reston, VA: National Association of Secondary School Principals.

Jenlink, P. M. (2014, November). An examination of self-authoring ethical dilemma cases as dramatic rehearsal for moral leadership. Paper presented at the UCEA (University Council for Educational Administration) Annual Convention. Washington, DC.

National Policy Board for Educational Administration (NPBEA) (2015). Professional standards for educational leaders 2015. Reston, VA: NPBEA.

Niesche, R., & Keddie, A. (2016). *Leadership, ethics and schooling for social justice*. New York: Routledge.

Rest, J. R., Narvaez, D., Bebeau, M. J., & Thoma, S. J. (1999). *Postconventional moral thinking: A neo-Kohlbergian approach*. Mahwah, NJ: Erlbaum.

Santoro, D. A. (2011). Good teaching in difficult times: Demoralization in the pursuit of good work. *American Journal of Education, 118*(1), 1–23.

Shapiro, J. P., & Stefkovich, J. A. (2016). Ethical leadership and decision making in Education: Applying theoretical perspectives to complex dilemmas (4th ed.). New York: Routledge.

Strike, K. (2007). *Ethical leadership in schools: Creating community in an environment of accountability*. Thousand Oaks, CA: Corwin Press.

Strike, K. A., Haller, E. J., & Soltis, J. F. (2005). *The ethics of school administration* (3rd ed.). New York: Teachers College Press.

Superville, D. R. (2015, June). School-leader standards to get more revision, *Education Week*. Retrieved June 10, 2015 from: www.edweek.org/ew/articles/2015/06/10/school-leader-standards-to-get-more-revision.html?qs=School-Leader+Standards+to+Get+More+Revision

Thoma, S. (2006). Research on the Defining Issues Test. In M. Killen & J. Smetena (Eds.), *Handbook of moral development* (pp. 67–91). Hillsdale, NJ: Erlbaum.

Vanneman, A., Hamilton, L., Anderson, J. B., & Rahman, T. (2009). Achievement Gaps: How Black and White Students in Public Schools Perform in Mathematics and Reading on the National Assessment of Educational Progress. Statistical Analysis Report. NCES 2009–455. National Center for Education Statistics.

Young, M. (2016). National Educational Leadership reparation (NELP) Standards: What they are, how they were developed, and what purpose they serve. In *UCEA Review* (pp. 4–5).

Young, M. D. & Mawhinney, H. (Eds.). (2012). *The research base supporting the ELCC Standards*. Charlottesville, VA: UCEA.

Young, M. D. & Perrone, F. (2016). How are standards used, by whom and to what end? *Journal of Research on Leadership Education, 11*(1), 3–11.

CHAPTER 1

Being an Ethical Leader Means Taking Responsibility for Students' Academic and Social Success

William C. Frick, Steven J. Gross, and Alison S. Wilson

CHAPTER OVERVIEW

In this chapter we seek to provide varying definitions of ethical leadership and bring to light the important balance of attending to school children's academic and social wellbeing, while adhering to professional ethical standards. Leaders in educational settings at all levels are continually confronted with complex ethical challenges that require deep reflection and understanding. In order to respond effectively to such complex problems, leaders must have an expanded understanding of a range of ethical reference points. This means being able to reason and act pluralistically with Multiple Ethical Paradigms (MEP) including the ethics of justice, care, critique, community, profession, and virtue. Further, students of educational leadership must see the moral situations and ethical dilemmas they face in the context of varying degrees of turbulence, ranging from light, moderate, severe, and extreme as well as the underlying forces of stability, cascading, and positionality that can raise or lower the level of instability of a given situation or constellation of phenomena. This chapter also includes a case study that illustrates the tension between accountability and responsibility for students' academic and social success that educational leaders can experience when faced with an ethical dilemma. Key sections are followed by opportunities for aspiring educational leaders to apply the concepts and tools for ethical decision making presented throughout the chapter to the case study as well as their own educational practice.

INTRODUCTION

As indicated by Standard 2 of the Professional Standards for Educational Leaders (PSEL) (2015), 21st-century school leadership requires administrators to accept responsibility for all aspects of students' development (see Standard 2c) and foster a sense of this responsibility among all members of their school community (see Standard 2f). The language of "responsibility", as indicated in the title of this chapter and addressed more fully in the following sections, is qualitatively different than the language of "accountability." This requires leaders to have a clear understanding of the ever-increasing neoliberal political and policy context in which public schools currently function in addition to both a broad and deep awareness of the students and communities they serve (see Standard 2e), including the commitment and capacity to support them (see Roosevelt, 2006). Moreover, as we recognize the transition to the PSEL (2015) (formerly the ISLLC Standards), we would like to highlight the differences between key elements of the "Ethics" standard. According to the ISLLC Standards (2008), an educational leader promotes the success of every student by *ensuring a system of accountability for every student's academic and social success.* In its more recent iteration in PSEL (2015), this standard calls for effective educational leaders who adhere to ethical principles and professional norms that *place children at the center of education and accept responsibility for each student's academic success and well-being.* As you are likely to clearly see, these elements (as italicized) are not necessarily commensurate and therefore we set to the task of examining both very closely. On another note, the importance of language and the power of meaning it conveys cannot be overstated; as such, we are pleased with how this element and its associated meanings have undergone a change that is more representative of the foundational moral purposes of schooling and its operation.

We would also be remiss if we did not mention our keen awareness of how standardization has penetrated the profession of educational administration, as it has for education as a professional field generally, in addition to the standardization influence on the institutionalized bureaucracy of schooling per se. This has a lot to do with accountability, and we will discuss more about this later in the chapter. Are standards (model policy, preparation, professional association, etc.) good or bad? Our intention is not to provide a critique of ISLLC or PSEL Standards or other standards that are informed by their various iterations, but we do want our readers to be aware that standards of most kind (understood as benchmarks rather than criteria of excellence, see Strike, 2007) can be superficial, mechanistic, and depict the minimum of some criterion or aspiration, and this is particularly so when we seek to standardize the morally humanistic dimension of professional work in school leadership. Standards are not sufficient and all encompassing, even with an informed and educatively oriented textbook such as this. By no means do we wish to reinforce the legitimacy of benchmarks, but we do wish to elaborate and nuance the possible meaning of moral excellence. Standards therefore should not be simply employed expediently and uncritically in the sense that external and distal powers drive expectations for the profession and therefore we must assiduously prepare to meet those expectations. We believe this is wholly the wrong approach to thoughtful professional formation, both in craft skill and in moral commitments. We hope this chapter, and the book as a whole, breaks what can be viewed as an artificial mold of standardization and encourage readers to look deeper, reflect robustly, and adopt dispositions and commitments that are praiseworthy of the profession.

We begin by introducing a case that will serve to direct and promote the development of thinking over specific content presented in this chapter. With the case as setting and backdrop, a progression of various learning activities and summary tables will be presented at critical junctures in order to encourage interactive meaning making with ideas, assertions and challenges so as to promote the application of informed administrative practice.

CASE STUDY 1.1: WHEN ETHICS AND POLICY COLLIDE

It had been a typical spring day for first-year assistant principal Richard Inman at Rocket Junior High. By 7:20 a.m., while waiting for Bus 50, Richard walked through the courtyard speaking with the students. Bus 50 dropped off students from the south side of town. A south-side kid himself, Richard had an agenda to reach this group of students. By staying late and playing basketball after school with the toughest of the bunch, he had cultivated a relationship with Juan, a muscular, heavily tattooed young man of 15 who was the undisputed leader of the group. His extra effort to cultivate a relationship was paying off. Juan and his devoted followers had improved their grades, mingled with others, and Juan himself had not been involved in a fight for months, a record for him.

Later in the day, he was not so optimistic. Richard called Juan to the office to follow up on his third tardy of the week. Juan's fifth-period teacher immediately called him back stating that she had witnessed Juan giving something to another student in the hall (just after he had been summoned to the office). The teacher believed drugs might have been exchanged and said that the other boy, David Ramos, a slightly built young scholar who participated in honors' classes and was a standout trombonist in the band, seemed quite nervous. Richard contemplated what to do with David Ramos.

In this school of 900 students, the only discourse Richard could recall having with David was a congratulatory remark after the Christmas band concert. Decision made, he reached again for the phone and asked the school police officer to escort David out of class and bring him to the office.

Juan arrived first and David soon after. Richard brought both boys and the officer (a decision of inclusion he would later doubt) into his office and asked them what had taken place. Juan said he had just given David something to hold for him. When David was questioned about the exchange (in the presence of the officer), he began to shake, tears welled up in his eyes, and he refused to say anything. The officer searched David and discovered a pair of brass knuckles, a prohibited weapon, the possession of which constituted a felony offense. The officer immediately handcuffed David.

At this point, David began to cry and suddenly Juan said, "Hey, I told him I would kick his ass if he didn't hold the knucks for me. Those are mine; I was going to use them after school to take care of some personal business."

Richard felt a swell of pride. Standing up and admitting that he had coerced the small, honor student to hold the weapon for him was a HUGE breakthrough for Juan! His joy immediately turned to sadness, regret, and guilt.

Richard thought the school police officer would take the cuffs off of David but that did not happen. He asked why and the officer said that he had to take both students to jail and charge them with felony possession of a prohibited weapon on school property. In addition, a zero-tolerance board policy demanded both students should be expelled for no less than 45 days into the district's disciplinary alternative education program (DAEP).

That was no big deal for Juan; he had been through this numerous times before. But not David. This kid had not been in any trouble and had not initiated what happened to him. The system was broken, and he himself had just become a victim along with a small boy who had not had the courage to stand up to a bully. What kind of society demanded courage from 11-year-old children? Richard felt sick as he realized his own thoughtlessness had contributed to both boys being cuffed and led from the room. He felt trapped between following policy, which he had been taught to do, and his deep obligation to do the very best he could for his students.

Within minutes, both boys were taken to the youth detention facility. Richard called the mothers of both boys and the reaction of the parents spoke volumes. Juan's mother responded with "Let him sit there for a few days; maybe he will learn his lesson this time." David's mother hung up on Richard and was in his office 15 min later. Richard explained the situation and promised David's mother he would do all he could to help. David's mother was angry, "If the other kid admitted he forced my son to do this, why is my son in trouble?" Richard had no logical or suitable answer for this question. He mutely gave her the address of the detention facility and watched as she took it, read it, broke into tears, then left. He stared after her and wondered again why he had not protected David.

He filled out the paperwork on Juan because he knew what school policy stated, but after he wrote David's name on a blank form, he hesitated. David was an innocent victim. His history as a honor student, musician, a student who had no discipline violations on his record, and Richard's own understanding of Juan's intimidation tactics on those he perceived as weak substantiated Richard's belief that David was innocent. David's mother had not even known this policy existed. What should he do? What would be best for or fair to David?

Richard tore up the blank form which had David's name on it and threw it away. He would not file the paperwork to have David expelled. It was a violation of policy, but sending David into a hellhole like the district DAEP program would be a mistake, one that would shatter David's future, his dreams, and his potential. The south side had already destroyed other young men. He would not let it reach out and destroy David as well.

One week later, David was back in class and Juan was in district DAEP. Richard got a call from the Director of Secondary Education who directed Richard to follow through with expulsion papers on David. Richard explained that he would not be able to comply with the directive and explained the situation. The director said he understood Richard's position but encouraged him to follow policy and let him know that he would have no choice but to write Richard an official reprimand, which would be included in his personnel file if he did not relent.

THE PHILOSOPHY OF ADMINISTRATIVE LEADERSHIP[1]

The point that school administrative decision making requires more than the mechanical application of existing rules, regulations and various levels of school and school-related policy has been well established (Hoy & Miskel, 2013). The essential aspects of school leadership are more than simply possessing and carrying out certain technical skills to ensure effective and efficient management of organizational operations (Sergiovanni, 2009). The emphasis and preoccupation with bureaucratic scientism and management perspectives is counterbalanced with the importance of value, moral, and ethical bases for educational leadership decision making. There is an ever-increasing recognition that putatively value-free administrative decisions and actions are actually "value-laden, even value-saturated enterprises(s)" (Hodgkinson, 1978, p. 122; see also Willower & Licata, 1997; Aviv, 2014) that undergird our understanding of what Greenfield (1985, 1999), and others (Green, 1990) have articulated in more precise terms as the careful location of purpose and worth in things, or, in other words, moral education and moral leadership.

This recognition of value-driven, moral leadership action, according to Hodgkinson (1978), is an "administrative logic" of a different order. Herbert Simon (1957) can be credited for helping us understand the importance of negotiating the value-laden, value-saturated nature of administrative practice in his conception of "economic man" where value compromises within modern organizational life are increasingly necessary, and therefore make being "good enough" rather than perfect rationality the distinctive mark of organizational leadership (Lakomski, 1987).

Negotiating compromises, or what is commonly referred to as "satisficing," becomes the essential leadership skill. The mix of values, beliefs and assumptions from a myriad of interested parties, particularly in U.S. schooling writ large and those within an immediate geospatial context, creates "messy, complicated, and conflict-filled situations" that require difficult choices between competing, highly prized conceptions of what is desirable "that cannot be simultaneously or fully satisfied" (Cuban, 2001, p. 10). This leadership context is what Begley (2000) refers to as value praxis.

School administration is not purely art or science, nor is it art and science; it is art, science and philosophy involving habits of mind, hand and heart. There are three prominent ways of knowing and dealing with the world—three modes of action. These modes are theoria, techne, and praxis. There is no true dichotomy between theory and practice—each is a different modality of a single continuum. Praxis, on the other hand, is ethical action in the political context of purposeful human conduct (Adkins, 1978). Praxis focuses on behavior guided by purpose, intention, motive, normative morality, emotions, and values in addition to the facts or "science" of the case (Hodgkinson, 1991) and has been referred to by others as valuation (Willower, 1994). Therefore, praxis calls forth the reflective practice of school administration in deep deliberation over what we take to be important in relation to one another in community (see also Freire's (1986) use of the concept as an action-reflection dialectic). This level of professional reflexivity (the conscious act of self-reference where examination or action bends back on, refers to, and affects the person instigating the action or examination) is paramount in the life world of the educational leader. This is especially so when sorting through the various forms of accountability and how they are distinct from responsibility.

LEARNING ACTIVITY 1.1

- In the case study, how does Richard demonstrate "professional reflexivity," and how does this influence his decision-making process?
- Consider this situation from the perspective of the various stakeholders involved—Richard, Juan, David, Juan's mother, David's mother, and the Director of Secondary Education. Discuss potential conflicts in what these stakeholders consider to be in the best interest of the students involved. How do you explain these conflicts?

THE DECONSTRUCTION AND REINTERPRETATION OF ACCOUNTABILITY

Accountability in U.S. schooling is not, historically speaking, a near recent event cast as educational reform (Mehta, 2013). There have been many waves of what has been referred to as a technocratic logic penetrating the educational field. In fact, perhaps the earliest formal attempts to evaluate the performance of schools took place in Boston in 1845. As Madaus and colleagues indicate, "this event is important

. . . because it began a long tradition of using pupil test scores as a principal source of data to evaluate the effectiveness of a school or instructional program" (Madaus, Stufflebeam, & Scriven, 1983, p. 5). In our contemporary context, because there is so much emphasis on standards and on testing in the U.S., we are inclined to think of accountability largely as an issue of meeting benchmarks for academic achievement as defined by test scores (Strike, 2007). Unfortunately, the entire test-based accountability movement has not paid attention to the evidence of systemic reform as originally conceived (Smith & O'Day, 1991), and The National Research Council, after review of research on high-stakes accountability, found few benefits to such approaches to school improvement (Hout & Elliott, 2011; see also Welner & Mathis, 2015). But this is only one form of accountability that educational leaders need to consider. There is actually a challenging interaction of multiple, simultaneous accountabilities that administrators are obliged to juggle, and these accountabilities are in many ways contradictory and conflicting (Gross, Shaw, & Shapiro, 2003).

Firestone and Shipps (2005) lay out a typology of five different kinds of external and internal accountability—political, bureaucratic, market, professional, and moral (see Table 2.1) that leads them to a concluding hypothesis supported by Carnoy, Elmore, & Siskin (2003): Leaders can contribute to student learning by interpreting external and internal accountabilities to help educators promote a shared sense of ethical obligation, that is "internal accountability" (p. 82).

Table 1.1 Typology of Leaders' Accountabilities

	Type	Manifestations (examples)	Objectives	Leader's Expected Response
External	**Political**			
	Local	Citizen Pressure	Satisfaction	Coalition Builder
	State/Federal	Legal Mandates	Obedience	Negotiator
	Bureaucratic			
	Process	Regulations	Compliance	Functionary
	Outcome	Goals/Incentives	Alignment	Knowledgeable Advocate
	Market			
		Competition	Efficiency/ Creativity	Manager/ Entrepreneur
External and Internal	**Professional**			
		Practice	Preferred	Expert Educator
		Consensus	Practice	
	Moral			
		Beliefs	Value Commitments	Consistent, Empathetic Defender of Justice

Accountability in a general sense is a commitment to answer to the norms of legitimate authority in our society, and school leaders should be informed by an understanding of accountability that takes into account these multiple authorities so as to assume the role of active intermediary (Strike, 2007). These authorities are varied and include the legislature, parents, the profession, and the immediate social surround of the community. Hyper-accentuated external accountability can promote "vices"—goal displacement, goal reduction, motivational displacement, gaming, and quite possibly demoralization (Santoro, 2011). Ultimately, the antidote to external accountability is a thoroughgoing understanding of what is meant by responsibility (or internal accountability). Accountability (external) is primarily focused on the ledger whereas responsibility is focused on moral commitment and intent (Starratt, 2006).

Accepting and assuming responsibility signals that school leaders have internalized a value system that guides their practice and that ultimately influences the moral commitments of a school or system (Starratt, 2008). Moral leadership is not about personal taste in the values that one adopts, but rather serves as a foundational countermeasure to the mixed signals of accountabilities that might jeopardize fairness, communal values, empathy for others, social justice, a well-rounded education, and the best interests of students (Firestone & Shipps, 2005; Frick, 2011). Mixed signals are the terrain of administrative leadership and indicative of institutional and environmental turbulence (this idea of turbulence will be discussed in detail later in the chapter; Gross, 2014). Ultimately, moral leadership (responsibility/internal accountability) inspires internal compunctions (Sergiovanni, 1992), the deeply felt obligations to resist technical rationalities and banal representations of what schooling should mean and be measured by in a free, open, and democratic society (Greene, 1995).

LEARNING ACTIVITY 1.2

- Use the Typology of Leaders' Accountabilities (see Table 2.1) to analyze the case study. Identify the various types of accountability and how each contributes to the situation, decision making, and potential outcome in this scenario.
- How does this situation illustrate the distinction and tension between "accountability" and "responsibility"?

NURTURING THE DEVELOPMENT OF SCHOOLS THAT PLACE CHILDREN AT THE HEART OF EDUCATION

Rothstein (2004), Rose (2009), and Kirp (2011), among other researchers, practitioners, and public policy laborers, contend that schools must focus on a wider range of educational objectives in order to provide students with the ability to lead productive and meaningful lives. The complexity of the human condition requires a focus on the whole child (Kirp, 2011; Scherer, 2009) not only to create strong local programs, but also to serve the good of the larger community. A developed understanding of the centrality of students' best interests (both individual and collectively) could be a way to nurture schools as places where the heart of education is squarely about children and youth, constituting a paramount professional moral commitment. Engendering communal allegiance to shared moral and professional responsibility for children's best interests at both the school site and district level is imperative and cannot be achieved without strong, fully operating communities of practice focused on both the normative and practice dimensions of the profession (Knapp, Copland, & Talbert, 2003; Talbert, 2011; Wenger, 1998).

With this in mind, all schooling stakeholders need to consider the important implication that David Kirp (2011) presents to us, a "golden rule" of a particular kind, "that every child deserves what's good enough for a child you love" (p. 8). The injunction can easily get lost in the midst of competing issues and agendas, but attending to and hopefully living and working by the golden rule might not be the responsibility of school workers in particular but rather a central social obligation of all members, groups, and institutions of our society in general. In that sense, placing children at the heart of education can only be realized, in its fullest and most meaningful sense, by broad, wide-ranging public support and purposeful activity that results from a coordinated policy and professional agenda.

THE VARIOUS UNDERSTANDINGS OF ETHICAL EDUCATIONAL LEADERSHIP[2]

There exist multiple ethical paradigms, or what could be referred to as moral reference points, that inform and ostensibly guide the work of educational leadership in schools (see Table 2.2). When considering normative ethical frameworks in education, moral philosophy provides a broad backdrop to situate and better understand the distinct theoretical perspectives of ethical and moral leadership within educational administration. As such, there are primarily six ethical themes or standpoints considered in the field of educational leadership. These moral perspectives, typically articulated as theories of duty, guidance for individual ethical decision-making, expressions of relational morality, or guidance for establishing moral school environments, comprise the basis from which much of the literature exists. For this particular chapter, a separate consideration of each of the theoretical standpoints is important because it informs our understanding of what an "Ethics" Standard for the profession might mean and how it might be applied in practice.

Justice

A justice perspective, or what has been referred to in the literature and practice within the profession as an "ethic of justice", is clearly expressed in the work of Strike, Haller, & Soltis (1998). This perspective focuses on ethical concepts that constitute the foundational principles of liberal democracies. Taken as a whole, they can be described as a "civic ethic" where it is believed that all persons irrespective of culture, race, or other defining categories possess the capacity for a sense of justice and the ability to conceptualize what is their own good. People have the capacity to critique their notion of justice and the good life and are capable of transcending cultural contexts in order to achieve analytic distance when testing principles such as due process, freedom, equality, and the common good.

There is a fundamental tension within the perspective of observing justice. Two broad schools of thought occupy the continued discussion over a civic ethic. One position places the individual person as an independent reality prior to social relationships. Individuals are motivated by self-interest and engage in social relations for their own benefit. Social contracts that support societies and governments are essentially individuals agreeing to surrender some liberty in return for amicable relations with others or protection from others' self-interest. The basis for these beliefs appears to have emerged from two competing perspectives of public discussion in Western culture. One view held that everything people have— including political rights and freedoms—originates with God. Another view supposed that God had granted humanity the moral freedom to construct its own societies and that rights and freedoms are the result of social contracts based on human reason and experience. Regardless of the basis for these beliefs, justice is viewed as contractual and legal engineering to bring about harmony between the needs and wants of self-serving individuals (Rawls, 1993).

The second position situates social relationships and society as a prior reality to the individual person. This perspective places the common good of the community as a superior concern over individual self-interest. It is only through living in relation to others that personhood is achieved and moral lessons of communal protection and care are realized. The common good is accomplished by justice that emerges from a community's choice to act and govern fairly for all its members (Sullivan, 1986). Efforts to harmonize the two positions within the justice perspective are evident in the work of Taylor (1994). Sergiovanni and Starratt (1993) express the tension another way by saying,

> Whether . . . ethical systems are understood as grounded in Natural Law (somewhat the way engineering principles are based on laws of physics . . .) or understood as socially constructed guides derived from pragmatic and humanitarian concerns and interests of the civil community is a question long argued by philosophers and social theorists.
>
> (p. 78)

The justice tradition has a longstanding history in the West. Fundamental human rights and the protection of those rights by means of justice are central concepts of postindustrial, liberally democratic, constitutional nation states. But rights and justice do not tell us the whole story about the moral life. Laws and governmental processes can, have been, are, and will be immoral based upon other ways of viewing our collective moral life together. And that collective life can be viewed parochially, but ever increasingly, must be viewed globally. Justice and rights fall short because they view the moral realm as an institutional and political process whereby a moral minimum is established for relations between people. This perspective tells us little about how we relate to one another as a happy and flourishing community, or do more than the morally minimal.

Care

A care perspective, or what has been referred to in the literature and practice within the profession as an "ethic of care", is clearly expressed in the work of Noddings (1988), Beck (1994), and Gilligan (1982). Interpersonal in nature, this moral perspective focuses on the demands of relationship from a position of unconditional positive regard, or described elsewhere as a deep awareness of "the other" as persons in community with ourselves as subjects. This position asserts that as human beings (and females perhaps, in particular) we have the capacity to feel deep respect or love for other people, and especially people different from ourselves. Our attitudes toward others "are determined in part by an understanding of who and what they are: in this case, that they are human beings, persons, and that as persons they possess an inner integrity, a self-determination, a capacity for free and spiritual activity that we also sense in ourselves" (Gilkey, 1993, p. 79). This level of empathy and self-understanding applied to the other can become the foundation for treating persons as ends and not as means, and can, in large part, provide the inner basis of an outward social order.

To be in relationship with others where care, nurturance, respect, compassion, and trust are the dominant characteristics is to be fully human. The integrity of human relation(ship) and connection is paramount for this perspective; and consideration of rights, principles, and laws are secondary to the primacy of beneficence for seeking resolution of moral issues. Acts, dispositions, and thinking that are conducive to the well-being of others and a "commitment to receptive attention and a willingness to respond helpfully to legitimate needs" is the bedrock of moral striving (Noddings, 1996, p. 265). Rather than restricting the moral domain to considerations of duty and obligation, an ethic of care asks a more foundational question: How shall we live? Care theory "is relation-centered rather than agent-centered, and it is more concerned with the caring relation than with caring as a virtue" (Noddings, 2002, p. 2). Both relation(ship) and virtue are acknowledged, but relation(ship) is primary and "credits the cared-for with a special contribution, one different from reciprocal response as carer" (Noddings, 2002, p. 2). The cared-for contribute significantly to relational morality, and "social" virtues are defined situationally within the space of personal interaction.

Close relationships are a central feature of the moral life and constitute another aspect of moral community that lends an additional vantage to our understanding of practical ethics. Although a focus on the dyadic relationship of care provides insights into the "I–Thou" existential experience of humankind as a legitimate voice of mutual encounter with the other as a person possessing inner integrity, there appears to be more to the moral story. The emphasis on relation with the singular other can disrupt and warp a "thoroughgoing consideration of care" (Noddings, 1993, p. 48) where one's entire web of relations, both as the carer and the cared-for, are robustly considered.

Critique

A critique perspective, or what has been referred to in the literature and practice within the profession as an "ethic of critique", is clearly expressed in the work of Foster (1986), Giroux (1992), and Apple (1982). These authors draw their arguments from critical theory and the body of literature derived from the Frankfurt School of philosophers. The critique perspective within educational leadership deals with issues beyond interpersonal relations and serves as a moral posture, and examination of larger social and institutional dimensions of human life. Particularly, issues of competing interests, power, the nature and structure of bureaucracy, the influence and force of language, and redress for institutionalized injustice are the focus of critical concern as it relates to the legitimacy of social arrangements.

The disproportionate benefit of some groups over others as a result of political, economic, and judicial hegemony are moral concerns that transcend the naive perspective that societal structures and properties are simply the way things are. Reasoning and acting ethically also entails the inherent paradoxes of leading and managing within an institutional position, on one hand, and being an activist against practices and procedures that do not support democratic processes, freedom and social justice, on the other (Kozol, 2005).

The moral focus of a critique perspective is concerned with making known and acting upon those circumstances that silence, oppress, or discriminate. As Giroux (1992) states:

> Leadership poses the issue of [ethical] responsibility as a social relationship in which difference and otherness become articulated into practices that offer resistance to forms of domination and oppression. This raises the need for a discourse on leadership that prompts a discriminating response to others, one that makes students, for example, attentive to their own implication in particular forms of human suffering and to the oppression of others whose voices demand recognition and support.
>
> (p. 7)

A discriminating leadership response to others calls for an elevated critical consciousness about our larger social world, its institutions, and the dynamics of power and privilege in framing structures of social reality that can be, if desired, re-envisioned. In its most direct and obvious form, the morality of critique is manifest in a politics of recognition and redistribution (Gutmann, 1994; Hursh, 2007).

Although the critical perspective provides insights into the moral life, especially as it pertains to issues of social justice, identity politics, and corporatist privatization, there is an aspect inherent to theoretically critical ethical standpoints that disallow a clear answer for the problematic social arrangements of our immediate social surround and the larger world. This is especially true when a substantive, robust, and publicly enculturated democracy, as a "powerful script for human freedom" (Giroux, 1992, p. 37) is employed without specific and workable remedies for the claimed re-envisioning of possibilities through struggle. Some important work that makes reference to actionable initiatives within this "paradigm" is emerging and can be described as *emancipatory leadership* (Kozleski & Thorius, 2014; Simmons, 2014).

Community

A community perspective, or what has been referred to in the literature and practice within the profession as an "ethic of community," is clearly expressed in the work of Furman (2003a, 2003b, 2004) and Bellah et al. (1985). According to this viewpoint, moral choices are best made in communitarian settings rather than a traditional focus on the experiences internal to an individual agent (see also Dionne, 2012). Moving away from the Western notion of individual as leader and moral agent, community-building and communities of practice are emphasized. Community is not defined as an entity but rather an ongoing set of processes that include communication, dialog, and collaboration. This position purports that being and acting ethically cannot be achieved without collective commitment to the constructive methods of communal process. The community rather than the individual person is the moral agent and educational leaders are obliged to practice and also engender communal processual skills in others taking part in the work of schools. The term "processual" is unusual, likely because it is a shift in ontological perspective regarding community. Community, within this tradition, is not necessarily a thing (tangible entity) but rather a "sense" achieved by "ongoing processes of communication, dialogue, and collaboration and not on a set of discrete indicators such as 'shared values' . . ." (Furman, 2002, p. 285). Community is not viewed as a measured product or object, but rather a continuous, ongoing process where moral weight is given to inspiring commitment to courses of interpersonal exchange over an end product or something tangible.

A commitment to the processes of community, continuous and recursive, that focus on interpersonal and group awareness, respectful listening, empathetic knowing and understanding of others, effective communication, partnering and working together, and supporting and encouraging dialog in open and equal forums, is the foundational value to be internalized and acted upon (see Habermas, 1992). The practice of community is prior and foundational to the moral aims and purposes of schooling, which include social justice, enactment of democracy and learning for all children.

A communitarian understanding of our collective life together provides a powerful insight about the moral life. What is ethical is not so much what the individual person does in relationship to others, but how the collective responds to environmental and membership needs where Western notions of atomistic individualism, celebrated autonomy, and Hobbesian self-interest give way to moral considerations consisting of egalitarian sentiments, the deep-seated human drive toward living in community with others, and by design, our collective attunement to one another through an awareness of our common humanity. Although powerful sentiments, this perspective is incomplete. How can we live our lives together with no clear sense of personal moral culpability? Communities, no matter how expertly or naturally they are constructed, cannot avoid the moral weight of the actions of the perpetrator and the suffering of the victim, no less the authorization of the bystander and rescuer. Not to acknowledge this moral weight would be, in our Western worldview, immoral.

Profession

A profession perspective, or what has been referred to in literature and practice within educational administration and leadership as an "ethic of the profession", is clearly expressed in the work of Shapiro and Stefkovich (2001, 2005, 2011), Stefkovich and O'Brien (2004) and Stefkovich (2006, 2014). This perspective argues for an ethical paradigm that considers the "moral aspects unique to the profession" of education and educational leadership in particular (Shapiro and Stefkovich, 2005, p. 18). The ethic of the profession considers the ethical frameworks of justice, care, and critique not as totally distinct, incommensurable moral reasoning, but as complementary—a "tapestry of ethical perspectives that encourages . . . rich human response to . . . many uncertain ethical situations" (Starratt, 1994, p. 57). The ethic of the profession, although informed by other moral theory, is distinct unto itself as a framework to guide and inform educational leadership as a practical and moral activity.

The ethic of the profession indicates that a disparity often exists between professional codes meant to inform decision-making and conduct, and the personal moral values of administrators who guide their judgment and behavior. An attempt to integrate professional and personal codes of ethics can lead to moral dissonance, or a "clashing of codes." In responding to this inevitable discord, the ethic of the profession is grounded in a reasoned consideration of the educational shibboleth "the best interests of the student" (Walker, 1998).

The student's best interests are the focal point of the ethic of the profession. A model for determining the best interests of the student consists of a robust focus on the essential nature of individual student rights, the duty of responsibility to others for a common interest, and respect as mutual acknowledgment of the other as having worth, value, and dignity unto themselves (Stefkovich and O'Brien, 2004; Stefkovich, 2006, 2014). The ethic of the profession, and more precisely the best interests of the student model (Stefkovich and O'Brien, 2004; Stefkovich, 2006, 2014), has been applied primarily to court decisions from case law pertaining to K-12 education, although there is a growing empirical account of what "best interests" might mean for practitioners (Frick, 2011; Frick, 2013; Frick & Tribble, 2012; Frick, Faircloth, & Little, 2013). Reflecting on students' best interests assists aspiring and practicing educational leaders to problematize their decision-making and to understand how professional choices are informed by one's moral reasoning and deliberation, personal values and beliefs, professional norms, and adherence to ethical principles.

A professionalized ethics in education, implicating those who are cultural workers at any and all institutional levels who are focused on developing and imparting knowledge, tools and dispositions to the next generation and beyond, has been viewed by some as a redundancy (Green, 1987). Professions are defined by the logic of their definitional relationships and goals to a larger public. By sheer virtue of a profession's internal character and structure, normative qualities emerge within it that either include or exclude those from practice. This is a very important consideration for the field. We must be concerned about the normative formation of educational administrators whereby, rather than spelling out narrow standards (preparation or otherwise) and simply offering free-standing courses in ethics, the moral commitments of the profession permeate the entire pre-service curriculum and/or are developed in an incumbent practicing profession. In addition, the very meaning of the maxim, "the best interests of the student," appears to be varied and indeterminable based upon a multiplicity of circumstance and setting.

Virtue

In addition to the five ethical themes considered in the field of educational leadership, there exists a literature that speaks directly to aretaic judgment of character. These works articulate specific traits and dispositions necessary to think and act morally as an educational leader. Starratt (2004) suggests that becoming a moral school leader requires the development of traits of responsibility, authenticity, and presence. Begley (2005), on the other hand, identifies the motivations and dispositions of reflective self-honesty, relational sensitivity, and dialogical openness as indispensable qualities of character that are necessary to lead in democratic yet diverse school communities.

Virtue is an important moral insight drawing back to the time of Aristotle's (1989) *Nicomachean Ethics*, 334–323 BCE, signaling that it is not necessarily what you do, but rather who you are that bears moral credit. Good deeds flow from good character formed through habit, and this basic moral premise finds its relevance in the arena of school leadership. A strict ethics of character is limited, though—it does not tell us how to act. Character must be complemented with action. What might be more suitable for this tradition? Possibly a complex understanding of what practical wisdom entails in order to educate and lead for the good— knowing that both characterological disposition and action are required in order to lead morally.

DRAWING TOGETHER AN INTEGRATED AND PLURALISTIC PERSPECTIVE

What do we take to be important in relation to one another? We assert that none of the aforementioned ethics either separately or together say enough about the purposes and processes associated with a moral, democratic community in schools (Furman & Starratt, 2002). Our assertion rests with the claims of others working for the support and operation of public schooling. Rudy Crew (2007), former superintendent of Miami-Dade County Public Schools (the fourth largest school system in the USA), argues for, among many things, the nuanced thought and activity required to bridge gaps, create consensus (not necessarily unanimity), and find equitable solutions to pressing educational issues. Schools can and should connect us as persons, communities, and cultures if we can get morally smart. This requires pluralistic ethical reasoning (Hinman 2008; Tuana, 2007). The theme of connectedness is expressed eloquently by Wagner (2001), who provides a practical theory of action for school leaders for positive change. Collaborative relationships among adults and youth are the key to the dilemma of school reinvention. For leaders, it is not about "selling" an idea, program, or reform model by "getting buy-in" but rather about engendering ownership and commitment for improved student outcomes, however conceived. Collective ownership and commitment goes to the level of moral purpose, and the "biggest challenge for educational leaders is to nurture engagement and commitment rooted in community" (Wagner, 2001, p. 385; see also Strike, 2007).

Beyond the school or school system itself, this idea of collective cohesion implicates the politics, economics, and moral order of whole communities if the work of schooling is itself to be worthy of its purposes. As Phillip Schlechty (2009) implores us:

> Civic capacity is dependent on the will of the leaders of community groups, local organizations, and public agencies to work together on behalf of the common good—and on the skill these leaders have, or develop, in pursuing such cooperative efforts. In brief, civic capacity has to do with the ability of [groups, associations, and agencies] that exist in a community to collaborate.
>
> (p. 193)

Ultimately, this perspective on public schooling is one that is deeply informed by the commitment that education in a democracy is neither a property right nor a civil right, but rather a moral imperative and cultural requirement in order to promote the common good and general welfare—to make communities more livable and an ever increasingly diverse culture such as ours more collectively vibrant. Schools therefore are not instruments to provide directed benefits to each individual student (although this is very important), rather public schools rightly function to promote and maintain the values and principles of social cohesion in service to our collective life together (Schlechty, 2009, p. 199).

Table 1.2 provides a summary of the various ethical reference points offered within our professional field. The summary serves to condense the preceding detailed explanation. In Learning Activity 1.3, make reference to Table 1.2 in contemplating the chapter case.

Table 1.2 Ethical Paradigms that Guide the Work of Educational Leadership in Schools

Ethical Theme	Key Sources	Focus	Issues
Justice	Strike et al. (1998)	Foundational principles of liberal democracies	• Due process • Freedom • Equality • Common good • Fundamental human rights
Care	Noddings (1988) Beck (1994) Gilligan (1982)	Demands of relationship from a position of unconditional positive regard	• Integrity of human relation(ship) and connection • Empathy and self-understanding applied to the other • Relationships marked by care, nurturance, respect, compassion, and trust • Primacy of beneficence
Critique	Foster (1986) Giroux (1992) Apple (1982)	Making known and acting upon those circumstances that silence, oppress, or discriminate	• Examination of larger social and institutional dimensions of human life • Legitimacy of social arrangements • Competing interests • Dynamics of power and privilege • Nature and structure of bureaucracy • Influence and force of language • Redress for institutionalized injustice • Politics of recognition and redistribution
Community	Furman (2003a, 2003b, 2004) Bellah et al. (1985)	Community (rather than the individual person) as the moral agent	• Community-building and communities of practice • Continuous and recursive processes of community • Interpersonal and group awareness • Respectful listening • Empathetic knowing and understanding of others • Effective communication • Partnering and working together • Supporting and encouraging dialog in open and equal forums
Profession	Shapiro & Stefkovich (2001, 2005, 2011) Stefkovich & O'Brien (2004) Stefkovich (2006, 2011)	Student's best interests	• Essential nature of individual student rights • Duty of responsibility to others for a common interest • Respect as mutual acknowledgement of the other as having worth, value, and dignity unto themselves • Problematized decision making • Understanding of professional choices as informed by one's moral reasoning and deliberation, personal values and beliefs, professional norms, and adherence to ethical principles
Virtue	Starratt (2004) Begley (2005)	Character traits and dispositions necessary to think and act morally as an educational leader	• Responsibility • Authenticity • Presence • Reflective self-honesty • Relational sensitivity • Dialogical openness

THE DIMENSION OF TURBULENCE THEORY AND ITS APPLICATION

Students and practitioners of educational leadership must see the moral situations and ethical dilemmas they face in the context of varying degrees of turbulence. To further this understanding Gross (1998, 2004, 2014) developed Turbulence Theory. Specifically, turbulence can be seen in one of four levels, ranging from light, moderate, severe, and extreme (see Table 1.3). Understanding the levels of turbulence and being able to frame these within a context through a turbulence gauge (Gross, 2004) is useful since this allows educational leaders to escape from the unrealistic concept that all turbulence is of equal magnitude. In a similar way, it is critical that educational leaders understand that turbulence is neither a purely positive nor a negative entity but rather a constant force in our environment that one strives to work with. In order to attain this level of responsiveness with turbulence, it is vital for leaders to understand the drivers of turbulence. These include positionality, or the perspective that each person in a given situation has regarding the current turbulence; cascading, or the events surrounding the current turbulence that have an impact on how that turbulence is perceived; and stability, or the strength or weakness of a given organization or relationship that is experiencing turbulence (Gross, 2014).

Finally, Multiple Ethical Paradigms (MEP), as defined by Shapiro and Stefkovich (2010), can be used with Turbulence Theory to help guide responses to ethical dilemmas (Shapiro and Gross, 2013). In this case, educational leaders learn to gauge current levels of turbulence in a given situation. Consider which of the ethical lenses best informs a possible response, and predict changes in turbulence that might result.

LEARNING ACTIVITY 1.3

- Examine the case study scenario according to each of the ethical themes (justice, care, critique, community, profession, and virtue). Consider how Richard might have handled the situation differently by applying each theme separately. For example, how would applying the ethic of justice have affected Richard's decision making? How would this differ if applying the ethic of care? Critique? Community? Profession? Virtue?
- After examining each ethical theme separately, consider whether a single ethical theme or combination of themes would be most appropriate for guiding Richard's decision making in this scenario. Explain your reasoning.
- Using Table 1.3, gauge the levels of turbulence in this situation and predict how various responses to the situation might change the levels of turbulence.
- Based on your analysis, how should Richard respond to the Director of Secondary Education?

Table 1.3 Degrees of Turbulence found in Educational Institutions

Degree of Turbulence	General Definition
Light	Associated with ongoing issues, little or no disruption in normal work environment, subtle signs of stress.
Moderate	Widespread awareness of the issue, specific origins.
Severe	Fear for the entire enterprise, possibility of large-scale community demonstrations, a feeling of crisis.
Extreme	Structural damage to the school's normal operation is occurring. Collapse of the reform seems likely.

Source: From Gross, S. J. (2014). Using turbulence theory to guide actions. In Bransons, C. M., Gross, S. J. (Eds.). *Handbook on Ethical Educational Leadership* (pp. 246–262). New York: Routledge.

In this way, educators have a practical yet theoretically informed process with which to reflect and act in the midst of ethical dilemmas.

LEADERSHIP RESPONSIBILITY VS. MANAGERIAL HEROISM

We challenge prospective and incumbent leaders to understand, reflect, and act upon a high level of ethical awareness in an educational environment that is turbulent and filled with dilemmas and contradictions. On one hand, there is the pathway of the traditional, transactional administrator who follows the dictates of her/his organization and the state. On the other hand is the direction of the transformative leader who understands the foundations of education deeply and also knows how to navigate his/her school and school system in an era typified by ethical dilemmas. Table 1.4 demonstrates the difference between and tensions inherent between these two approaches (Gross, 2009; Gross & Shapiro, 2016).

While we accept the premise that leadership is rarely either/or, we believe that educational leaders who aspire toward the New DEEL vision in Table 1.4 are more likely to achieve the goal of supporting academic and social success for students. One reason for this belief is that this approach to leadership is an example of replacing accountability with responsibility, which in our view is a more dynamic a force.

In addition, the leadership profiled in Table 2.4 requires building the kinds of alliances within and especially beyond the school's boundaries that make academic and social success for students at least a potentially achievable goal. School leaders can add considerably to the academic and social success of students, but they cannot do so in isolation. We agree with Welner and Mathis (2015) when they assert:

> Well-supported schools with substantial resources can make an important difference in these children's lives, but it is not realistic to expect schools to be the nation's primary anti-poverty program. Doing so is as unfair to children as it is to educators. It is a false promise.
>
> (p. 3)

Table 1.4 New DEEL Vision

New DEEL (Democratic, Ethical Educational Leadership) Vision for Leaders[1]	Behavior of Traditional School Administrators
Transformational	Transactional
Guided by inner sense of responsibility to students, families, the community and social development on a world scale.	Driven by an exterior pressure of accountability to those above in the organizational/political hierarchy.
Leads from an expansive community-building perspective. A democratic actor who understands when and how to *shield* the school from turbulence, and when and how to *use* turbulence to facilitate change.	Bound by the system and the physical building. A small part of a monolithic, more corporate structure.
Integrates the concepts of democracy, social justice, and school reform through scholarship, dialogue, and action.	Separates democracy and social justice from guiding vision and accepts school improvement (a subset of school reform) as the dominant perspective.
Operates from a deep understanding of ethical decision making in the context of a dynamic, inclusive, democratic vision.	Operates largely from a perspective of the ethic of justice wherein obedience to authority and current regulations is largely unquestioned despite one's own misgivings.
Sees one's career as a calling and has a well-developed sense of mission toward democratic social improvement that cuts across political, national, class, gender, racial, ethnic, and religious boundaries.	Sees one's career in terms of specific job titles with an aim to move to ever greater positions of perceived power within the current system's structure.

1. The New DEEL is a partner Center of the UCEA Consortium for the Study of Leadership and Ethics in Education. It is an action-oriented partnership dedicated to inquiry into the nature and practice of democratic ethical educational leadership through sustained processes of open dialogue, right to voice, community inclusion, and responsible participation toward the common good. Members of the organization strive to facilitate democratic ethical decision-making in educational theory and practice.

Source: From Gross, S. J., & Shapiro, J. P. (2016). *Democratic ethical educational leadership: Reclaiming school reform*. New York: Routledge.

LEARNING ACTIVITY 1.4

- Reflect on a situation that you have faced in which a policy conflicted with what you felt was in the best interest of an individual student or the larger community. Describe the competing interests involved.
- How might you have used the tools provided in this chapter to navigate the situation? Consider alternative decisions and solutions based on your understanding of ethical leadership as presented in this chapter.
- Locate the vision statement and related goals for your school or district. Evaluate how these statements reflect an ethical commitment to supporting

students' academic and social success. Consider important school or district policies in relation to these vision and goal statements. Identify potential conflicts related to accountability vs. responsibility for students' academic and social success.

- Make a list of potential community resources and partners who could help further your school or district's vision for student success.

CONCLUSION

The PSEL (2015) rightly emphasize the need for collective responsibility (moral accountability) for *every* student's academic and social success and a "system" by which to realize this aspiration. Even more central to this apparent injunction is the commitment to adhere to ethical principles and professional norms that nurture the development of schools that place children *at the center* of education.

SUMMARY OF KEY POINTS

- Professional reflexivity can help educational leaders negotiate competing and often conflicting interests and accountabilities.
- Responsibility, or internal accountability, reflects an educational leader's internalized value system and serves as an antidote to the multiple external accountabilities that might compromise students' best interests.
- Multiple ethical paradigms can help guide educational leaders' decision making, although none of these paradigms (separately or together) can fully speak to the purposes and processes associated with moral, democratic school communities.
- In addition to evaluating the competing accountabilities contributing to an ethical dilemma, educational leaders can gauge the levels of turbulence in a given situation to inform their decision making.
- Moral, democratic school communities require attention to collaborative relationships between adults and youth, collective ownership and commitment, and the role of whole communities in the work of schooling.

IMPORTANT RESOURCES

Investigate these important organizations:

Broader, BOLDER Approach to Education In affiliation with Economic Policy Institute

- Sign up for the BBA e-newsletter
  Mailing address:
  Broader, Bolder Approach to Education
  1333 H Street NW
  Suite 300, East Tower
  Washington, DC 20005
  Website: www.boldapproach.org/

Coalition of Essential Schools

- Sign up for the CES e-newsletter
  Mailing address:
  Coalition of Essential Schools
  482 Congress Street, Suite 500A
  Portland, ME 04101
  Website: http://essentialschools.org/

National Education Policy Center

- Sign up for the NEPC e-distribution list
  Mailing address:
  National Education Policy Center
  School of Education, 249 UCB
  University of Colorado
  Boulder, Colorado 80309–0249
  Website: http://nepc.colorado.edu/contact

Listen to a constructive debate about many of the issues presented in this chapter:

The Diane Rehm Show
WAMU 88.5 | American University Radio | National Public Radio (NPR)
"Rethinking Standardized Testing"
Broadcast on Wednesday, 18 February 2015, 11 am (Eastern)
Website: http://thedianerehmshow.org/shows/2015–02–18/rethinking_
standardized_testing

Locate the following articles within UCEA's *Journal of Cases in Educational Leadership* (JCEL) for additional opportunities to apply the concepts and tools presented in this chapter:

Brinson, Lovett, & Price (2004). *A Matter of Principle*.
Kearney & Smith (2009). *Taps for the High Stakes Test*.

Mackenzie (2005). *Who Should Make Decisions?: A High School Wrestles With Tracking*.

Salmonowicz (2008). *Grades and Graduation: An Ethical Dilemma*.

Try applying Tuana's (2007) ethical sensitivity and reasoning process that informs one's moral literacy. The circular and deliberative cycle is much different than the typical staged, linear solution identification and action planning approach to problem solving.

NOTES

1. Portions of this section are taken from Frick, W. C. (2009). Principals' value-informed decision making, intrapersonal moral discord, and pathways to resolution: The complexities of moral leadership praxis. *Journal of Educational Administration, 47*(1), 50–74.
2. Portions of this section are taken from Frick, J. E., & Frick, W. C. (2010). An ethic of connectedness: Enacting moral school leadership through programs and people. *Education, Citizenship, and Social Justice, 5*(2), 117–130. DOI: 10.1177/1746197910370729.

REFERENCES

Adkins, A. W. H. (1978). "Theoria" versus "praxis" in the Nicomachean Ethics and the Republic. *Classical Philology, 73*, 297–312.

Apple, M. (1982). *Education and power*. Boston, MA: Routledge Kegan Paul.

Aristotle (1989). *Nicomachean ethics*. Trans. M. Ostwald. New York: Macmillan Publishing Company. (Original work, 334–323 BCE).

Aviv, R. (2014, July 21). Wrong answer: In an era of high-stakes testing, a struggling school made a shocking choice. *The New Yorker*, 54–65.

Beck, L. G. (1994). *Reclaiming educational administration as a caring profession*. New York: Teachers College Press.

Begley, P.T. (2000). Values and leadership: Theory development, new research, and an agenda for the future. *The Alberta Journal of Educational Research, 46*(3) 233–249.

Begley, P. T. (2005). Ethics matters: New expectations for democratic educational leadership in a global community. University Park, PA: Rock Ethics Institute.

Bellah, R., Madsen, R., Sullivan, W., Swidler, A, & Tipton, S. (1985). *Habits of the heart: Individualism and commitment in American life*. Berkley, CA: University of California Press.

Carnoy, M., Elmore, R. F., & Siskin, L. S. (2003). *The new accountability: High schools and high stakes testing*. New York: RoutledgeFalmer.

Crew, R. (2007). *Only connect: The way to save our schools*. New York: Farrar, Straus and Giroux.

Cuban, L. (2001). *How can I fix it? Finding solutions and managing dilemmas: An educator's road map*. New York: Teachers College Press.

Dionne, E. J. (2012). *Our divided political heart: The battle for the American idea in an age of discontent*. New York: Bloomsbury USA.

Firestone, W. A., & Shipps, D. (2005). How do leaders interpret conflicting accountabilities to improve student learning. In W. A. Firestone, & C. Riehl (Eds.), *A new agenda for research in educational leadership*. New York: Teachers College Press.

Foster, W. (1986). *Paradigms and promises: New approaches to educational administration.* Buffalo, NY: Prometheus Books.

Freire, P. (1986). *Pedagogy of the oppressed.* New York: Continuum.

Frick, W. C. (2011). Practicing a professional ethic: Leading for students' best interests. *American Journal of Education, 117*(4), 527–562.

Frick, W. C. (Ed.). (2013). *Educational management turned on its head/Exploring a professional ethic for educational leadership: A critical reader.* New York: Peter Lang.

Frick, W. C., & Tribble, J. T. (2012). An investigation of elementary public school administrators' ethical reasoning in considering "the best interests of the student". *Scholar-Practitioner Quarterly, 6*(3), 307–328.

Frick, W. C., Faircloth, S. C., & Little, K. S. (2013). Responding to the collective and individual "best interests of students": Revisiting the tension between administrative practice and ethical imperatives in special education leadership. *Educational Administration Quarterly, 49*(2), 207–242.

Furman, G. C. (2002). *School as community: From promise to practice.* Albany, NY: SUNY Press.

Furman, G. C. (2003a). The 2002 UCEA presidential address: Toward a 'new' scholarship of educational leadership. *UCEA Review, 45*(1), 1–6.

Furman, G. C. (2003b). Moral leadership and the ethic of community. *Values and Ethics in Educational Administration, 2*(1), 1–7.

Furman, G. C. (2004). The ethic of community. *Journal of Educational Administration, 42*(2), 215–235.

Furman, G. C., & Starratt, R. J. (2002). Leadership for democratic community in schools. In J. Murphy (Ed.), *The educational leadership challenge: Redefining leadership for the 21st century* (pp. 105–133). Chicago, IL: National Society for the Study of Education.

Gilkey, L. (1993). *Nature, reality, and the sacred.* Minneapolis, MN: Augsburg-Fortress Press.

Gilligan, C. (1982). *In a different voice.* Cambridge, MA: Harvard University Press.

Giroux, H. A. (1992). *Border crossings: Cultural workers and the politics of education.* New York: Routledge.

Green, T. F. (1987). The conscience of leadership. In L. Shieve, & M. Schoenheit (Eds.), *Leadership: examining the elusive. 1987 Yearbook.* Alexandria, VA: Association for Supervision and Curriculum Development.

Green, T. F. (1990). The value of 'values'. *Career Development Quarterly, 38*(3), 208–212.

Greene, M. (1995). *Releasing the imagination: Essays on education, the arts and social change.* San Francisco, CA: Jossey-Bass.

Greenfield, W. D. (1999). Moral leadership in schools: Fact or fancy? Paper presented at the Annual Meeting of the American Educational Research Association, Montreal, Quebec, Canada, April.

Greenfield, W. D. (1985). Moral, social, and technical dimensions of the principalship. *Peabody Journal of Education, 63*(1), 130–149.

Gross, S. J. (1998). Staying centered: Curriculum leadership in a turbulent era. Alexandria, VA: Association of Supervision and Curriculum Development.

Gross, S. J. (2004). Promises kept: Sustaining innovative curriculum leadership. Alexandria, VA: Association of Supervision and Curriculum Development.

Gross, S. (2009). (Re-)constructing a movement for social justice in our profession. In A. H. Normore (Ed.), *Leadership for social justice: Promoting equity and excellence through inquiry and reflective practice* (pp. 257–266). Charlotte, NC: Information Age Publishing.

Gross, S. J. (2014). Using turbulence theory to guide actions. In Branson, C.M., Gross, S. J. (Eds.), *Handbook on ethical educational leadership* (pp. 246–262). New York: Routledge.

Gross, S. J., & Shapiro, J. P. (2016). *Democratic ethical educational leadership: Reclaiming school reform.* New York: Routledge.

Gross, S. J., Shaw, K., & Shapiro, J. P. (2003). Deconstructing accountability through the lens of democratic philosophies: Toward a new analytic framework. *The Journal of Research for Educational Leadership, 1*(3), 5–27.

Gutmann, A. (Ed.). (1994). *Multiculturalism: Examining the politics of recognition.* Princeton, NJ: Princeton University Press.

Habermas, J. (1992). *Autonomy and solidarity: Interviews with Jügen Habermas* (rev. ed.). London: Verso.

Hightower, B., & Klinker, J. (2012). When ethics and policy collide. *Journal of Cases in Educational Leadership, 15*(2), 103–111.

Hinman, L. M. (2008). *Ethics: A pluralistic approach to moral theory.* Belmont, CA: Thomas Wadsworth.

Hodgkinson, C. (1978). *Towards a philosophy of administration.* Oxford: Basil Blackwell.

Hodgkinson, C. (1991). *Educational leadership: The moral art.* Albany, NY: SUNY Press.

Hout, M., & Elliott, S. W. (2011). *Incentives and test-based accountability in education.* Washington, DC: National Academies Press.

Hoy, W. K., & Miskel, C. G. (2013). *Educational administration: Theory, research, and practice.* (9th ed.). New York: McGraw-Hill.

Hursh, D. (2007). Assessing No Child Left Behind and the rise of neoliberal education policies. *American Educational Research Journal, 44*(3), 493–518.

Kirp, D. L. (2011). *Kids first: Five big ideas for transforming children's lives.* New York: Public Affairs.

Knapp, M. S., Copland, M. A., & Talbert, J. E. (2003). *Leading for learning: Reflective tools for school and district leadership.* Seattle, WA: Center for the Study of Teaching and Policy.

Kozleski, E. B., & Thorius, K. K. (Eds.). (2014). *Ability, equity and culture: Sustaining inclusive urban education reform.* New York: Teachers College Press.

Kozol, J. (2005). *The shame of the nation: The restoration of apartheid schooling in America.* New York: Crown Publishers.

Lakomski, G. (1987). Values and decision making in educational administration. *Educational Administration Quarterly, 23*(3), 70–82.

Madaus, G. F., Scriven, M., & Stufflebeam, D. L. (Eds.). (1983). *Evaluation models: Viewpoints on educational and human services evaluation.* Boston, MA: Kluwer-Nijhoff.

Mehta, J. (2013). The penetration of technocratic logic into the educational field: Rationalizing schooling from the progressives to the present. *Teachers College Record, 115*(5), 1–36.

Noddings, N. (1988). An ethic of caring and its implications for instructional arrangements. *American Journal of Education, 96*(2), 215–230.

Noddings, N. (1993). Caring: A feminist perspective. In K. A. Strike, & P. L. Ternasky (Eds.), *Ethics for professionals in education* (pp. 43–53). New York: Teachers College Press.

Noddings, N. (1996). On community. *Educational Theory, 46*(3), 245–267.

Noddings, N. (2002). *Educating moral people: A caring alternative to character education.* New York: Teachers College Press.

Rawls, J. (1993) *Political liberalism.* New York: Columbia University Press.

Roosevelt, G. (2006). The triumph of the market and the decline of liberal education: Implications for civic life. Teachers College Press, *108*(7), 1404–1423.

Rose, M. (2009). *Why school? Reclaiming education for all of us.* New York: The New Press.

Rothstein, R. (2004). *Class and schools: Using social, economic, and educational reform to close the black–white achievement gap.* New York: Teachers College Press.

Santoro, D. A. (2011). Good teaching in difficult times: Demoralization in the pursuit of good work. *American Journal of Education, 118*(1), 1–23.

Scherer, M. (2009). *Engaging the whole child: Reflections on best practices in learning, teaching, and leadership.* Alexandria, VA: Association for Supervision and Curriculum Development.

Schlechty, C. (2009). *Leading for learning: How to transform schools into learning organizations.* San Francisco, CA: Jossey-Bass.

Sergiovanni, T. J. (1992). *Moral leadership: Getting to the heart of school improvement.* San Francisco, CA: Jossey-Bass.

Sergiovanni, T. J. (2009). *The principalship: A reflective practice perspective* (6th ed.). Boston, MA: Allen & Bacon.

Sergiovanni, T. J., & Starratt R. J. (1993). *Supervision: A redefinition.* New York: McGraw-Hill.

Shapiro, J. P., & Gross, S. J. (2013) *Ethical educational leadership in turbulent times: (Re)solving moral dilemmas* (2nd ed.). New York: Routledge.

Shapiro, J. P., & Stefkovich, J. A. (2001). *Ethical leadership and decision making in education: Applying theoretical perspectives to complex dilemmas.* Mahwah, NJ: Lawrence Erlbaum.

Shapiro, J. P., & Stefkovich, J. A. (2005). *Ethical leadership and decision making in education: Applying theoretical perspectives to complex dilemmas* (2nd ed.). Mahwah, NJ: Lawrence Erlbaum Associates.

Shapiro, J. P., & Stefkovich, J. A. (2011). *Ethical leadership and decision making in education: Applying theoretical perspectives to complex dilemmas* (4th ed.). New York: Routledge.

Simmons, J. M. (2014). The pedagogy of emancipatory leadership: Reinventing Freire to neutralize and deconstruct the current neoliberal educational climate. *UCEA Review, 55*(3), 24–26.

Simon, H. (1957). *Models of man.* New York: John Wiley & Co.

Smith, M. S., & O'Day, J. (1991). Systemic school reform. In S. Furman & B. Malen (Eds.), *The politics of curriculum and testing* (pp. 233–268). Philadelphia, PA: Falmer Press.

Starratt, R. J. (1994). *Building an ethical school: A practical response to the moral crisis in schools.* London: Falmer.

Starratt, R. J. (2004). *Ethical leadership.* San Francisco, CA: Jossey-Bass.

Starratt, R. J. (2006). Cultivating the moral character of learning and teaching: A neglected dimension of educational leadership. Keynote speech presented at CCEAM Conference. www.topkinisis.com/conference/CCEAM/wib/index/outline/Starratt%2OR.pdf

Starratt, R. J. (2008). Responsible leadership. *The Educational Forum, 69*(2), 124–133.

Stefkovich, J. A. (2006). *Best interests of the student: Applying ethical constructs to legal cases in education.* Mahwah, NJ: Lawrence Erlbaum.

Stefkovich, J. A. (2011). *Best interests of the student: Applying ethical constructs to legal cases in education* (2nd ed.). Mahwah, NJ: Lawrence Erlbaum.

Stefkovich, J. A. (2014). *Best interests of the student: Applying ethical constructs to legal cases in education* (2nd ed.). New York: Routledge.

Stefkovich, J., & O'Brien, M. (2004). Best interests of the student: An ethical model. *Journal of Educational Administration, 42*(2), 197–214.

Strike, K. A. (2007). *Ethical leadership in schools: Creating community in an environment of accountability.* Thousand Oaks, CA: Corwin Press.

Strike K. A., Haller E. J., & Soltis J. F. (1998). *The ethics of school administration* (2nd ed.). New York: Teachers College Press.

Sullivan, W. M. (1986). *Reconstructing public philosophy.* Berkley, CA: University of California Press.

Talbert J. E. (2011). Collaborative inquiry to expand student achivement in New York City Schools. In J. O'Day, C. Bitter, & L. Gomez (Eds.). *Education reform in New York City: Ambitious change in the nation's most complex school system.* Cambridge, MA: Harvard Education Press.

Taylor, C. (1994) The politics of recognition. In A. Gutmann (Ed.), *Multiculturalism* (pp. 25–73). Princeton, NJ: Princeton University Press.

Tuana, N. (2007). Conceptualizing moral literacy. *Journal of Educational Administration, 45*(4), 364–378.

Wagner, T. (2001). Leadership for learning: An action theory of school change. *Phi Delta Kappan, 82*(5), 378–383.

Walker, K. (1998). Jurisprudential and ethical perspectives of "the best interests of children." *Interchange, 29*(3), 287–308.

Welner, K. G., & Mathis, W. J. (2015). Reauthorization of the Elementary and Secondary Education Act: Time to move beyond test-focused policies. NEPC Policy Memo. Boulder, CO: University of Colorado.

Wenger, E. (1998). *Communities of practice: Learning, meaning, and identity.* Cambridge, UK: Cambridge University Press.

Willower, D. J. (1994). Values, valuation, and explanation in school organizations. *Journal of School Leadership, 4*, 466–483.

Willower, D. J., & Licata, J. W. (1997). *Values and valuation in the practice of educational administration.* Thousand Oaks, CA: Corwin Press.

CHAPTER 2

Modeling Ethical Leadership

Being an Ethical Leader Means Modeling Principles of Self-Awareness, Reflective Practice, Transparency, and Ethical Behavior

Marla Susman Israel and Lisa Bass

CHAPTER OVERVIEW

In this chapter, the authors discuss the importance of the school leader's role in promoting ethical leadership through self-awareness, reflective practice, transparency and ethical behavior. Authors emphasize how ethical leaders strive to lead by example and this chapter illuminates the habits of mind and behaviors such leaders display in their daily practice in schools. Within this chapter, the narrative and activities are designed to help the student of educational leadership clarify his or her own beliefs in a wider context and consider ways of reasoning through challenging ethical dilemmas in the volatile environments that typify the 21st-century educational milieu. Clarifying the competing interests within an ethical dilemma along with the act of moral reasoning create the foundation for transparency in one's leadership practices. Flowing from this self-awareness, self-authorship, enhanced ethical reasoning, and authentic leadership are approaches to leadership that define transparency. This transparent, moral leadership includes a commitment to shared governance, an open process in decision-making and agenda setting, and an inclusive orientation to the wider community beyond the school walls.

This chapter is intended to provide future and practicing administrators with a mindful framework for constructing the questions necessary to realize the moral dimensions that are currently at stake in our educational institutions in order to build reasoning, motivation, and implementation strategies to solve these ethical dilemmas as they arise within our schools (Rest, et al., 1999). It is the intent that the aspiring leader will be able to display and to eventually own "preferred patterns of professional practice" (Ozar, 1994), not only in relation to student academic outcomes, but also in the critical areas of students' social emotional learning and democratic citizenship development, which are not measured through the current high-stakes college and career ready assessments that drive today's accountability systems. This chapter rests on the belief that when an educational leader practices professional ethical behavior that is aligned with his/her own personal ethical belief system, that this leader will act with integrity and transparency truly fulfilling his/her vocation. This vocation is the call to lead schools with "moral purpose writ large—principled behavior connected to something greater than ourselves that *relates* to human and social development" (Fullan, 2002, p.14)

INTRODUCTION

Today's schools demand that educational leaders think deeply and act ethically in their roles as advocates for "the best interest of the child" (Stefkovich, 2013). Leaders in educational settings at all levels are continually challenged with complex ethical dilemmas that require deep reflection and understanding. As our profession looks to refine and revise its standards, this deep reflection resulting in ethical action is articulated through the expansion of the National Educational Leadership Standards (NELP) for building leaders, Standard 2.1. Professional Norms states: "Program completers *understand and demonstrate* the capability to enact the professional norms of integrity, fairness, transparency, trust, collaboration, perseverance, learning and continuous improvement in their actions, decision making and relationships with others." Likewise, Professional Standards for Educational Leaders (PSEL) Standard 2 b.) states: "Effective leaders act according to and promote the professional norms of integrity, fairness, transparency, trust, collaboration, perseverance, learning and continuous improvement." This intentional articulation of three distinct behaviors of mind and practice signals the importance of the educational leader as an individual who not only is self-aware of the ethical dilemmas he/she wrestles with on a daily basis, but is also an individual whose leadership behavior is transparently modeling the ethical ideals that drive the work to serve children, parents and their communities.

Aspiring leaders need to see themselves as educational thinkers and doers who understand the responsibility inherent in educating other people's children. Equally, they need to be aware of, and utilize, the multiple perspectives of ethical reasoning to enhance their practice especially under less than ideal conditions. Finally, educational leaders need to value the elements of shared governance and open decision-making that lead to transparency of actions. Working in concert with a professional code of ethics is the individual's own epistemology, specifically as it relates to the role of education for children, families and the community. Yet in an era that focuses on, and rewards, accountability and compliance rather than responsibility and fidelity, deep thinking and transparent decision-making are often pushed aside for the sake of expediency. Far from seeking to establish one best or ideal perspective, the intention of this chapter is to help each aspiring and current educational leader to understand her or his own way of understanding the world and then to link these core values to the profession's code(s) of ethical behavior in order to act in "the best interest of the child."

In order to respond effectively to such problems, leaders must have an expanded understanding of ethical lenses. This means being able to reason, utilizing the Multiple Ethical Paradigms (MEP) (Shapiro & Stefkovich, 2005), including the ethics of justice, care, critique, and the profession as well as the ethic of the community which have been discussed in the previous chapter. Further, students of educational leadership must see the ethical dilemmas they face within the context of today's students, teachers and communities in which they come to serve. Educational leaders must act with integrity, or rather they must integrate their ethical reasoning with their ethical behavior in order to model this deep thinking and action for others in the school community.

Within educational leadership there are multiple influences that have the power and authority to "lead us away from the path that best embodies who we were meant to be" (Neafsey, 2003, p. xi). With conflicting federal, state and judicial mandates, and an ever-increasing diverse and global population to educate within our public schools, school leaders are often faced with ethical dilemmas concerning students, their families, and the educational community at large within an environment of diminishing resources and education-bashing. To begin to address these ethical dilemmas, and the multiple influences vying for attention, the educational leader must be able to articulate to him/herself and for others (the important stakeholders within the school community) what is morally at stake in the situation and must possess ethical reasoning and self-awareness skills, leading to judgments about what ought to be done, given what is morally at stake in the situation (Ozar, 2001a and b). In short, an aspiring leader who wants to model ethical leadership for others must develop self-authorship, authenticity and ethical reasoning skills in order to demonstrate consistent ethical behavior.

Unpacking the Standard: Implications for School Leaders

NELP 2.1: Program completers understand and demonstrate the capability to enact the professional norms of integrity, fairness, transparency, trust, collaboration, perseverance, learning and continuous improvement in their actions, decision making and relationships with others.
PSEL 2b. Effective leaders act according to and promote the professional norms of integrity, fairness, transparency, trust, collaboration, perseverance, learning, and continuous improvement.

Building a Self-Authored Leader. As educational administrators continue to feel increased pressure to meet the demands of state and national accountability through the Common Core State Standards and the national standards and assessment movement, ethical decision-making has become increasingly difficult. High-stakes testing is inextricably linked to funding, jobs, and prestige and therefore places pressure on administrators to perform at high levels or perform unethically to meet those standards (Israel & Marks, 2011). This is evidenced by the increase in the changing of grades on standardized tests in Georgia schools and most recently in

Washington, DC (Kerchner, 2013). At the time of publication, investigations were ongoing in Washington State, New Jersey, and Pennsylvania.

Neill, Grisbond & Schaeffer (2004) posited that standardized testing first mandated by NCLB, and later, the Common Core, added undue burden to public schools because of their inauthentic accountability standards. For these reasons, not every state adopted these standards, and among those that did, many rapidly repealed them. These standards, less than perfect for promoting inclusive practices, may make it even more difficult to reach students in urban schools and schools with higher populations of second-language learners, racial minority populations, and low socioeconomic status families (Abedi 2004; Boaler, 2003). Abedi and Dietel (2004) noted: "NCLB establishes high expectations for all students and seeks to reduce the achievement gap between advantaged and disadvantaged students. These are worthy goals, which require extraordinary improvement in student learning. These challenges for English language learners are especially difficult" (p. 1).

These increased pressures call on educational administrators to act ethically in creating opportunities for student growth and instructor success through meaningful support systems. Additionally, educational leaders must act authentically and ethically in reporting gains in educational attainment on standardized testing regardless of the personal costs, such as sanctions and possible job loss (Israel & Marks, 2011). Fulfilling these tasks requires educational leaders to have a deep understanding of their values and beliefs, their relationships with others in educational organizations, and, in turn, align their actions with those values and beliefs. Self-authorship, first explored by Kegan (1994), but applied to college students by Baxter Magolda (2004) provides a model for understanding how people congruently align their values with their actions. Additionally, authentic leadership, as an inextricable actionable behavior emerges from one's ability to be a self-authored individual. These combined frameworks map onto the ethical decision-making processes of educational leaders as they navigate experiences within their school contexts. Baxter Magolda's framework (2004) is highlighted here because it aligns well with the intentions of NELP Standard 2.1, as well as with the aims and purposes of this chapter. It lays a foundation for self-awareness, which is integral to values espoused in NELP Standard 2.1 as well as PSEL Standard 2b.

Self-Authorship Meaning-Making. While the model was initially designed for college students, Baxter Magolda (2008) recognized that self-authorship begins during college and continues to be developed across time through professional and personal engagements beyond a person's formal education. Therefore, university instructors have the ability to directly affect the development of students in educational leadership preparation programs through programming and curriculum.

There are three dimensions to self-authorship (see Figure 2.1). Each of these dimensions answers a section of a broader question: How do I know who I am and how do I want to construct relationships with others? The three components are: a) epistemological (how do I know); b) intrapersonal (who I am); and c) interpersonal (and how I want to construct relationships with others). The epistemological dimension regards one's ability to examine knowledge and from where knowledge comes. People critically analyze perspectives other than their own

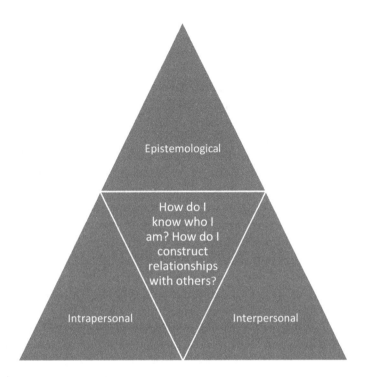

Figure 2.1 Dimensions of Self-Authorship

and reconcile new ideas with their own. The intrapersonal dimension requires one to reflect on their values. This dimension requires one to understand "one's particular history, confidence, the capacity for autonomy and connection, and integrity" (Baxter Magolda & King, 2004, p. 9). Last, the interpersonal dimension requires one to examine and appreciate differences and others' values. One is no longer threatened by difference. It allows one to engage in authentic relationship building.

Baxter Magolda (2008) described three elements in the building of a self-authored system. *Trusting the internal voice* describes a student's recognition that "reality, or what happened in the world and their lives, was beyond their control, but their reactions to what happened was within their control" (p. 279). Students in this phase must recognize, create, and own their emotions based on how they want to respond to a given situation. This allows them to control the situation, rather than having the situation control them. Students must trust their internal voices within the realms of self-authoring their lives (i.e., epistemologically, intrapersonally, interpersonally). Baxter Magolda (2008) noticed, "confusion, ambiguity, fear, and even despair as individuals struggled to analyze and reconstruct some aspect of their beliefs, identity, or relationships in various contexts" (p. 280); however, as the instructor supported the students, they began to build internal foundations.

Building internal foundations refers to creating a personal philosophy to guide one's reactions to the external situations affecting them. This phase requires students to coalesce all dimensions of self-authorship into a cohesive identity. Students may continue to refine their beliefs, values, and identity, but eventually come to a place where they have a core self-authored identity that connected their intellectual and emotional selves, and these selves begin to align with their actions.

The last element is *securing internal commitments.* Baxter Magolda (2008) noted that in this element "participants integrated their internal foundations and infrastructure with their external personal realities" (p. 281). Whereas in the previous element, students begin to align thoughts with action, in this element students live out those convictions in all aspects of their lives. Fear of the unknown and inability to control situations no longer paralyze action, and students are open to continual learning.

It is important to note that these elements are not linear, but rather cyclical as people interact with new people or are faced with new challenges. Meaning-making relies on personal support networks and may be experienced differently based on one's various social identities within a given context (e.g., sexual orientation, race, gender, ability, immigration status). Moving through these phases "initiates a reframing of relationships that become more authentic because they honor one's internal commitments" (Baxter Magolda, 2008, p. 282). This author believes that the process of self-authorship meaning-making must occur not only for college students, but also for educational leaders if they are to become self-authored leaders who know themselves and their ethical responsibilities to children, families and communities.

Authentic Leadership Development. Gardner, Avolio, Luthans, May and Walumbwa (2005) defined authenticity as "both *owning* one's personal experiences (values, thoughts, emotions and beliefs) and *acting* in accordance with one's true self, (expressing what one really thinks and believes and behaving accordingly)" (p. 344). Thus, there is a congruence of thought and action within all aspects of one's life. Importantly, authenticity is shaped by interactions with others, but is a result of one's perception of self within that social construct. Hence, Avolio and Gardner (2005) described authenticity in terms of achieving relative "levels of authenticity" (p. 320).

Expanding on the work of other authentic leadership researchers, Avolio and Gardner (2005) identified components of developing authentic leaders including *positive psychological capital, positive moral perspective, leader self-awareness, leader self-regulation, leadership processes/behaviors, follower self-awareness/regulation, follower development, organizational context,* and *veritable and sustained performance beyond expectations* (see Figure 2.2).

Positive psychological capital refers to "capacities of confidence, optimism, hope, and resiliency" (Avolio & Gardner, 2005, p. 322). This positive capital enables leaders to continue to formulate their self-awareness and self-regulatory behaviors. There is an inherent ethical and moral dimension to authentic leadership that they call *positive moral perspective.* This perspective refers to the "moral capacity, efficacy, courage, and resiliency" (p. 324). Important in this concept is that authentic leaders must act with a moral compass that points towards ethical decision-making, as one could theoretically be a *bad* authentic leader if their values are harmful and those values align with destructive behaviors. One gains *leader self-awareness* through

Figure 2.2 Components of Developing Authentic Leaders

reflection in an attempt to "gain clarity and concordance with respect to their core values, identity, emotions, motives and goals" (Gardner, et al., 2005, p. 347). What Avolio and Gardner (2005) add to the conversation is not that people only understand themselves, but that they understand themselves in relation to others (e.g., how they behave and are perceived). This leads to *leader self-regulation* or an alignment of value and actions. These actions turn into positive modeling, positive emotion, and optimism, defined as *leadership processes and behaviors*. This component is additionally characterized "when leaders display unbiased processing of self-relevant information, personal integrity, and an authentic relational orientation, leader–follower relationships will be characterized by high levels of respect, positive affect, and trust" (p. 326).

Authentic leadership is not only defined by a leader's ability to be authentic, but the cyclical and interlocking relationship between leader and follower (or "the other" as that one should not immediately assume superior-subordinate relations). The two following components of leader development are, in fact, the development of others. The two components mirror leader development in that there is *follower (other) self-awareness/regulation*, or the identification of values and identity, and in turn *follower (other) development*, or an internalization of those values that leads to their development over time.

Lastly, authentic leaders are developed by their *organizational contexts*. Contexts can be toxic; however, Avolio and Gardner (2005) suggested that for "leaders and followers to be effective, leaders must promote an inclusive organizational climate that enables themselves and followers to continually learn and grow" (see also Gardner et al., 2005; Luthans & Avolio, 2003). These positive, authentic learning environments turn into *veritable and sustained performance beyond expectations*. This performance is non-financial and refers to "tacit knowledge, including building human, social and psychological capital, and considering how the organization is fundamentally run, including psychological contracts with employees" (p. 328).

Ethical Leadership Development. The concepts of self-authorship and authentic leadership are clearly and inextricably linked. With self-awareness as the key component to both frameworks, it becomes even more important that people explore what their personal beliefs, values, morals, and identity mean to them as leaders. What Avolio and Gardner (2005) add to the conversation is not that people only understand themselves, but that they understand themselves in relation to others (e.g., how they behave and are perceived). This interplay of self and others requires leaders not only to define themselves in relation to their own personal beliefs, but rather to relate to the contexts in which they exist, including personal and organizational beliefs. Additionally, this relationship, between self and others, ties directly to the ethical decision-making capacity building of aspiring educational leaders. The opportunities that educational leadership educators provide to reflect on these values, beliefs, and identities, to construct meaning, and apply knowledge to actual lived contexts becomes extremely important to the development of self-authored authentic leaders.

Baxter Magolda (2004) noted that while self-authorship can happen over time, it occurs more intentionally through educational initiatives, or learning partnerships between instructor (or peers) and student. They forwarded The Learning Partnerships Model as a model for providing support in this development. The model has three assumptions and three principles. The first assumption is that knowledge is complex and socially constructed. Second, knowledge construction occurs when one can learn in relation to the self. Last, there is a mutual construction of knowledge between student, authorities, and peers. The author noted: "these three assumptions were not usually explicitly stated . . . they were, instead, enacted through the approach educators, employers, or other adults used [them]" (Baxter Magolda, 2004, p. 42). Therefore, all leadership development should occur through applying three principles to the learning experience of students.

The first principle is that colleagues within a profession must validate each other's capacity to know. This provides the capacity for a learner to construct knowledge with respect from peers and instructors. Second, learning is situated in the learners' experiences. Therefore, learning must occur in a context that is relevant and related to what the learner is experiencing outside the classroom by using expertise and knowledge to support learning. Last, there is a mutual construction of meaning. There is no authority on the subject. Rather, conversation, challenge, and support provide an opportunity for all learners (e.g., student, peers, instructors) to equally learn and grow from conversations in the classroom. The intent of this chapter is to provide the aspiring educational leader the time and space to construct self-authorship, authentic leadership, and ethical leadership in order to that the educational leader can then model these habits of mind and behaviors for others.

THE NATURE OF A PROFESSION

Dr. William Frick, quoting Robert Marzano, during his Brock Prize acceptance speech declares: "Education is so important and fundamental that the profession should have an oath" (public communication on April 5, 2008). And while educational leadership does not have an oath such as medicine "to do no harm," one could say that the professional oath for educational leaders would require that one always put "the best interests of the child" at the center of ethical decision making (Shapiro & Stefkovich, 2011). But whose child does one put at the center of the decision making? And when multiple children have competing interests, which child's needs (or interests) are put first? Are some needs privileged over others, and why? For example, a special education child may need multiple resources to provide her with the Least Restrictive Environment (LRE). This is not only an ethical decision, it is a legal mandate. But what about the gifted child who may also need multiple resources to provide her with the "least restrictive environment?" Note that the gifted child's least restrictive environment is not the law but rather an aspiration. Does one child's needs get trumped by the other child's needs because of limited finances and a legal mandate?

This is where *The American Association of School Administrators (AASA) Code of Ethics for Educational Leaders* may be helpful to the aspiring educational leader in understanding and prioritizing the often competing needs of the "best interests of multiple children." The *AASA Code of Ethics* reads as follows:

The educational leader:

1. Makes the education and well-being of students the fundamental value of all decision making.
2. Fulfills all professional duties with honesty and integrity and always acts in a trustworthy and responsible manner.
3. Supports the principle of due process and protects the civil and human rights of all individuals.
4. Implements local, state and national laws.
5. Advises the school board and implements the board's policies and administrative rules and regulations.

6. Pursues appropriate measures to correct those laws, policies, and regulations that are not consistent with sound educational goals or that are not in the best interest of children.

7. Avoids using his/her position for personal gain through political, social, religious, economic or other influences.

8. Accepts academic degrees or professional certification only from accredited institutions.

9. Maintains the standards and seeks to improve the effectiveness of the profession through research and continuing professional development.

10. Honors all contracts until fulfillment, release or dissolution mutually agreed upon by all parties.

11. Accepts responsibility and accountability for one's own actions and behaviors.

12. Commits to serving others above self.

(CCSS0, 2008)

Now immediately one can see that the best interest of the students is the #1 priority of these twelve statements within the profession's ethical code. And yet, this first statement lists students in the plural and not the student in the singular. So, what is one to do when there are competing, multiple student needs? Additionally, often in the best interest of the students, the educational leader needs to remove a teacher whose performance is unacceptable. And yet, the code states in both statement #3, through due process, and statement #4, that the educational leader must uphold local, state and national laws. This explicitly means that one must provide the teacher displaying unacceptable performance due process and a full remediation plan of action before one can dismiss for unacceptable teaching. And yet, the children only get to be in third grade once while the teacher's remediation process may last multiple months and even years. How is this putting the "best interests of the child" at the "center of the decision making?" (Shapiro & Stefkovich, 2011). So, what should the educational leader do?

As was stated previously, self-reflection, through the development of self-authoring, is critical for the aspiring educational leader to begin this ethical decision-making process. It is important for an educational leader to understand his/her core values and the school district's core values in which he/she works. For the purposes of this chapter, the core values are the guiding principles (often called "the school/district mission"), and the personal and professional codes of ethics, that articulate what is right or wrong for the person, the professional, and the profession in the context of the organization and the community at-large.

LEARNING ACTIVITY 2.1

To begin to reveal and articulate one's core values as a process of self-authoring, the reader is encouraged to engage in the following self-reflection.

Ethical Codes and Mission

1. Find your school or district's mission.

   • What core values do you believe are highlighted in the mission?
   • What core values do you believe are missing from the mission?

   Review the AASA Code of Ethics for Educational Leaders. From this review answer the following questions:

   • Which statements do you agree with?
   • Which statements do you question? And why?
   • Which statements seem mutually exclusive to enact at the same time?
   • Which statements support your school's/district's mission?

2. Discuss your answers with a colleague.

   • Where do you find common agreement?
   • Where do you find differences in your discussion?

PROFESSIONAL OBLIGATIONS, VIRTUES, AND SACRIFICES

Rest's model of moral reasoning (1984, 1994, 1999), asks the individual to first become aware that there *is* a moral dilemma, and then requires the individual to develop reasoning skills and the motivation to implement a resolution. The first step of awareness is similar to self-authoring in that the educational leader needs to become aware of what he/she values, or holds dear as an educator, and uncover what the organization and the profession value, as well as recognize and understand where there are inherent competing values and tensions within and between each of these ever-widening concentric circles of the self who interacts with others (Begley, 2006). Often, internal confusion within the educational leader occurs when his/her core values align with some but not all of the multiple stakeholders' core values.

   Moral reasoning through religious teachings and virtues underscores a model of the "perfect man" with virtues such as goodness, kindness, honesty and even self-sacrifice (which is actually stated as item #12 in the aforementioned educational leadership code) as the touchstones for understanding core values and the ethical behavior that leaders should emulate (Gini & Green, 2013). The difficulty with using religious teachings and virtues as a foundation for core values is that they are often grounded in beliefs and habits of mind that are culturally or religiously driven and therefore offer competing visions of what these virtues really mean and what these behaviors actually look like for mere mortals in the 21st century.

Moral reasoning through the "iceberg of culture" asks the educational leader to understand diversity above and below "the water" (Lindsey, Roberts, & Campbell-Jones, 2013) in order to understand the core values for both the individual and the organization. One is to look deeper than food, fashion and festivals (above the water) to understand and uncover core values. One is asked to look below the water and understand the deeper culture, and hence core values, through the lens of cultural awareness and sensitivity. But again, as in the other forms of moral reasoning, using culture as a way to uncover core values is fraught with difficulties. Issues of respect, punishment and "duty to home" are just a few examples of culturally driven core values that can become ethical dilemmas within today's Western eurocentric educational environment.

Charlotte Danielson's (2002) "four circles model" for understanding ethics, leadership behavior and subsequent educational policy-making is another model of moral reasoning. Danielson asks the educational leader to look at what one believes from experience, knows through educational research, and wants for the students and community in order to craft a resolution for what ought to be done. Again, this model of moral reasoning asks the educational leader to self-reflect and self-author a path of behavior to guide positive polices for students and families in schools. But as one looks to who leads in today's schools, one can easily understand how individual core values and beliefs, as well as the research one cares to privilege, can alter the final ethical decision and subsequent behaviors and policies that ensue. Therefore, through self-reflection and self-authorship, it is critical for the educational leader to understand that what he/she may want for students and the community may not be aligned to actual community values and may translate to others as paternalistic policy regardless of original intent. This is where the transparency of the educational leader's ethical reasoning becomes so important.

Finally, Ozar (1994) defines nine categories of questions about professional obligations to use as a platform for moral reasoning. For purposes of this chapter, they have been customized to fit the profession of educational leadership and students in schools. They are the following:

1. Who is (are) the profession's chief client(s) and what do we owe these clients?
2. What are the central values of this profession in the best interest of students?
3. What is the ideal relationship between a member of this profession and a client?
4. What sacrifices are required of members of this profession and in what respects do the obligations of this profession take priority over other morally relevant considerations affecting its members?
5. What are the norms of competence for this profession?
6. What is the ideal ethical relationship between members of this profession and co-professionals?
7. What is the ideal ethical relationship between members of this profession and the larger community?
8. What ought the members of the profession of educational leaders do to make access to the profession's services available to everyone who needs them?
9. What are the members of the profession obligated to do to preserve the integrity of their commitment to its values and to educate others about them?

LEARNING ACTIVITY 2.2

Nine Categories of Questions about Professional Obligations

- Answer the aforementioned nine questions for how you envision the profession of educational administration.
- Discuss your answers with a colleague or classmate. Note the similarities and differences between your answers. Is there common ground?

LEARNING ACTIVITY 2.3

Writing Your own Professional Code of Ethics

- Review and reflect upon your readings, answers and conversations with others in regards to learning activities 2.1 and 2.2.
- Write a first draft of your own professional code of ethics. Compare your professional code of ethics with the current professional code (2008). You will revisit this draft code throughout this chapter.

CASE STUDY 2.1: CAN YOU KEEP ME SAFE?

It was 8:25 a.m. and the day was just beginning at the primary school. Each teacher met her students outside to escort them to the classroom. From the onset of the day, the co-teachers of one of the second-grade classrooms knew this wasn't going to be an ordinary day when Pablo walked into the school sobbing. The young boy could barely utter a few Spanish words when he was warmly greeted by his English-speaking teachers. Both the general education teacher and the special education teacher looked at each other with bewilderment, not knowing how to begin to assist the upset 8-year-old boy.

The child in this case is Pablo Guzman, a new English language learner (ELL) recently arrived from Ecuador. Pablo, born in the United States, has lived with his mother and older brother in South America since the parents' deportation four years ago. Currently the boy and his father rent a room from a neighborhood family as the two adjust to their new living arrangements, getting to know each other on a daily basis. The parents agreed that it was in the child's best interest to return to the U.S. because his schoolteachers were physically abusing Pablo due to his inappropriate behavior at the Ecuadorian public school. The father recounted that he could no longer afford to send his wife enough money to cover his son's medical expenses, since the boy was seeing therapists regularly. On several occasions Pablo had also mentioned that his older brother didn't love him and would often beat him when their mother wasn't home.

Needless to say, Pablo's transition has been anything but smooth, particularly because he has difficulty communicating in his native language, doesn't speak any English yet, has trouble following directions, trusting others, and socializing with his peers. Pablo disrupts his class several times a day, is disrespectful to his teachers, has pulled down his pants in class, and has shown aggressive behavior towards his classmates. While many of the Spanish-speaking children are eager to translate for Pablo and his teachers, the amount of off-task time for all the students is immense.

In an effort to assist the classroom teachers, both the English as a Second Language (ESL) and Spanish teachers have been serving as translators/guidance counselors/deans on a daily basis. At the teachers' requests, the father has been extremely cooperative in providing previous school records, medical documentation, and demonstrating complete willingness to work collaboratively with the school to assess the child's educational and neurological needs. Within the few short months Pablo has been at the primary school, the young boy is showing willingness to learn English and shown some academic and social progress in small groups.

Early that Monday morning, the special education teacher shuffled Pablo into a building, and coincidentally ran into the Spanish teacher in the stairwell. She kindly requested a translation to understand her student. Pablo told the Spanish teacher that his father had hit him with a belt the night before and again that morning because he wouldn't eat his meals. Although the boy's speech wasn't clear, the teacher could decipher the child's accusation. The Spanish teach knew for a fact that Pablo has never expressed this concern since his arrival at the primary school. As a Latina and mother, she understood the Hispanic culture's acceptance of spanking, empathized with the father's frustrations, and recognized that this could be an isolated incident. Based on her encounters with the father, she strongly believed that this was not a suspected case of child abuse. However, she also acknowledged that her colleague was expecting to hear an accurate translation of what the boy had stated.

The Spanish teacher knew what the consequences would be upon translating the boy's accusation and she feared what the father's reaction would be if this case was reported to the Department of Youth and Family Services (DYFS). She immediately recalled that during a previous meeting, Mr. Guzman had appeared defeated by the challenges of raising a special needs child alone in this country. He was so distraught that he had mentioned the possibility of sending Pablo back to live with his mother in Ecuador. Fearing for the boy's ultimate safety, she hesitated before translating her conversation with the little boy.

The Spanish teacher wondered if the father's illegal immigrant status might indeed cause him to send the boy back to Ecuador if he felt threatened after the school reported the case to the DYFS. Besides, what constituted "real" child abuse' an occasional spanking from his concerned father or the daily abuse at the hands of his Ecuadorian schoolteachers and older brother? She was sure that if she addressed this concern with the father herself, it could be handled without reporting it to the DYFS.

Lost in Translation: from Shapiro, J.P. & Stekovich, J.A. (2011). *Ethical leadership and decision making in education: Applying theoretical perspectives to complex dilemma* (3rd ed.). New York: Routledge (pp. 90—92).

LEARNING ACTIVITY 2.4

Case Role-Play for Lost in Translation

With classmates, act out the case Lost in Translation (or engage in "Readers' Theatre") to highlight each stakeholder involved. The following parts need to be filled:

1. Narrator
2. Pablo
3. Pablo's father
4. Special education teacher
5. Spanish teacher
6. Principal (off-stage)
7. Superintendent (off-stage)
8. The Bilingual Advisory Parent (BAP) Council (off-stage)
9. U.S. Congressman, Luis V. Gutierrez

LEARNING ACTIVITY 2.5

Case Analysis for Lost in Translation

Using the aforementioned MEP question constructs, answer the following questions for discussion:

1. How might the dilemma be resolved through the lens of utilitarianism—for the greater good?
2. How might the dilemma be resolved through the lens of deontology—the rule of law?
3. How might the dilemma be resolved through the lens of care—Care of Palo? Care of Pablos's father? Care for the Spanish teacher?

4. How might the dilemma be resolved through the lens of critique?—Whose voices are not heard? What is needed to be done so all voices involved are heard?

5. How might the dilemma be resolved through the lens of the profession?— What is expected of us as educational leaders? What is expected of us as educational leaders within the school and within the greater community?

LEARNING ACTIVITY 2.6

Defending an Ethical Position

For the case Lost in Translation, choose one ethical lens and answer the following questions. Be prepared to orally defend this analysis with the chosen ethical lens to the whole.

1. State the dilemma through your chosen ethical lens.
2. Identify all possible resolutions using this lens.
3. What ought to be done—using this ethical lens.
4. What is not considered using this ethical lens?

In Chapter 2 of this text, you read about Turbulence Theory (Gross, 2014; Gross in Shapiro and Gross, 2013) including the concepts of contextual forces, positionality, degree of turbulence, and possible consequences. For the purposes of this chapter, beginning self-authorship, authentic leadership development, and ethical leadership development, the following questions will be used as constructs for applying turbulence theory to the aforementioned case so that you can begin to articulate, make transparent, and model ethical reasoning and subsequent ethical behavior.

LEARNING ACTIVITY 2.7

Adding Turbulence Theory to the Case

1. First, review the website www.enriquesjourney.com to understand today's current immigration issues for children like Pablo and adults like Pablo's parents.
2. Then, for the case Lost in Translation, answer the following questions in light of today's current immigration reform context:

- What are the current contextual forces possibly affecting this case?
- What is at stake for each of the players in this case? What is at stake for the educational leaders involved in this school system?
- What are the possible consequences for each of the players in this case? What is at stake for the educational leaders involved in this school system?
- In light of your analysis of this case through the multiple ethical lenses of justice, care, critique and profession, and in light of your answers based on turbulence theory, how would you resolve this ethical dilemma? Be able to defend your resolution with others.

LEARNING ACTIVITY 2.8

Ethical Analysis Refined

1. Review your resolution from Learning Activity #6.
2. Review your Draft Professional Code of Ethics. Answer the following questions:

- Which pieces of your draft professional code of ethics did you not uphold (or actually broke) in your final resolution for Lost in Translation?
- Based on reviewing your resolution with your draft professional code of ethics would you modify your resolution? If so, how would you change your resolution and why?

LEARNING ACTIVITY 2.9

Ethical Codes Revisited

1. Reflect upon your draft professional code of ethics.
2. Keep and/or reconstruct all or part of your code.
3. If appropriate, rank order your values listed within your professional code.
4. Explain why you have kept or revised all or part of your code and its rankings in light of what you have learned.
5. Be sure that your code articulates and integrates your personal values of the ideal leader you want to be.
6. Articulate this code in both a written narrative form and then in a PowerPoint presentation that you would present to your faculty.

CONCLUSION

The purpose of this chapter was to help you, the aspiring leader become an ethical leader who models the principles of self-awareness, reflective practice, transparency and ethical behavior. Now, let's see how you can put all of this theory into practice with the next case study.

CASE STUDY 2.2: REALLY, YOU CAN KEEP ME SAFE?

Mrs. Alec Dean sat there with the loaded revolver in her hand and wondered what she would do now. Her school, P.S. 12 was now "a receiving school" after 54 schools had been closed in the City of Chicago for under-enrollment and poor academic performance. P.S. 12 was a "receiving school," one of the few on the west-side of the city where a disproportionate number of schools had been closed. P.S. 12 now received students from the original attendance area plus four other attendance areas. It was well-known that children from 7 different gangs now attended her K-8 elementary school. In order to ensure that children walking or taking the bus to school were safe crossing gang lines, the Board of Education had hired thousands of people to patrol the streets and provide safe-passage. But extra security personnel were not hired for inside the school walls where students were beginning to "stake out and claim" territory. Nor were extra security hired for children who chose to stay after school for extra help or extra-curricular activities.

Samaj Johnson was a likeable 11-year-old boy. He was one of the 300 new students now attending P.S. 12 after the mandated school closings. Of those 300 students, over 85% of these children were reading at 3 or more years below grade level. But not Samaj—he was a 5th grader reading at an 8th grade level. He was bright, studious, and a hard-worker. At his original home school, only two blocks away from his home, he had never been in any trouble. Now, while still living in the same housing project (pictured below) he needed to travel approximately 3 miles to get to P.S. 12, his new school. He now took a bus 2.5 miles and then walked the last .5 miles to his new school. He traveled alone to school as he was from a single-parent home and his dad worked the night shift as a security guard.

And now, Mrs. Dean sat there with a loaded revolver in her hand and Samaj crying on her couch. The policies and procedures were quite clear. A student bringing a loaded weapon into a school resulted in an automatic expulsion, a police investigation, and either jail time or a placement at one of the "juvenile detention schools."

Mrs. Dean looked at Samaj and uttered, "why?" Samaj looked straight at Mrs. Dean and replied: "I never got in trouble at my old school. But look at my face. Look at this slice on my head. I've been beaten up every day going home from school. I've been beaten up in the bathrooms here at school; I got to hold it all day. I've been told that if I don't join the Bull Dogs, they will kill me. I'm tired Mrs. Dean. I just wanted to keep going to school and someday go to college. You gonna keep me safe Mrs. Dean? Cause I don't see it. So I took my daddy's gun from work. I had no choice if I was going to keep going to school and learn. With a gun, they won't dare to bother me now.

(Self-authored from the Chicago school closings that occurred in August 2012)

LEARNING ACTIVITY 2.10

From Theory to Practice

NELP 2.1: Program completers understand and demonstrate the capability to enact the professional norms of integrity, fairness, transparency, trust, collaboration, perseverance, learning and continuous improvement in their actions, decision making and relationships with others.

For the case study above, formulate a carefully reasoned judgment about how the issue should be resolved based on: 1) one or more of the ethical lens (including and educational leaders' obligations through these lens(es); 2) Turbulence Theory; and 3) specifically on the basis of your revised code of professional ethics. Be sure that your judgment and resolution demonstrate professional integrity—the ability to think and act in an integrated manner that honors your personal and professional ethical values and honors the people you work for and with day in and day out in school. Remember, when one acts with integrity, one is true to one's calling: "we act in a way in which our deep gladness and the world's deep hunger meet (Buechner, 1993).

REFERENCES

Abedi, J. (2004). The No Child Left Behind Act and English language learners: Assessment and accountability issues. *Educational Researcher, 33*(1), 4–14.

Abedi, J., & Dietel, R. (2004). Challenges in the No Child Left Behind Act for English-language learners. *Phi Delta Kappan, 85*(10), 782–785.

American Association of School Administrators. (2008). *Statement of ethics for school administrators.* Retrieved January 4, 2009 from: http://web.odu.edu/webroot/instr/ed/bcunningham.nsf/pages/ethicsstatement

Avolio, B. J., & Gardner, W. L. (2005). Authentic leadership development: Getting to the root of positive forms of leadership. *The Leadership Quarterly, 16*(3), 315–338.

Baxter Magolda, M. (2004). Self-authorship as the common goal of 21st-century education. In M. Baxter Magolda, & P. M. King (Eds.). *Learning partnerships: Theory and models of practice to educate for self-authorship* (pp. 1–36). Sterling, VA: Stylus.

Baxter Magolda, M. B. (2008). Three elements of self-authorship. *Journal of College Student Development*, *49*(4), 269–284.

Baxter Magolda, M. B. & King, P. M. (Eds.). (2004). *Learning partnerships: Theory and models of practice to educated for self-authorship*. Sterling, VA: Stylus.

Begley, P. T. (2006). Self-knowledge, capacity and sensitivity: Prerequisites to authentic leadership by school principals. *Journal of Educational Administration*, *44*(3), 6–43.

Boaler, J. (2003). When learning no longer matters: Standardized testing and the creation of inequality. *Phi Delta Kappan*, *84*(7), 502–506.

Buechner, F. (1993). *Wishful thinking: A seeker's ABC*. San Francisco, CA: Harper.

Council of Chief State School Officers (CCSSO) (2008). Educational leadership policy standards: ISLLC 2008. Retrieved from: www.aasa.org/content.aspx?id=1390

Danielson, C. (2002). *Enhancing student achievement: A framework for school improvement*. Alexandria, VA: ASCD.

Fullan, M. (2002). Moral purpose writ large. *School Administrator*, *59*(8), 14–17.

Gardner, W. L., Avolio, B. J., Luthans, F., May, D. R., & Walumbwa, F. (2005). "Can you see the real me?" A self-based model of authentic leader and follower development. *The Leadership Quarterly*, *16*(3), 343–372.

Gini, A., & Green, R. (2013). *Ten virtues of outstanding leaders: Leadership and character*. Malden, MA: Wiley & Son.

Gross, S. J. (2014). Using turbulence theory to guide actions. In Branson, C., M., & Gross, S. J. (Eds.), *Handbook on Ethical Educational Leadership* (pp. 246–262). New York: Routledge.

Israel, M. S. & Marks, W. (2011). Federal accountability and compliance: The need to build ethical resiliency with current and future educational leaders. *Teaching ethics: Society for Ethics Across the Curriculum*, *12*(1), 113–140.

Kegan, R. (1994). *In over our heads: The mental demands of modern life*. Cambridge, MA: Harvard University Press.

Kerchner, C. T. (2013). Education Technology Policy for a 21st Century Learning System. Policy Brief 13–3. *Policy Analysis for California Education, PACE*.

Lindsey, R. B, Roberts, L. M. & Campbell-Jones, F. (2013). *The culturally proficient school: An implementation guide for school leaders*. Thousand Oaks, CA: Corwin.

Luthans, F., & Avolio, B. J. (2003). Authentic leadership: A positive developmental approach. In K. S. Cameron, J. E. Dutton, & R. E. Quinn (Eds.), *Positive organizational scholarship* (pp. 241–261). San Francisco, CA: Barrett-Koehler.

Neafsey, J. P. (2003, August). Discerning our calling: Guidelines for reflection and discussion. Paper presented for Project EVOKE Loyola Faculty Workshop, Chicago, IL.

Neill, M., Grisbond, L., & Schaeffer, B. (2004). *Failing our children: How No Child Left Behind undermines quality and equity in education*. Cambridge, MA: Fair Test.

Ozar, D. T. (1994). Profession and Professional Ethics. In *Encyclopedia of Bioethics* (Vol. 4, pp. 2103–2112). Boston, MA: Macmillan, McGraw-Hill.

Ozar, D. T. (2001). Learning outcomes for ethics across the curriculum programs. *Teaching Ethics*, *2*(1), 1–27.

Rest, J. R. (1984). The major components of morality. In W. Kurtines, & J. Gewirtz (Eds.), *Morality, moral behavior, and moral development* (pp. 24–38). New York: Wiley.

Rest, J. R. (Ed.). (1994). Background: Theory and research. In J. R. Rest & D. Narváez (Eds.), *Moral development in the professions: Psychology and applied ethics* (pp. 1–26). Hillsdale, NJ: Lawrence Erlbaum Associates.

Rest, J. R., Narvaez, D., Bebeau, M., & Thomas, S. (1999). *Postconventional moral thinking: A neo-Kohlbergian approach*. Hillsdale, NJ: Lawrence Erlbaum.

Shapiro, J. P. & Gross, S. J. (2013). *Ethical educational leadership in turbulent times:(Re)solving moral dilemmas* (2nd ed.). New York: Routledge.

Shapiro, J. P., & Stefkovich, J. A. (2005). Viewing ethical dilemmas through multiple paradigms. In J. Shapiro, & J. Stefkovich, *Ethical leadership and decision making in education: Applying theoretical perspectives to complex dilemmas*, (pp. 10–26). Mahwah, N.J.: Lawrence Erlbaum.

Shapiro, J. P. & Stefkovich, J. A. (2011). *Ethical leadership and decision making in education: Applying theoretical perspectives to complex dilemma* (3rd ed.). New York: Routledge.

Stefkovich, J. A. (2013) *Best interests of the student: Applying ethical constructs to legal cases in education* (2nd ed.). New York: Erlbaum (Taylor & Francis Group).

CHAPTER 3

Supporting Democratic and Ethical Schools

Susan C. Faircloth

CHAPTER OVERVIEW

This chapter instructs pre-service, as well as practicing administrators, on the principles of democratic and ethical schooling. It delves deep into defining exactly what
democracy is in education, and explores what ethical practice means to a school
leader. The purpose of schooling is discussed, followed by the ethic of critique,
and notions of equity, and inclusion, democratic leadership, a principal's response,
social justice leadership, ethics in education, leading in the best interest of children, and making sense of the conflict between democratic leadership and ethical
schools. This chapter concludes with implications for school leaders and learning
activities.

INTRODUCTION

Chapter 4 addresses the role of school leaders in "safeguard[ing] the values of
democracy, individual freedom and responsibility, equity, social justice, community,
and diversity" as called for in Standard 2 ("Effective educational leaders act ethically and according to professional norms to promote each student's academic
success and well-being.") of the Professional Standards for Educational Leaders[1]
and further elaborated on in Standard 2 of the draft version of the National
Educational Leadership Preparation Standards for School Leaders, which instructs
leadership preparation programs to ensure that graduates "understand and demonstrate the capability to promote the success and wellbeing of each student, teacher,
and leader by applying the knowledge, skills, and commitments necessary for: (1)
professional norms; (2) decision-making, (3) educational values; and (4) ethical
behavior. Although Standard 2 calls for school leaders to act in an ethical manner
toward all members of the school environment, this chapter focuses on the school

leader's relationship with and responsibility to students as they are potentially the most vulnerable and directly impacted group within the school. In doing so, I argue that ethical leadership is predicated upon the school leader's enactment of democratic leadership practices that serve to establish and maintain a fair and just learning environment. Such practices help to facilitate student access to a wide variety of educational opportunities and increase the likelihood of positive post-school outcomes for students.

Leading ethically and democratically in today's schools is a daunting task as school leaders negotiate the challenge of educating an increasingly diverse student population while upholding the democratic principles upon which the United States was founded. The task is complicated by the fact that this nation is still grappling with how best to create integrated and equitable educational structures where students from diverse backgrounds produce similar academic outcomes. As difficult as this task may be, it is imperative to safeguard the democratic ideals that promote equity and help to prepare students for productive citizenry.

To understand what democratic leadership within schools might look like in practice, it is helpful to reflect on Dewey's 1916 address calling for the nationalization of the U.S. educational system. In this address, Dewey argued that

> our nation and democracy are equivalent terms; that our democracy means amity and good will to all humanity (including those beyond our border) and equal opportunity for all within. Since as a nation we are composed of representatives of all nations who have come here to live in peace with one another and to escape the enmities and jealousies . . . to nationalize our education means to make it an instrument in the active and constant suppression of the war spirit, and in the positive cultivation of sentiments of respect and friendship for all men and women wherever they live. Since our democracy means the sub-stitution of equal opportunity for all for the old-world ideal of unequal opportunity of different classes and the limitation of the individual by the class to which he [or she] belongs, to nationalize our education is to make the public school an energetic and willing instrument in developing initiative, courage, power and personal ability in each individual. . . . So I appeal to the teacher . . . to remember that they above all others are the consecrated servants of the democratic ideas in which alone this country is truly a distinctive nation.
>
> (pp. 427–428)

Although Dewey's address spoke specifically to teachers, this call for action can and should arguably be extended to school leaders as they are instrumental in the shaping of school cultures and climates, and the adoption and enactment of the school's vision, mission, and ultimately its actions toward it students, their families and the communities in which they live, work and play.

According to Giroux (1992): "democracy is both a discourse and a practice that produces particular narratives and identities informed by the principles of free-dom, equality, and social justice" (p. 5). If we believe Giroux's characterization of democracy, we as school leaders, then, are called upon to be mindful of the ways in which the narratives we create help to establish and sustain equitable, fair and just schooling structures and practices.

LEARNING ACTIVITY 3.1

1. To facilitate a deepened awareness and understanding of the ways in which individual and professional ethics impact the role of the school leader, readers are asked to:

- Review and become familiar with the new Professional Standards for Educational Leadership, paying particular attention to references to ethical practice.

2. The following cases are published in the *Journal of Cases in Educational Leadership.* These cases specifically address democratic leadership in schools. It is recommended that readers select and review one or more of these cases, paying particular attention to the questions and guiding activities included at the end of each case. After reviewing these cases, readers are asked to develop a detailed plan for addressing the ethical dilemmas posed in each of these cases. Readers are also asked to consider the ways in which democratic leadership is fostered in your response to the issues posed in these cases.

> Bergmark, U., Salopek, M., Kawai, R., & Lane-Myler, J. (2014, March). Facilitating democracy in a testing culture: Challenges and opportunities for school leaders. *Journal of Cases in Educational Leadership*, *17*(1), 32–44.
>
> Mackenzie, S. V. (2005, June). Who should make decisions?: A high school wrestles with tracking. *Journal of Cases in Educational Leadership*, *8*(2), 17–33.
>
> Mette, I. M., & Scribner, J. P. (2014, December). Turnaround, transformational, or transactional leadership: An ethical dilemma in school reform. *Journal of Cases in Educational Leadership*, *17*(4), 3–18.
>
> Shields, C. M. (2007, March). A failed initiative: Democracy has spoken – has it? *Journal of Cases in Educational Leadership*, *10*(1), 14–21.

3. Read and respond to the following scenario using the ethical frameworks presented by Shapiro and Stefkovich (2010)—the ethics of critique, justice, best interest, and the ethic of the profession.

> **Scenario:** At a large urban elementary school in a rural southeastern state, each school day begins with a moment of silence and the reciting of the Pledge of Allegiance. What are the potential ethical and legal implications of such actions? How would you, as a school leader, respond? Reference Standard 2 (Ethical Leadership) in responding to these questions.

4. Survey the faculty and staff in your school building/district to identify their definitions of key concepts including individual liberty/freedom, democratic values, social justice, and equity. Reflect on the extent to which these definitions reflect or differ. Ask faculty and staff to use these terms to develop their own philosophies of democratic leadership. Review these philosophies and discuss how they either concur with or differ from your own philosophy and practice of democratic leadership. Reference Standard 2 (Ethical Leadership) and Standard 6 ("Effective educational leaders develop the professional capacity and practice of school personnel to promote each student's academic success and well-being").

THE PURPOSE OF SCHOOLING?

As Giroux and McLaren (1986) argue, "schools do not merely teach academic subjects, but also, in part, produce student subjectivities or particular sets of experiences that are in themselves part of an ideological process" (p. 228). This belief is reaffirmed by Calabrese (1990), who argues that schools are tasked with doing much more than preparing students academically; rather, they are tasked with preparing students to uphold and preserve beliefs. The essence of his sentiment is that schools have a responsibility not only to educate the academic minds of students but also to foster the development of creative and reflective practices that will enable these students to live full lives post-school, ideally to contribute to the betterment of the nation. The tricky part here is that, as Giroux and McLaren (1986) argue, education and teaching can be very politicized endeavors as teachers are, in general, expected to teach students about a particular way of life/living—in the case of the United States, the particularities of democratic ideals and values.

Giroux and McLaren characterize school as "a place where classroom and street-corner cultures collide and where teachers, students, and school administrators often differ as to how school experiences and practices are to be defined and understood"(p. 229). To counteract these potential conflicts, faculty within colleges and schools of education are tasked with acknowledging the "cultural politics" of educator preparation—for both future teachers and school leaders—and "to create conditions for student self-empowerment and self-constitution as an active political and moral subject" (p. 229). This process has the potential to empower students to question what is going on around them rather than simply reproducing it. This questioning should then be transferred beyond the confines of educator preparation programs into the classrooms and school buildings in which these graduates will eventually find themselves teaching and leading. The challenge for us, as educational leadership faculty, is to foster open and safe learning environments—both within and outside of the walls of our classrooms. Educational leadership faculty should encourage and support future school leaders as they work to try on what it might look like to engage in democratic leadership practices, to reflect on their own personal and professional codes of ethics and the ways in which these codes, or elements of these codes may collide and conflict, and the ways in which they work to ensure that all students have the opportunity to fully engage in and benefit from their education. Future school leaders can then realize the ultimate goal of enabling students to live productive and meaningful lives beyond school.

RETHINKING THE PURPOSE OF SCHOOLING AND THE PRACTICE OF LEADING

As demonstrated above, engaging in democratic school leadership practices may require school leaders to engage in an intense examination and potentially a major rethinking of the purpose of schooling. The act of rethinking the purpose and process of schooling and the practice of school leadership also necessitates an understanding of a number of key terms often infused within education-related dialogue, yet rarely explicitly defined or operationalized. A sampling of these key terms is presented below.

Citizenry

Westheimer and Kahne (2004) note the existence of three types of citizens: (1) those who are *personally responsible* or active in the community through volunteering and service; (2) those who are *participatory* or civically engaged; and (3) those who are *justice-oriented* or committed to social justice and action. They also point out the limitations of the personal responsibility typology, which emphasizes individual rather than collective action.

Productive citizenry

A productive citizen is viewed as one who contributes economically or otherwise to the well-being and betterment of society. According to Johnson and Deshpande (2000):

> Society faces a collective and moral imperative to engage schools, communities, and families in guiding our children to use knowledge acquired in school to make informed, intellectually driven decisions that will lead to a productive lifetime of health and wellness.
>
> (p. 66)

In the United States, this work is typically done within a larger framework of the values and principles associated with a democracy.

Democracy

According to Dewey (1916, p. 87), "a democracy is more than a form of government; it is primarily a mode of associated living, of conjoint communicated experience" (p. 3). If this is true, it then raises questions regarding what this shared experience of democracy looks and feels like and who is empowered to design and shape this experience. Similar questions may be asked of leadership preparation as well as leadership practice (e.g., who is tasked with designing leadership preparation and who has the privilege of engaging in leadership practice within schools?)

Individual Liberty/Freedom

With citizenship or citizenry comes certain rights and freedoms. An undergirding principle of most democracies is a belief in and commitment to individuals' right to life, liberty, and the pursuit of happiness—a concept defined in the Bill of Rights. According to Black (1960), "The use of the words, 'the people,' . . . in the [9th and 10th] Amendments and strongly emphasizes the desire of the Framers to protect individual liberty" (p. 871). Black goes on to write, "The Framers were well aware that the individual rights they sought to protect might be easily nulli-fied if subordinated to the general powers granted to Congress. One of the reasons for the adoption of the Bill of Rights was to prevent just that" (p. 875). In essence, individuals have the right to make certain decisions for themselves and to exercise certain practices such as religion without the undue influence of the government and its actors. However, the limits of individual liberty and freedom are tested within the confines of the school building where children and youth are subjected to the will of those who are tasked with educating and leading them during the school day.

Democratic Leadership

Starratt (2001, cited in Furman & Starratt, 2002) refers to democratic leadership as promoting a climate in which members of the school community are encouraged to exchange information and ideas, be honest and open, able to change depending upon the nature of the issue at hand, and embodying a sense of compassion and empathy for others. Building on this notion of democracy both promoting and emanating from co-constructed and shared dialogue and decision-making, Klinker (2006) argues that education and the process of schooling are critical to the contin-ued existence of a democratic government. According to Klinker, in a democracy, citizens are given: (1) freedoms, (2) "political equality", and (3) control of policies and policy makers. In effect: Democratic leadership empowers all to voice their opinions but also negotiate differences to work in concert (McCombs, & Quiat, 2002; Woods, 2003 [as cited in Ruffin & Brooks, 2010, p. 243]). Democratic leader-ship opens the boundaries of leadership and respectfully accepts that all beings have an ethical right to participate in decision-making processes (Donaldson, 2006; Woods, 2004; Ruffin & Brooks, 2010, p. 243).

To achieve democratic leadership, Ruffin and Brooks (2010) point to the centrality of coalition building. In the case of schools, it can be argued that the coalition extends beyond the physical walls of the school into the community. As communities continue to diversify, it is imperative that key stakeholders are actively and meaningfully engaged in decision-making and the day-to-day life of the school. This emphasis on coalition building is in keeping with Furman and Starratt's (2002) characterization of democratic leadership as a communal responsibility, with individuals taking on more or less responsibility depending upon the context. Thus, the development of a democratic school community requires open and ongoing dialogue, intentional consideration and action, and a willingness and ability to accept the "messy and idiosyncratic nature of leadership" (p. 124) in schools.

This is further reinforced by Rusch's (1995) depiction of democratic leadership in schools as being dependent upon individuals' ability and willingness to come together as a community. According to Rusch, challenges to democratic school leadership include the need to restructure or break down "hierarchical lines and then redeployment of bureaucratic mechanisms" (p. 4). Rusch argues that building and sustaining a democratic community within a school is not easy, yet it is essential. For this to occur, school leaders must be cognizant of and responsive to the context of the school and its surrounding community. It is also important to establish good working relationships between university leadership preparation programs and schools as well as teacher preparation programs and schools.

Democratic schooling practices

Calabrese (1990) argues that democratic schools are characterized by the following:

1. The ethic of justice is upheld;
2. Everyone is treated equitably;
3. Integrity is key;
4. The school community is involved in decision making;
5. Everyone is included;
6. Resources are distributed equitably; and
7. Individuals are supported in addressing grievances.

For each of these to become and remain foundational elements of the school, leaders must do more than talk or teach about democratic principles; they must live these principles for others to see in an authentic and real manner (Furman & Shields, 2005).

Ethic of Critique

According to Furman and Starratt (2002), democratic leadership is a moral and value-laden process. As Maxcy (1998) writes, democratic leaders must think and act critically and must be aware of the values they bring to the decision-making process as well as the values of those they lead and serve. This is in keeping with the ethic of critique, which Starratt (1991) describes as being "aimed at its own bureaucratic context, its own bureaucratic mind-set" (p. 189). The ethic of critique goes beyond critiquing social structures and inequalities to begin to enact changes aimed at upsetting structural imbalances and giving voice to those impacted by these imbalances. According to Starratt (1991):

> The ethic of critique poses the fundamental ethical challenge to the educational administrator: how to construct an environment in which education can take place ethically. The ethic of critique reveals that the organization in its present forms is a source of unethical consequences in the educational process.
>
> (p. 190)

To address these inequalities and injustices requires deep changes in the overall structure and operation of schools in order to create a more socially just and ethical schooling structure. One of the challenges for school leaders is to acknowledge their role in sustaining inequitable and unjust educational struc-tures while simultaneously working to dismantle these structures. In doing so, the school leader's responsibility and actions shift from the school and its students to society at large as the school leader transforms into an advocate for and agent of social justice.

Social Justice Leadership

According to Furman and Shields (2005, as cited in Normore & Jean-Marie, 2008), social justice and democratic leadership are inextricably linked. Both principles are concerned with "individual rights and the good of the community" (Normore & Jean-Marie, p. 186). However, Normore and Jean-Marie (2008) argue that the sole responsibility for social justice and democratic leadership does not rest on the shoulders of the school leader; in contrast, it is a joint venture involving the community "in promoting social justice, democratic and equitable schooling, and positive relationships" (p. 199).

Theoharis (2007) describes social justice leaders as individuals who "make issues of race, class, gender, disability, sexual orientation, and other historically and currently marginalizing conditions . . . central to their advocacy, leadership practice, and vision" (p. 223). In effect, social justice leaders firmly believe that the purpose of schooling goes well beyond simply teaching students the basics of reading, writing, and math. In reality, it gets at the heart of who our students, their families, and communities are, and the ways in which they will eventually come to help shape the world in which future generations live and learn. Social justice leadership is discussed further in Chapter 5.

Equity in Education

Among the many values they uphold, social justice leaders are concerned with equity. Unterhalter (2009) points out that although the term "equity" is often used in policies and recommendations regarding education, rarely is this term explicitly defined, thus making it difficult to establish and implement equitable policies and practices, particularly within schools. According to Unterhalter, equity may be considered in terms of fairness; however, fairness is still a somewhat nebulous and subjective concept. In an attempt to reconcile this lack of a clear definition, Unterhalter proposes a model in which there are three levels of equity:

1. **Equity from below**—emphasis on working across differences to ensure that all parties have a voice in decision-making. A related goal is one of facilitating individual and collective agency.
2. **Equity from above**—rules based, emphasis on rights and freedom and ultimately justice.
3. **Equity from the middle**—based on "social arrangements" that promote the fair distribution of resources across social, economic and other groups—but also recognizes that there are limits on available resources and that the simple distribution of resources does not, in and of itself, result in equity.

In pointing out the different ways in which equity may be enacted, Unterhalter reminds us that each of these definitions is inherently related to the notion of equality. While Castelli, Ragazzi and Crescentini (2012) describe equality as "promoting the same treatment for all" (p. 2245), Brayboy, Castagno, and Maughan (2007) caution us that although "equality reaches the goal of sameness, . . . it does not necessarily mean justice" (p. 164). This raises both an administrative and ethical dilemma for school leaders charged with treating students in both an equitable and just manner.

ETHICAL CHALLENGES FOR SCHOOL LEADERS

As Calabrese (1990) points out, the formal structures of schools have not been organized to function as just or ethical communities. They have different sets of standards for administrators, teachers, and students based on their distribution and application of power. In short, a school cannot teach students ethical values and the meaning of participation in a democratic society through the teaching of civic and ethical principles. The school community must live these principles and infuse them into the school's culture. The school can respond by examining its culture and making a determined effort to build an ethical community (p. 12).

   In building a more ethical community, school leaders are often tasked with making decisions that, both willingly and unwillingly, pit the individual interests and needs of a student against the collective interests and needs of students at large. In some cases, this raises an ethical and administrative dilemma as school leaders work to balance their responsibility for the individual student against their responsibility for all students.

Acting in the Best Interest(s) of Students

As noted above, school leaders are tasked not only with meeting the collective needs of student groups, but also the needs of individual students, which often times differ significantly from the needs of the larger group. While the term "best interest" applies to the individual student rather than a group of students, there is an inherent assumption that what is done in the best interest of one student will not purposefully hurt or add injury to a larger group of students. In writing about the concept of best interest, Stefkovich and Begley (2007) emphasize the principles of "fairness, justice, and caring" (p. 212).

Although grounded in legal principles, there has been a great deal of variation in how the term "best interest" has been applied in both courts and schools. To address this variation, Stefkovich and Begley (2007) propose an approach by which school leaders are better able to act in the best interest of the child/student. This approach emphasizes "rights, responsibility, and respect" (p. 215). According to Stefkovich and Begley:

1. Students have a right to education, freedom from harm, dignity, and equality;
2. Students have an obligation to act responsibly; and
3. Students have a right to be respected and a responsibility to treat others with respect.

In implementing this approach, school leaders recognize that education is a property right and that any attempts to deny students' access to this right must be accompanied by the exercise of due process by which the student has the right to be informed, to be heard and to take action if the denial of access is found to be unwarranted. The best interest of students is discussed further in Chapter 5 of this text.

According to Stefkovich (2014), when "confronted with difficult situations, school leaders frequently rely on the rule of law to guide their work" (p. 3). However, many, if not most, of the situations that these educators face on a day-to-day basis require ethical rather than, or in addition to, legal decision making" (p. 3). In these cases, it is imperative that school leaders are able to reflect back on and learn from their administrative preparation and training and its emphasis on ethical decision-making as outlined in Standard 2 of the National Educational Leadership Preparation Standards.

LEARNING ACTIVITY 3.2

As discussed in brief above, school leaders are called upon to balance their own individual ethical beliefs with the ethical codes and expectations of the profession. Recognizing this expectation, readers are asked to reflect on the following:

*   What are the values, dispositions and practices that help to promote and sustain educational inequalities among students of different racial/ethnic/

cultural/social/economic and other groups? What are the values, dispositions and practices of school leaders that can help to lessen and alleviate
these educational inequalities?

- When faced with competing individual and collective student interests, how
  might the practice of democratic leadership help to resolve tensions that
  may emerge? What might you do to mediate the tensions that emerge when
  your own personal code of ethics comes into conflict with the ethics of
  then profession of school leadership?

TEACHING DEMOCRATIC VALUES AND IDEALS TO AN INCREASINGLY DIVERSE CITIZENRY

According to McFarland et al. (2017):[1]

1. There are approximately 50.3 million children (PK-12) enrolled in public
   schools.
2. There are 91,430 traditional public schools.
3. Approximately 50% of school-age children are identified as White, 16% Black,
   25% Hispanic, 5% Asian/Pacific Islander, 3% two or more races, and 1%
   American Indian/Alaska Native.
4. Fifty-nine percent of public schools have more than 50% White student enrollment, approximately16% have more than 50% Hispanic student enrollment,
   and 9% have more than 50% Black student enrollment.
5. Nine percent of all students are classified as English Language Learners.
6. Twenty percent of families with children between the ages of 5 and 17 live in
   poverty, with the lowest percentage living in poverty in New Hampshire (10%)
   and the highest percentage in Mississippi (31%).
7. Twenty-four percent of children in public schools attend high poverty schools—
   schools in which the majority (75% or more) of students are eligible for free
   or reduced price lunch.
8. More than six million (6.6 million) children—13% of all students—between
   the ages of 3 and 21 are identified as students with disabilities.
9. Eight-three percent of all students graduated with a regular high school diploma,
   while approximately 6% dropped out before completing high school.

These data reflect the increasing racial, ethnic, socioeconomic, linguistic, and other
diversity of the student population. The next chapter is devoted to issues of diversity.
Data for the 2011–12 school year indicate the following:

1. There are approximately 116,000 principals in both public and private schools
   in the U.S.

2. Eighty percent of public school principals identify as White, 10% Black or African American, 7% Hispanic, and 3% other race/ethnicity.
3. Slightly more than half (52%) of all principals are female, with higher percentages of females (64%) in primary schools and fewer in high schools (30%).
4. Sixty-two percent of principals have completed a master's degree.
5. Typically, principals work nearly 60 (58.1) hours each week, with more than one quarter of their time spent directly working with students.
6. Most principals have an average of 7.2 years of experience as a school leader; and 80% are involved in developing discipline policies for students.

(Bitterman, Goldring, & Gray, 2013)

These data raise important questions regarding the extent to which school leaders reflect the racial, ethnic, cultural, linguistic, social, economic, gender, and other diversity of the U.S. population. If not, schools and districts, as well as educational leadership preparation programs must ask what steps should be taken to ensure a more representative educator and leadership pool? An equally important question is the extent to which colleges and schools of education are preparing educators to work in and with increasingly diverse schools and communities. It must also be acknowledged that to simply diversify the educator ranks is to place a temporary fix on a long-standing and complex issue.

EDUCATIONAL LEADERS RESPONDING TO THE CHANGING DEMOGRAPHICS OF EDUCATION

Greenberg (1992) reminds us that children and families do not leave their "roots" (i.e., cultures) behind once they enter the educational arena. The task of educational leaders is to find ways in which children's and families' cultures can be incorporated into and respected by the formal and informal structures of schooling. Unfortunately, much too often culture and difference are at the root of many disputes and disagreements in schools. This is particularly evident during the holidays when schools work to balance the Christian religious tenets upon which many argue this nation was built, against the increasingly diverse religious traditions of this nation's populous. This also raises questions related to the ethical principle of "best interest" as it relates to balancing the rights and responsibilities of the individual student with the rights and responsibilities of students at large—not an easy task for any school leader, but one made even more complex when the school leader's personal and/or ethical codes of ethics and beliefs is challenged.

Leading democratically and ethically sounds good; however, actually embodying these ideals may be difficult, if not impossible for some leaders. As an American Indian female professor of Educational Leadership and Administration, I will grapple with these terms as I work to prepare future generations of school leaders to work within an educational system that for more than 500 years has worked to assimilate and acculturate this nation's original inhabitants in its quest for the democratic ideal. In doing so, I concur with Westheimer and Kahne (2004), two authors who raise questions about what productive citizenry and democratic ideals really mean and the propensity to teach these concepts from a limited, and often biased and subjective, perspective in schools—to the exclusion and marginalization of those whose cultural, ethnic or other backgrounds differ from those typically in power within schools. Unfortunately, "the notion of democracy occupies a privileged place in U.S. society" (Westheimer & Kahne, 2004, p. 237) and is not experienced by many, including the most vulnerable of all, this nation's students. Students of educational leadership should consider their own backgrounds (as I have here), and how their background and experiences impact their ability to lead diverse schools. Chapter 5 offers suggestions for school leaders toward addressing issues of diversity.

CASE STUDY 3.1

After reflecting on the increasing diversity of schools and the implications of such diversity for readers are asked to read and respond to the following case:

"Beyond Feathers and Fluff: Teaching About American Indians in the Early Grades"

Three years ago, the parents of a young American Indian child relocated to a mid-sized town in southern state. In preparation for this move, they researched local school ratings and decided to purchase a home in an area of the city with the highest rated elementary school. Although this school was known for its academic rigor and excellence, the parents were also aware that the school lacked racial and ethnic diversity. This meant that their daughter would be one of, if not the only American Indian child in her school. They were troubled by this realization, but rationalized the decision to send their daughter to this school, by focusing on the academic advantages they assumed she would receive.

As the school year began, the parents met with their daughter's teacher and spoke briefly with her regarding their daughter's American Indian heritage. Careful not to over-step their boundaries, the parents did not speak at length about their concerns nor did they lecture the teacher on the importance of culturally relevant teaching and learning practices. As educators themselves, this was a particularly difficult challenge, yet they wanted the teacher to know that they respected her and her professional knowledge and expertise.

For most of the first half of the school year, there were few issues; however, as the holidays approached, the parents became increasingly concerned that their daughter's teacher and other teachers in the school would engage in culturally inappropriate teaching practices related to the Thanksgiving story, pilgrims, and Indians. Unfortunately, their concerns increased when they perused a social media site and found photos, from the previous school year, of children from their daughter's school dressed in paper headbands and feathers, standing beside a tipi. The parents looked at each other in stunned silence before discussing how to approach this situation. Although their daughter's teacher assured them that this type of activity would not take place in her classroom, they had no assurance that similar acts would not take place in other class-rooms across the school.

After much consideration, the parents scheduled a meeting to discuss this matter with the school's principal and the district's social studies curriculum coordinator. Upon entering the principal's office, the parents sat on one side of the table and the principal and curriculum coordinator sat on the other side of the table. As could be expected, there was an uneasy atmosphere in the room, with each party doing their best to present their issues and concerns while listening to the other side. After exchanging pleasantries, the principal asked the parents to discuss their concerns. They explained that they were concerned about the potential for myths and stereotypes about American Indian peoples to be perpetuated if teaching approaches, such as the making and wearing of Indian "costumes" were used. They also explained that their daughter was American Indian and that they wanted her and her classmates to see American Indian peoples not as relics of the past but as modern-day peoples. They also wanted their daughter to be proud of her cultural heritage and her classmates to learn about and appreciate the cultural and linguistic diversity of the nation's 600-plus tribes. Finally, they explained that there were a number of resources that could be utilized to incorporate American Indian history, culture, literature, music, etc. into the classroom, and that they would be happy to work with the school to identify such resources.

As the parents came to the end of their opening remarks, the principal sat back in her chair, folded her arms, and turned to the curriculum coordinator, who she identified as also being an American Indian. The curriculum coordinator then explained to the parents that she was involved in the development and implementation of the current social studies curriculum at their daughter's school and that she saw no issues or concerns with the curriculum. According to her, if the parents were not happy with the curriculum, they had the option of removing their daughter from the classroom during the teaching of these activities.

As the parents listened to the curriculum coordinator, tears began to well up in the mother's eyes, and the father's face became increasingly red as he struggled to maintain his composure. Eventually, the parents regained their voices and explained to the principal and curriculum coordinator that the removal of their child was not an acceptable option. The father also explained the importance of feathers to American Indian peoples. According to the father, "teaching students that something so sacred to American Indian peoples can be replicated with construction paper and tape, is a blatantly disrespectful of American Indian peoples and their cultures."

After listening to the parents, the principal ended the meeting by thanking them for meeting with her. She then stood up and prepared to leave the room. The mother then spoke up and asked how the school would handle the parents' concerns. The principal responded, "We will think about what you've said. Have a good day." The mother then asked, "Should we expect to hear from you?" The principal replied, "As I said, we will think about what you have said. Have a good day."

The parents left the school with little hope that the principal would respond to their concerns. However, a few weeks later, the parents received an email from the principal.

Now answer the following questions:

1. What are some ways in which traditional Westernized approaches to schooling might conflict with American Indian values and beliefs? How might this conflict be mediated?

2. Are there any ethical dilemmas presented in this case? If so, what are these specific dilemmas? What ethical frames (e.g., justice, care, critique, community)

3. How might the principal best respond to the parents' concerns?

4. How might the curriculum coordinator work with the parents to address their concerns while also respecting the principal's role as the leader of the school?

5. As a member of the leadership team at your school, how would you resolve this situation, taking into consideration Standard 2 (Ethical Leadership) and Standard 3 ("Effective educational leaders strive for equity of educational opportunity and culturally responsive practices to promote each student's academic success and well-being")?

CASE STUDY 3.2: MAKING SENSE OF THE CONTRADICTIONS OF DEMOCRATIC LEADERSHIP AND ETHICAL PRACTICE: INTROSPECTION AND CONCLUDING THOUGHTS

Throughout the writing of this chapter, I was struck by the complex notions of such terms as individual liberty, democratic values and productive citizenry. For months, I have grappled with how to make sense of these terms in such a way as to be useful for aspiring and practicing school leaders tasked with "safeguard[ing] the values of democracy, individual liberty, equity, justice, community, and diversity" as outlined in Standard 2 of the Professional Standards for Educational Leaders. I came to the conclusion that each of these values could be written about in their own chapter or book without ever giving adequate treatment to any of these values. Yet, this was the task at hand when I agreed to write this chapter. As I grappled with this task, I reflected on my own lived experience as an American Indian woman, the first in my family to earn a doctoral degree and to enter the hallowed halls of the academy as a professor—one deemed worthy of imparting meaningful knowledge onto others. This led me to reflect even further back to my own schooling experiences as a young child in the new South— a South still reeling from the Civil Rights movement of the 1960s, forced integration of schools, and historical and continuing patterns of racial segregation both within communities and schools. One image that played vividly over and over in my mind was an image of my kindergarten classroom in which there were two American Indians, a handful of Whites, and a majority of African American students. On first glance, this image might seem as innocuous, as it had to me, for most of my life; however, a second more intentional glance at this image offers a portent of things to come for me in my own educational experience within the public school system—an experience charac- terized by limited access to educational opportunities commonly afforded to others and minimal expectations for life beyond the school house doors. In the eyes of my school system, success for me would have been graduating from high school and going to work in the same hog slaughtering factory where my mother had worked for 37 years— 36 years longer than she ever intended. In the eyes of the school, she was a marginally productive citizen and that was enough. She complied with the law, went to work every day, paid taxes, and sent her children to school. What more could she or society ask for from her? Yet, underlying this notion of productive citizenry—a term I am confident my mother and her family never heard, nor did I, until becoming an academic—was a lack of any questioning of my mother about who she wanted to be or what she wanted her children to become.

As the mother of a six-year-old kindergarten student, I, along with my husband, have had the luxury of purchasing a home in an affluent community enabling our daughter to attend the best-ranked school in the district. In exchange for this stamp of academic excellence, we have had to turn our heads to the fact that our daughter is one of very few American Indians in her school, and that diversity for her at this school will rarely, if ever, be associated with race, ethnicity, or culture. This is something that has caused me great consternation as I herald the importance of racial, ethnic, religious, socioeconomic, gender, sexual orientation, and all other forms of diversity in the lives of my family and our community. Yet, I have made a conscious choice—to privilege standard notions of academic excellence and rigor over something much more difficult to quantify or qualify—the importance of diversity. What I describe here is related to the development of a productive citizenry and the exercise of my own individual liberty to choose where my child is educated. This choice is equally related to the uneasy pairing of such terms as democratic values, equity, and leadership within the context of traditional schooling structures.

As I work to prepare the next generation of school leaders, I share these stories with them, just as I share the story of a recent meeting with a school leader in which I relayed to her the inappropriateness of instructing young children to dress up and pretend to be American Indians as a way of learning about the Pilgrims and Indians and the first Thanksgiving. For me, this conversation was as much about my own child as it was all of the other children who are being taught that it is morally and ethically fair and just to essentialize a racial or ethnic group down to the wearing of feathers or other stereotypical costumes.

To effectively teach about and/or engage in the practice of democratic and ethical school leadership, we must first acknowledge that the United States is a nation born on the backs of slave labor and forced assimilation, acculturation and relocation of its own indigenous peoples, yet it is a nation heralded around the world as the beacon of equity, justice, fairness and liberty for all. This also requires asking hard questions and engaging in difficult conversations with ourselves and our students. This is the first of many steps in acknowledging and coming to terms with the tumultuous and conflicting history of this nation, and its schools, rather than sweeping it under the carpet and pretending that it does not exist. I believe strongly that acknowledgment of this history does not mean lessening one's belief in or support of the fundamental democratic values of this nation, yet what it does do is to better enable those who lead this nation's schools to recognize that these dearly held values cannot be adequately sustained if we do not first acknowledge that the absence of such values may return us to the very thing from whence this nation was born—a desire to escape intolerance, servitude, injustice, and lack of liberty. For educators, much of the responsibility for this change rests in the hands of the schools and colleges of education that are preparing the next generation of teachers and school leaders. Giroux (1992, p. 5, as cited in Maxcy, 1998) argues that universities have the responsibility of "educating people with a vision, people who can rewrite the narrative of educational administration and the story of leadership by developing a public philosophy whose purpose is to animate a democratic society" (p. 219). The recently revised standards for educational leaders and those who prepare these leaders lay the groundwork for this change to occur.

As we rethink what it means to prepare future educators and school leaders in a democratically inclined nation, we must, as Noddings (1995) suggests, also ask, "What do we want for our children? What do they need from education, and what does our society need?" (p. 365). In contrast to pundits who call for increased emphasis on academic and technical skills, Noddings calls for a society in which children are cared for—a society in which children learn to become "competent, caring, loving, and lovable people" (p. 365). This has important implications for the ways in which educational systems can and should operate, and the ways in which school leaders choose and are empowered to lead in a more democratic, just and ethical manner.

Equally important, Noddings (1995) points out that democratic schooling, like equitable schooling, is not synonymous with treating all individuals the same; rather, democratic education entails providing children with the opportunities and supports necessary for them to thrive. In many cases what these students need is not the same because all students and all schools are not the same, yet they are all deserve to be treated equitably, justly, fairy and ethically. As we work to achieve these goals, Noddings (1995) challenges us to rethink what it means to be "an educated person" and challenges us to consider the possibility of adopting multiple meanings and constructions of this term. I would argue that leaders should also be challenged to rethink what it means to lead in a democratic, just, and ethical manner.

SUMMARY OF KEY POINTS

- School leaders play a critical role in *"safeguard[ing] the values of democracy, individual freedom and responsibility, equity, social justice, community, and diversity."*

- As schools become increasingly diverse, it will be more important than ever for school leaders to reaffirm their commitment to leading in the best interest(s) of all students.

NOTE

1. Data represent the 2014–15 and 2015–16 school years.

REFERENCES

Black, H. L. (1960). The Bill of Rights. *New York University Law Review, 35*(4), 865–881.

Bitterman, A., Goldring, R., & Gray, L. (2013). Characteristics of public and private elementary and secondary school principals in the United States: Results from the 2011–12 schools and staffing survey (NCES 2013–313). Washington, DC: U.S. Department of Education, National Center for Education Statistics. Retrieved from: http://nces.ed.gov/pubsearch

Brayboy, B. M. J., Castagno, A. E., & Maughan, E. (2007). Equality and justice for all? Examining race in education scholarship. *Review of Research in Education, 31*(1), 159–194.

Calabrese, R. L. (1990). The school as an ethical and democratic community. *NASSP Bulletin,* (October), 10–15.

Castelli, L., Ragazzi, S., & Crescentini, A. (2012). Equity in education: A general overview. *Social and Behavioral Sciences, 69*(2012), 2243–2250. Available online at: www.science direct.com

Dewey, J. (1916). Nationalizing education. *The Journal of Education, 84*(16), 2102, 425–428. Stable URL: www.jstor.org/stable42807817

Furman, G. C., & Shields, C. M. (2005). How can educational leaders promote and support social justice and democratic community in schools? In W. A. Firestone & C. Riehl (Eds.), *A new agenda for research in educational leadership* (pp. 119–137). Columbia, New York and London: Teachers College Press.

Furman, G. C., & Starratt, R. J. (2002). Leadership for democratic community in schools. In S. Stringfield & D. Lane (Eds.), *Educating at-risk students: One hundred –first yearbook of the National Society for then Study of Education* (pp. 105–133). Chicago, IL: University of Chicago Press.

Giroux, H. (1992). Educational leadership and the crisis of democratic government. *Educational Researcher, 21*(4), 4–11. Stable URL: http://.jstor.org/stable/1177205

Giroux, H. A., & McLaren, P. (1986). Teacher education and the politics of engagement: The case for democratic schooling. *Harvard Educational Review, 56*(3), 213–239.

Greenberg, P. (1992). How to institute some simple democratic practices pertaining to respect, rights, roots, and responsibilities in any classroom (without losing your leadership position). *Young Children, 47*(5), 10–17. Stable URL: www.jstor.org/stable/42726569

Johnson, J., & Deshpande, C. (2000). Health education and physical education: disciplines preparing students as productive, helathy citizens for the challenges of the 21st century. *The Journal of School Health, 70*(2), 66.

Klinker, H. (2006). Qualities of democracy: Links to democratic leadership. *Journal of Thought, 41*(2), 51–63.

Maxcy, S. J. (1998). Preparing school principals for ethno-democratic leadership. *International Journal of Leadership in Education, 1*(3), 217–235. doi: 10.1080/1360312980010301

McFarland, J., Hussar, B., de Brey, C., Snyder, T., Wang, X., Wilkinson-Flicker, S., Gebrekristos, S., Zhang, J., Rathbun, A., Barmer, A., Bullock Mann, F., & Hinz, S. (2017). The condition of education 2017 (NCES 2017–144). U.S. Department of Education, Washington, DC: National Center for Education Statistics. Retrieved from: https://nces.ed.gov/pubsearch/pubsinfo.asp?pubid=2017144

Noddings, N. (1995). A morally defensible mission for schools in the 21st century. *The Phi Delta Kappan, 76*(5), 365–368. Stable URL: www.jstor.org/stable/20405342

Normore, A. H., & Jean-Marie, G. (2008). Female secondary school leaders at the helm of social justice, democratic schooling and equity. *Leadership & Organization Development Journal, 29*(2), 182–205.

Ruffin, V., & Brooks, J. S. (2010). Democratic leadership for community schools. *Journal of School Public Relations, 31*, 238–250.

Rusch, E. (1995). Leadership in evolving democratic communities. Paper presented at the Annual Meeting of the American Educational Research Association, San Francisco, CA, April 18–22, 1995. ERIC Document Reproduction Services No. 392 117.

Shapiro, J. P., & Stefkovich, J. A. (2010). *Ethical leadership and decision making in education: Applying theoretical perspectives in complex dilemmas* (3rd ed.). New York: Taylor & Francis.

Starratt, R. J. (1991). Building an ethical school: A theory for practice in educational leadership. *Educational Administration Quarterly, 27*(2), 185–202.

Stefkovich, J. A. (2014). *Best interests of the student: Applying ethical constructs to legal cases in education* (2nd ed.). New York: Routledge/Taylor & Francis.

Stefkovich, J., & Begley, P. T. (2007). Ethical school leadership: Defining the best interests of students. *Educational Management Administration & Leadership, 35*(2), 205–224. doi: 10.1177/1741143207075389

Theoharis, G. (2007). Social justice educational leaders and resistance: Toward a theory of social justice leadership. *Educational Administration Quarterly, 43*(2), 221–258. doi: 10.1177/0013161X06293717

Unterhalter, E. (2009). What is equity in education? Reflections from the capability approach. *Studies in Philosophy and Education, 28*, 415–424.

Westheimer, J., & Kahne, J. (2004). What kind of citizen? The politics of educating for democracy. *American Educational Research Journal, 41*(2), 237–269.

Safeguarding the Values of Diversity and Equity

Lisa Bass and Karen Stansberry Beard

CHAPTER OVERVIEW

This chapter discusses issues related to diversity, equity, and inclusion in schools. It consists of seven sections, a case study, and learning activities. The section titled "Understanding Diversity: A School Leader's Role and Responsibility," proposes actions for the 21st-century school leader toward effectively managing diversity. The next section, "Cultural Incompetence and the Increasing Education Debt," discusses the tremendous cost of cultural incompetence toward the mounting education debt to disenfranchised students. This debt is viewed in the context of the opportunity gap (e.g., Akiba, LeTendre, & Scribner, 2007; Milner, 2012) and reflects what is known as the achievement gap (see Ladson-Billings, 2006). The section titled "The Social Justice Leader" discusses the intersection and overlap in the missions of social justice leaders and leaders who champion viable diverse learning environments. The chapter ends with a section titled "Inclusive Leadership: From Desegregation to Integration." This section exposes the reality of the misnomer known as desegregated schools, and reintroduces the ideal of *truly integrated* schools. While decision making is value laden (Hoy & Miskel, 2013) school leaders have a variety of motivations for their actions and the decisions they make. A school leader's decisions and ensuing activities should be undergirded by ethical principles and guided by ethical frameworks.

Ethical frameworks are used in educational leadership to describe decision-making processes, and are the basis upon which these decisions are made. Among the frameworks most commonly cited in the educational leadership literature are the ethic of justice (Strike, Haller, & Soltis, 2005), the ethic of care (Bass, 2009; Beard, 2012; Beck, 1994; Gilligan, 1982; Noddings, 1988), the ethic of critique (Foster, 1986; Giroux, 1992), and the ethic of community (Furman, 2003, 2004). Ethical frameworks are delineated and discussed in detail by Frick & Gross in

Chapter 1, as well as in other key ethical leadership texts (e.g. Strike, Haller & Soltis, 2005; Shapiro & Stefkovich, 2016).

Decision making in the best interest of children is brought to the fore in recent literature (Stefkovich & O'Brien, 2004; Stefkovich & Begley, 2007), and is viewed as the moral foundation of all decision making in ethical leadership. If the well-being of all children becomes the basis of decision making for educational policy and practice, then schools should improve as beneficial policies and processes are implemented. Ethics and the best interest of the child frameworks shape conversations on ethics in educational leadership. They also inform the lenses through which school leaders view their world in order to make ethical decisions in their leadership praxis. Existing frameworks are quite extensive; however, they do not fully speak to how to address diversity, a growing area of focus in educational leadership. Although diversity is frequently mentioned in educational leadership, its meaning and implications are assumed. Because people make assumptions about diversity, the true purposes and intentions behind diversity initiatives are often unfulfilled. Key definitions are listed below to provide a context for the discussions in the remainder of this chapter.

INTRODUCTION

The purpose of this chapter is to discuss the role of the school leader in appreciating and managing diversity in schools. This chapter reminds the reader that appreciating and managing diverse populations is not only a responsibility, but also a moral imperative (e.g., Fullan, 2003; Strike, Haller & Soltis, 2005; Taylor, 2010) given the rapidly shifting demographic landscape of U.S. schools (Madsen & Mabokela, 2014; Maxwell, 2014). The prevalence of diversity in schools and the need to build up structures that advance educational attainment of diverse student subgroups are discussed. Definitions for diversity and related terms are provided, concluding with a discussion of the educational leader's role in promoting integrated, equitable and just learning spaces for all children. The goal of promoting integrated and equitable diverse schools is embedded in the newly developed National Standards for Educational Leaders (NELP) and the Professional Standards for Educational Leaders (PSEL), formerly the ISLLC Standards.

ALIGNMENT WITH NELP AND PSEL STANDARDS

The National Standards for Educational Leaders (NELP Standards) address ethics and ethical behavior in Standard 2: Ethics and Professional Norms. Diversity is specifically addressed in Element 2.3, Values, which states: "Program completers understand and demonstrate the capability to model essential educational values of democracy, community, individual freedom, and responsibility, equity, social justice, and diversity." Ethics and Professional Norms are also highlighted in

Standard 2 of the Professional Standards for Educational Leaders (PSEL). Within Standard 2, the charge to effective leaders is delineated in six points, a–f. Point e most clearly aligns with what is put forward in this chapter. Point e states that effective leaders "lead with interpersonal and communication skills, social-emotional insight, and understanding of all students' and staff members' backgrounds and cultures." In this chapter, both NELP and PSEL standards address leadership needing to understand the backgrounds of both students and staff members, and promoting equity in schools.

KEY DEFINITIONS

Diversity Being composed of different elements or qualities. Elements of diversity for schools and other organizations include race, ethnicity, religious, gender, ability, socioeconomic, sexual orientation, and political/ideological are considered when dealing with schools and (Merriam-Webster, 2016; Haring-Smith, 2012).

Inclusive education Inclusive education involves embracing human diversity and welcoming all children and adults as equal members of an educational community. This involves valuing and supporting the full participation of all people together within mainstream educational settings. Inclusive education requires recognizing and upholding the rights of all children and adults, and understanding human diversity as a rich resource and an everyday part of all human environments and interactions. Inclusive education is an approach to education free from discriminatory beliefs, attitudes and practices, including free from ableism. Inclusive education requires putting inclusive values into action to ensure all children and adults belong, participate and flourish (Cologon, 2013).

Leadership for diversity Leadership in schools and other arenas that facilitates and promotes the conditions necessary for all students to thrive in diverse learning environments (Coleman, 2012; Lumby & Coleman, 2010).

School desegregation The outcome of the *Brown v. Board of Education* decision, which outlawed *de jure* racial school segregation in American public schools. Prior to the Brown decision, black–white school segregation was absolute in the South, and very high in many school districts in other parts of the country (Reardon & Owens, 2014).

True school integration Schools where the leadership implements policies and practices that support and promote the inclusion of students from all groups and subgroups (i.e. sports and other extra-curricular activities, clubs, and lunch).

UNDERSTANDING DIVERSITY: A SCHOOL LEADER'S ROLE AND RESPONSIBILITY

School leaders must be conscious of the need to acknowledge diversity in their schools by expanding their knowledge of all forms of diversity (i.e. students and staff with learning differences, cognitive and physical disabilities, racial and ethnic diversity, sexual- orientation diversity, diversity of economic resources, and age diversity), and respectfully govern their buildings so that institutional policies and Fpractices demonstrate respect for all persons. Leaders also need to be aware of and acknowledge diversity even in cases when their student and/or staff characteristics *appear* to be similar. Differences may not be visible in socioeconomic status, sexual orientation, ability, and in cases where a student or staff members may not embody the dominant religious or political views. School leaders need to be aware of and sensitive to the needs of all their students and staff members. Without awareness of relevant issues and effective strategies to support diversity, leadership will fail in serving students and staff members from less represented backgrounds.

Coleman (2012) aptly points out that the key difficulty in managing organizations when diversity is present is not the actual differences, but that stereotypes are applied that cause automatic categorization and judgment of people on the basis of these differences (p. 597). Such stereotypes are most often ill conceived and do not accurately portray the persons or groups they were developed to describe. Negative stereotypes and categorizations stigmatize people who are not part of the dominant group, and can ultimately prove harmful to those bearing the label stigma. Therefore, the role of the school leader includes managing these stereotypes by instituting a zero-tolerance policy for the employment of deficit-based stereotypes.

School leaders are on the front line of managing the changing U.S. demographics, as schools are among the first institutions that experience demographic shifts and are also where the most diversity is found. Compulsory School Attendance laws require that all children attend school on average until the age of 16 (the age for mandatory education varies per state). Furthermore, all children, including those who are undocumented have the right to an education. Schools serve both the children of new U.S. residents and lifelong citizens of the country. Thus, leadership should strive to be proficient at meeting the needs of all diverse learners in order to foster the progression of the nation.

Current demographic trends indicate that our society is becoming increasingly diverse (Johnson, Scaefer, Lichter, & Rogers, 2014). The diversity, including race, gender, class, disability, sexual orientation, gender identification, religion, and other populations that have been marginalized in schools and society, are ever expanding and changing (see Figure 4.1). The changing demographic landscape stirs uncertainty, even fear and other negative emotions among many citizens. Many people, regardless of their background, consider the time when society was more homogeneous, familiar, safer, and more predictable.

If demographers' predictions hold true, students in U.S. schools will continue to change and grow to comprise a majority of people of color by 2042 (U.S. Census Bureau 2008; Johnson & Lichter, 2010). Figure A reflects the growth of diverse populations. There is a predicted decrease in White-only populations, and a con-tinuous increase in the population of all other groups, with a sharp increase in the Hispanic population leading the way. The statistics demonstrate the need for schools to become more proficient at educating non-White students. Many schools and school districts nationwide have great diversity among their student populations. It is therefore imperative that we implement and support leadership practices that demonstrate an appreciation of and equity for diverse populations. Students of color, particularly African American, Latino, and students who speak English as a second language, are often disenfranchised and underachieving (see Figure 4.1). There are currently no reform efforts that have adequately addressed the needs of these children and served to close the achievement gap between disadvantaged students of color and White students, as the achievement gap persists. In fact, the achievement gap has grown. If the problems' association with inequitable schooling are not adequately addressed, generations of disenfranchised youth will find themselves left behind and lost in an educational system that does not meet their needs.

LEARNING ACTIVITY 4.1

- What do you believe the role of school leaders should be in managing diversity?
- Design a professional development activity for teachers that instructs them on how to effectively work with diverse students.

(Percent of total population)

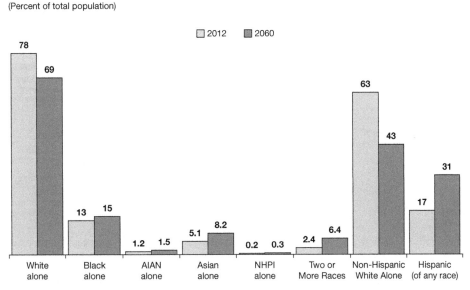

AIAN = American Indian and Alaska Native; NHPI = Native Hawaiian and Other Pacific Islander

Figure 4.1 Population by Race and Hispanic Origin: 2012 and 2060

If schools are to meet the needs of all their students, educators must devise strategies to reach and educate disenfranchised student populations while upholding a learning environment where diversity is celebrated and where learning conditions support equitable outcomes for all students. This will require a concerted and sustained effort on the part of all stakeholders involved, including policy makers, state and district-level administrators, principals and assistant principals, teachers, parents, local community stakeholders, and the students they serve. Both vertical and horizontal partnerships and collaborations will be required in order to tackle this longstanding, complex problem. Figure 4.2, demonstrates that schools are currently not serving non-White students well.

THE NEED TO FIGHT PERSISTENT DISPARITIES AND INEQUALITIES IN U.S. EDUCATION

Figure 4.2 provides a snapshot of the disparity in educational attainment. These figures are troubling for those interested in the achievement and trajectory of minority subgroups as well as those concerned with equitable educational attainment in the U.S. Hispanic (Saenz & Ponjuan, 2008) and Black (Milner, 2013) students are likely to remain of lower social standing and of lower socioeconomic status (see Figure 4.2). *Plyer* v. *Doe* (1982) argued that systematically denying education

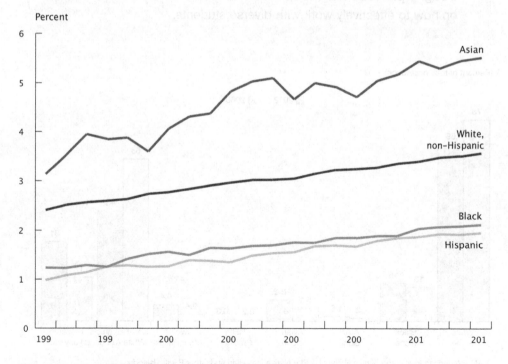

Figure 4.2 Percentage of the Native Population Aged 25
Source: U.S. Census Bureau, 1994–2015 Current Population Survey

was too great a deficit for any group to overcome. Though no racial or ethnic groups are technically denied education, years of ineffective instruction for disenfranchised subgroups yields the same outcome.

Persistent educational inequalities result in the presence of systemic and societal issues that must be addressed before the U.S. can become a progressive democratic society. This is especially true when the magnitude of the shifting demographics is considered. With almost 50 percent of the future U.S. population falling into the two categories of Black or Hispanic, the issue of their being less than proficient in reading and math, as well as the least likely to obtain education beyond high school, emerges as concerning and is problematic.

Segregated schooling is a factor in lower academic achievement (Beard, 2016, Forthcoming; Burris et al., 2004, 2005, 2006, 2007; Oakes, 2005; Persell et al., 1992; Reardon & Owens, 2014; Welner & Burris, 2006; Welner et al., 2008). Black and Hispanic students are more likely to attend schools that are majority minority (Kucsera & Orfield, 2014; Orfield, 2001). Segregation is harmful to students. Students who do not attend desegregated schools perform less well academically. However, truly integrated schools are even more impactful than desegregated schools.

INCLUSIVE LEADERSHIP: FROM DESEGREGATION TO TRUE INTEGRATION

Although legal segregation ended in 1954, de facto segregation persists in most schools. This segregation occurs because of district and neighborhood segregation (Orfield & Frankerberg, Chungmei & Orfield, 2003), or because of internal factors within schools and school districts (Tatum, 2003; Moody, 2001). Key findings indicated in Frankerberg, Lee, and Orfield's (2003) study on school segregation are as follows: Whites are the most segregated group in the nation's public schools. Most attend schools where at least 80 percent of the student body is White. At the same time, more schools are becoming non-White with the shifts in U.S. demographics. Orfield referred to these schools as apartheid schools. During the 1990s, the proportion of Black students in majority White schools decreased by 13 percent, to a level lower than any other since 1968. There is a dramatic shift in the numbers of Latino and Asian students, with Latinos often being segregated by both race and poverty. In short, Frankerberg et al. (2003) noted, "desegregation didn't reduce isolation, but has increased racial separation and white flight" (p. 9). Although principals have little to no direct impact on city/county planning or segregation within school districts, they do have the power to impact the internal racial climate of their own buildings.

Segregation is obvious in many diverse school buildings where you see s race groups consistently sitting together at lunchtime and during other discr times. For example, clubs or intramurals are often organized along r including sports teams and other extracurricular groups. Unfort schools also have a disproportionate distribution of students socioeconomic lines in both special education classes and gifted c' and English Language Learners are more likely to be labeled as special needs students, while White and Asian students are more likely to be tracked into academically gifted and college preparatory classes. Often, teachers will allow students to segregate in classrooms by where they choose to sit, and how they group themselves during small group work sessions. Within school segregation is a form of segregation that principals can dismantle by implementing pro-integration policies and practices. Some suggestions for integrating schools are made in the conclusion of this chapter where implications for practices are discussed.

Inclusion and integration are not just lofty ideals, but moral imperatives. It was decided that a diverse student body was important for the development of all students (Whitla et al., 2003). It was further determined that students of all racial backgrounds benefit from being part of integrated settings and experiencing integrated interactions at all aspects of their social and educational settings. Although many schools are desegregated, the benefits of desegregation cannot be fully realized unless students have meaningful interaction, productive patterns of communication, and parity on all levels throughout the school structure.

Although some schools are considered desegregated because they have diverse student bodies, desegregating schools is much less complex than integrating schools. *Brown* v. *Board of Education of Topeka* (1954) (*Brown*), determined that segregation was unconstitutional and mandated that districts organize schools to be inclusive of Black and White students. Consequently, organizational change occurred in schools across the country to varying degrees. Unfortunately, the policies that accompanied *Brown* to desegregate schools did not always cause students to interact with students who were from different racial and ethnic groups (Moody, 2001). Essentially, desegregation in of it itself was not the vehicle to integration.

Following the implementation of desegregation policies, many frightened and angry White citizens moved to areas far from inner cities to avoid having to comply with policies that required their children to attend school with Black children. This phenomenon, referred to as White flight, has influenced the make-up of most major cities and their schools. As White families migrated to suburban communities, many who wished for their children to attend public schools moved further away from urban areas in order to avoid sending their children to schools with Black and Hispanic children. Another method of avoidance or cocooning was the creation of exclusionary charter schools. These exclusive charters are selective and typically serve affluent White students.

Moody (2001) discussed the notion of homophily, or the inclination to form friendships with those most like oneself, as a framework toward better understanding why students most often cling to same-race groups. Beverly Tatum (2003) revealed similar findings when she discussed the same-race, familial clustering of students as a coping mechanism. Both Moody and Tatum discuss the important role of comfort and familiarity in the formation of friendships. Implications for leadership in creating policies and practices that integrate students are important, as Moody (2001) noted, "school organizational factors affect the probability of contact and the social significance of interaction" (p. 680). Tracking both separates students and creates a status differential between students who take different tracks (Beard, 2016,

Forthcoming; Burris et al., 2004, 2005, 2006, 2007; Oakes, 2005; Persell et al., 1992; Welner & Burris, 2006; Welner et al., 2008.

Integration is the process of promoting interaction between diverse students in a variety of social and educational contexts. This means placing students from diverse backgrounds (e.g., race, gender, ethnicity, sexual orientation, religion) in the same classroom, as well as purposefully including them in activities that will enhance discussion, collaboration, and collective problem-solving. Interactions in activities outside the classroom further encourage a common understanding between students from diverse backgrounds. As noted: "students who interact with diverse students in classrooms and in the broad campus environment will be more motivated and better able to participate in a heterogeneous and complex society" (Gurin et al., 2003, p. 18).

Developing citizens who understand and comply with the principles of justice in order to maintain a just and democratic society is needed. As noted, schools are the primary institution that all children and future citizens pass through. Diversity, ethics and justice are important for schools in two ways. The first is that diversity, ethics and social justice principles must guide ethical practices that demand an equitable education for all students. Second, we must teach students in word and in deed how to function in a diverse society, as well as the full appreciation of diversity in their daily lives. Schools are the most appropriate institution in which integration can take place, as students have the opportunity to meet, work, learn, partner, and socialize with students from diverse backgrounds. Interactions among diverse peer groups should start at a young age, so students have an opportunity to get to know others from diverse backgrounds before harmful prejudices and biases set in. However, familial and societal influences can create the need for interactions to be monitored and managed.

Messages from society and the media often perpetuate negative stereotypes. Families may intentionally or unintentionally reinforce negative stereotypes, fanning prejudices and misconceptions of diverse students in schools. Part of the mission of schools must become the dismantling of stereotypes and prejudices in their effort to build school climates and communities of learners that support unity among all groups.

LEARNING ACTIVITY 4.2

- Work with a partner on a detailed plan to redesign a segregated high school to encourage integration in an ethnically diverse high school. (Currently, the majority of the students in gifted classes are White and Asian, and lower level classes are occupied by African American and Hispanic students, most intramural clubs and extracurricular activities and some sports are segregated by race, and the lunchroom also reflects the lack of integration of students).

SOCIAL JUSTICE LEADERSHIP FOR DIVERSE SCHOOL SETTINGS: A CALL FOR EDUCATIONAL EQUITY

Many educational leadership scholars have explored social justice in education and educational leadership (Furman, 2012; Gerstl-Pepin & Aiken, 2012; Santamaria, 2014; Capper & Young, 2014), yet the concept remains nebulous and fluid. One of the more salient, yet succinct definitions of social justice is offered by George Theoharis, who defined social justice as observing principles of fairness and equity for all people and respect for their basic human rights. Theoharis (2007) also states that social justice principals are those that make issues of race, gender, class, disability, sexual orientation, and other historically and currently marginalizing conditions in the United States central to their advocacy, leadership practice and vision (p. 223).

School leaders are charged with making free and appropriate education accessible to *all students*, and promoting a school climate conducive to learning, such that all students can be successful, regardless of race, gender, class, disability, sexual orientation, gender identification, or other historically and currently marginalizing conditions. The actions noted above demonstrate an overlap between managing schools for diversity, and leadership based upon social justice principles. Social justice principals demand that school leaders are conscientious in their efforts to make all students and families welcomed and well served, regardless of their differences.

CULTURALLY RESPONSIVE SCHOOL LEADERSHIP

Gloria Ladson-Billings (1995a) introduced the notion of Culturally Relevant Pedagogy as it relates to effective teaching. She noted that Culturally Relevant Pedagogy was "just good teaching" (p. 159). Her work brought to light the notion that students respond better to educational experiences in which their culture is considered and even used to guide the education process and classroom management (Ladson-Billings, 1995b). Culturally responsive school leadership is the antecedent of culturally responsive teaching. Khalifa, Gooden, & Davis (2016) noted that Gay (2010) made the point that although culturally responsive teaching is important, the complexity of the challenges faced by minoritized students requires all aspects of education to be transformed, including funding, policy making, and leadership.

Khalifa, Gooden & Davis (2016) purport that culturally responsive school leadership is necessary because such leadership orientation is necessary in order to close persistent racialized opportunity gaps. They further noted that opportunity gaps arise out of cultural misunderstandings, which lead to a deviation from dominant cultural norms on behalf of Black and Hispanic students. When students do not comply with cultural norms and expectations, they are penalized more often for disciplinary infractions, often resulting in time spent in a discipline cycle, away from the learning that occurs within the classroom. Therefore, the achievement and disciplinary gaps grow. Leaders who are not properly trained in culturally responsive leadership are likely to perpetuate the status quo, continuing the downward cycle of low expectations and lower academic achievement among Black and Hispanic students. Principals who are adequately prepared are tooled to produce different results.

The Culturally Responsive School Leadership framework suggested to produce culturally responsive school leaders includes four identified behaviors (Khalifa, Gooden, & Davis, 2016). The first is that leaders must be critically self-aware, or acutely aware of their personal feelings and biases related to diversity in schools and society. The second tenet of the framework is that leaders must support the development of culturally relevant curricula and teacher professional development. As such, instructional leadership must include training in cultural relevance and require teachers to employ the principles of cultural relevance in their teaching. Third, culturally responsive school leadership means promoting a culturally responsive and inclusive school environment. This refers to using institutional care to develop policies and practices that ensure an inclusive and inviting school culture for all students. And finally, culturally responsive leaders engage students and parents in community contexts. In doing so, principals gain insight into the culture of the community and engage in a continuous dialogue and resulting activities that improve unity and cultural oneness between the school and the community. When schools practice this tenet, they honor the community context and frame the school culture such that it honors the culture of the community.

Principals who adhere to cultural responsiveness are social justice leaders who are equipped to work toward promoting learning for all students under their purview, regardless of race and the implications that all too often follow. Culturally responsive leaders reject the status quo and low expectations imposed on some student (groupings). They are capable of uniquely providing an environment where all students can succeed. The implications for practice below combine the essence of the ideals expressed throughout this chapter in order to offer keys pushing for student success in diverse contexts.

IMPLICATIONS FOR PRACTICE

Principals can effectively lessen, and ultimately end within school segregation by establishing their expectations for managing diversity, and implementing policies and practices that espouse the appreciation of diversity. Principals can do this by sharing the benefits of integration with teachers, students, and parents, both formally and informally. Beyond sharing relevant research, principals can act to implement policies that encourage integration. The framework suggested by Furman (2012, pp. 196–197) provides a strong foundation for constructing school leadership that is inclusive, responsive, and proactive in promoting just and equitable schools. Qualities that are embodied by inclusive, responsive leaders are summarized below.

- *Action-oriented and transformative.* Social justice leaders should be "proactive change agents" (Furman, 2012). Such leaders institute policies and practices that create an environment where justice and equity can flourish. Students and teachers are able to excel in this type of environment because they can relax their defenses and concentrate on their performance as the leader proactively protects the school.

- *Committed and persistent.* The struggle to maintain socially just schools is difficult exhausting (Theoharis, 2007). This is because social justice is counterintuitive to the natural laws of U.S. society. Although there are many benevolent and morally upright Americans, the U.S. has a history of racism, bigotry, and hate that has left remnants in present-day ideology and societal practices. School leaders have to fight persistently to maintain an environment where diverse groups can find a sense of belonging and thrive.
- *Inclusive and democratic.* Educational leaders must create inclusive policies and practices in schools where every student's voice is equally heard and equally important. Both teaching and learning as well as political structures should be equitable and accessible to all students.
- *Relational caring.* All students are more inclined to connect with leaders and teachers who demonstrate care and establish relationships. Additionally, students who have been marginalized are more inclined to perform when they feel cared for (Bass, in progress).
- *Reflective.* Practitioners who are critically reflective position themselves to be in a state of continuous improvement. They are also more likely to see, acknowledge, and address their own biases (toward diverse entities), so that they do not cause harm to their students (Furman, 2012).
- *Oriented toward a socially just pedagogy.* School leaders who are oriented toward a socially just pedagogy will make leading with equity across constituents as their goal. When social justice is the primary focus, leadership enforces policies and practices that push for fairness for all students.
- *Practices a culturally responsive pedagogy.* School leaders who are culturally responsive realize that diversity must be addressed according to individual cultural needs. This requires principals to get to know their student and staff, and to provide leadership and resources that addresses their various individual needs.

The culturally responsive framework above can be broken further into the policies and practices deemed appropriate by the principal for their particular school. For example, teachers can be required to group their students with diversity as the central criteria for at least some of their lessons. The principal can let it be known that he or she expects to see mixed racial grouping during class group work. Grouping that requires same race and/or gender must be minimal and second to the goal of group integration.

The second way that a principal can encourage integration is to require that all intramural groups be racially mixed proportionate to the make-up of the student body, with the expectation that the student and teacher leaders of the group would be charged with recruiting diverse group members. If group membership is not diverse, then the group should be subject to being discontinued, despite its popularity. Exceptions would be groups based upon gender, or approved special interests that might be difficult to recruit members for. Sports teams would also be charged with attempting to recruit diversity. Individual students could also be encouraged and incentivized to be in partnership with students of difference. Activities should be suggested for partners, requiring that they spend time together, both inside and outside of school, including in one another's homes, in an attempt to learn to appreciate each other's differences with a prescribed curriculum and supervision.

School leaders are in a powerful position to establish an inclusive school culture where all students are free to thrive. Actions taken will be those of a social justice leader and one who appreciates diversity while implementing institutional care. The case study below demonstrates the struggles of a leader who is faced with a dilemma in how to practice social justice leadership and institutional care while his teacher(s) may be doing otherwise.

CASE STUDY 4.1: PROMISES KEPT OR OPPORTUNITIES LOST: A WICKED PROBLEM IN EDUCATIONAL LEADERSHIP

Abstract

A novice principal's decision not to intervene on an ill-conceived policy prompts a parent to pursue a line of questioning that administrators aren't prepared for. In this case, a young man working through a high school transition while preparing for college is met with unexpected challenges in motivation. What the principal initially perceives as inconsequential becomes a wicked problem when the parent questions the ethics and legalities of the policy, teachers' intent, and potential civil rights violations. Underscored are nuances in communication, decision making, motivation and ethics. As the elements of the case unfold, matters pertaining to school and community relations, policy, law, race and gender present themselves useful for discussing a variety of key issues related to school leadership.

Key Words

educational administration, decision making, policy, ethics, school and community relations, race, gender, Brown v. Board of Education

Case Narrative

Jeff James, a principal who came from within the teaching ranks of Woodstone River High School (WRHS),* enjoyed the respect of both teachers and parents. WRHS was steeped in tradition and was one of the highest performing schools in the state. It was not uncommon for teachers to offer interesting and unique incentives to students. A teacher, in a moment of exuberance at an assembly, offered an incentive to the entire sophomore class. This incentive created leadership dilemmas for Mr. James who took the principalship a year later. The case prompts questions of policy, decision making, race, gender, law, leadership and organizational dynamics.

The Context

The community from which the Woodstone student body comes is a rapidly growing suburban community located 20 miles northeast of a Midwestern State metropolis. This particular suburb has become attractive to young professionals and corporate executives with children. The population has expanded 41% in the last 15 years to over 44,000 residents. Ninety-nine percent of the residents possess a high school diploma or higher; 74% hold Bachelor's degrees; and 29% hold Graduate or professional degrees. The average annual income is $115,000 (almost triple Midwestern State average). As the corporate presence has increased, community diversity has also increased. Woodstone realized a loss in white residents (12+%) over the past ten years. At the same time, it saw an increase in Asian (8+%); Black, and Hispanic residents, and residents of two or more races (combined 7.7%).

The change in racial demographics has been profound. WRHS now has a 24% minority population. The district serves the third largest English Language Learner population in Midwestern State. While there is diversity among the larger staff (including custodians, cooks, and instructional aids) there is very little racial diversity among the teaching staff. The sophomore and junior teaching staff consisted of 40 (63%) Caucasian males and 23 (37%) Caucasian females. During those ten years, a Chinese female bilingual aid was hired and two additional English as a Second Language (ELL) teachers joined the staff.

Historically, WRHS has been able to boast many indicators of academic success. Recently, however, the rapidly growing diverse student population has posed some challenges. For example, school leadership shifted professional development efforts and resources toward effective teaching strategies primarily for ELL students (the largest growing subgroup). Although leadership noted achievement gaps for other demographic groups, these went largely unattended. Several parents and a few teachers voiced concerns about possible bias and questioned why so many resources were being used to heavily support only one segment of diverse learners.

First Year: The Sophomore Test Motivation

As in years past, the teachers of the sophomore class encouraged students to come to school well prepared to take the state proficiency exam. The teachers of the sophomore class held an informational night for parents, emphasizing the importance of test readiness. The Science teacher, Mr. Reed, told the parents, "it isn't only important for your children to perform well for their own record, but it is important they perform well for the school. We've presented the material; the rest of their success is up to them."

The teachers followed up the next day with a student assembly for the sophomore class. The then principal informed the sophomore class that they were well prepared and no one in the entire sophomore class had demonstrated a need for concern that hadn't been addressed by the teachers. "All that is left is for you to show up, well rested, and be prepared to show off what you already know; just show up and show off."

The principal gestured back toward the teachers as if to turn the microphone over and exited the auditorium. Mr. Reed, the Science teacher, then said, "We are so confident in you, that if you get a score of 'Advanced' in four of the five core subject categories, you can opt out of taking a final exam of your choice." The students roared in celebration, while the remaining teachers glanced at one another in disbelief. A few of the teachers' mouths fell open in surprise and one teacher noticeably shook his head, looked at the floor, and nervously shifted from one foot to the other and back again.

Year Two: There's A New Kid in Town

The year after the incentive was offered to the entire WRSH sophomore class, Gabriel (Gabe) George, a 15-year-old African American student transferred into the WRSH junior class. This was his third transfer since his second-grade year. This one, though, came with a much deeper sense of loneliness. His peers in this community seemed to know one another so well and for so long. He found himself, in his room thinking and asking questions about all sorts of things.

Working to fit in had become decidedly more difficult. In his previous move, Gabe realized that he was judged in some situations by the color of his skin and had to work exceedingly hard to gain the respect of some of his teachers. He felt the heaviness of needing to prove himself, yet again. It was all becoming less interesting. This year, for the first time, he worried about whether or not he would even make it to college.

By October, Gabe considered his Chemistry teacher, Mr. Reed, to be the most frustrating teacher he'd experienced. Mr. Reed's favoritism was so obvious in class that other students commented on it. One day, Gabe shared with his mother that he, another child of color, and a few of the girls in class were not among Mr. Reed's favored students: "Even when I work with the lab group and we get it right, or when I study, he treats everything I offer suspiciously, like he doesn't know if I really did it or if I'm really capable, and some of it I know is good".

Mrs. George found him in his room more often. She planned to attend parent–teacher conferences and asked the Chemistry tutor they hired from the local university to join her to see what they could learn to better support Gabe in Chemistry. At the conference, Mr. Reed seemed distracted and rushed, facing a full conference schedule. He suggested that Gabe's trouble wasn't with lab or homework, but with the tests. Mrs. George requested the opportunity for another conversation when he was less rushed, but Mr. Reed suggested that he just meet with the tutor to explain Gabe's gaps in understanding.

A Mother's Concern

Mrs. George and the tutor conferenced with Mr. Reed on two more occasions. On the second visit, Mrs. George suggested that maybe Gabe didn't understand the test format. She asked Mr. Reed to share her son's exam so they could assist in test-taking strategies. Mr. Reed told her this was the second year of a unique program. Hence, exam information simply wasn't available and he wasn't permitted to share anything about the test. Frustrated, Mrs. George left more confused than when she came. Her frustration, coupled with Gabe's sense of disrespect, prompted her to call Mr. James. He informed her that Mr. Reed was a chemist and had received additional training to teach this special curriculum Chemistry course. He assured Mrs. George that Gabe would be fine and would ultimately do well in Mr. Reed's course.

A Question of Fairness

Gabe came into the house in an uproar. He told his mother: "The teachers told the class that anyone who took the state test last year and scored Advanced in four categories didn't have to take a final of their choice this year."

"OK, so what are you worried about? You scored Advanced in all five categories."

"Yeah, that's it, me and Ana weren't here last year."

"Well that doesn't matter, you still met the criteria."

"That's it, Ana and I were told we don't qualify. They said it doesn't apply to us because it was a promise and incentive for last year's sophomore class."

"That doesn't make sense. Don't worry about it. I'm sure this is a misunderstanding," Mrs. George told Gabe. The next morning, Mrs. George called Mr. James to discuss what Gabe had shared.

Mr. James said, "Well, yes, that is true. The sophomore teachers did make this promise to the class last year, but we got our scores back so late in the year that the sophomore teachers couldn't keep their promise to that class, so they appealed to junior class teachers to release students from a final of their choice this year instead."

"I think that's fine," said Mrs. George, "but Gabe is under the impression that this grace doesn't apply to him and one other student. Is that true? Our son transferred over the summer. He scored high and surpassed requirements for participation in this opportunity, and yet you're opting to separate him from his peers? Furthermore, why would you want to exclude a child from the activities and criteria set forth for the entire class?"

"That's the thing, he wasn't part of the class last year," Mr. James responded.

Mrs. George felt herself becoming frustrated, "You're right. He wasn't here, but he is still part of the same graduating class and his exam scores merit the opportunity. The criteria set forth weren't about where he was; they were an incentive to hit the high mark on the state exam. He did that!"

"Mrs. George, I'm not able to help you understand, except to say, this was a promise made to WRHS students last year and the teachers this year are trying to keep their promise to those students. Your son isn't the only one exempt from this promise. Quite a few students were advanced in only three categories. Please know, the teachers set forth this policy and because it was set last year, I wasn't involved, and as far as I can tell, your son isn't losing anything, he just isn't getting the benefit."

"Excuse me, Mr. James, my son isn't getting the benefit he deserves and because of that, he *is* losing something."

"What is he losing?"

"He is being excluded from participating with his peers in a privilege he earned. He met the criteria established and yet is losing the opportunity to protect his GPA like his similarly situated peers. My son is African American and in *Brown* v. *Board of Education*, Chief Justice Warren said, 'to separate them from others of similar age and qualifications solely because of their race generates a feeling of inferiority as to their status in the community that may affect their hearts and minds in a way unlikely to ever be undone.' Mr. James, I'm not interested in raising a heartbroken boy or an angry young man. Haven't we enough of them?"

"Mrs. George, I didn't know your son was black. I am not separating him on the basis of his race. In your mind, this is a racial issue. In my mind, that was not the intent of the exclusion."

Mrs. George responded, "Even as an unintended consequence, this policy has a discriminatory effect. Mr. James, Gabe is the only African American boy in this program. How could you not know he is black? I suspect because he is the only African American may have something to do with why he's had so much trouble in Chemistry. Maybe Mr. Reed doesn't think Gabe should be in his class. I can assure you, Gabe belongs in every one of his courses, and in this elite curriculum."

Mr. James replied, "As I told you, I don't see how I cannot support my teachers on this. Their intent was to motivate the class to perform well. This isn't a race matter."

"Thank you, Mr. James, with whom shall I speak next?"

"Well that would be the superintendent, but I can assure you, he will be in support of our decision because it is a school policy, not a district policy."

On Sunday afternoon, Mr. James called Allen Petrie. Superintendent Petrie had been in the district for seven years. He was well regarded both as a district leader and in leadership organizations throughout the state.

James began, "Allen, I was blindsided on Friday by a parent who is upset because the teachers made a policy decision last year to offer an incentive which her son has been excluded from. I wasn't even here last year, so I'm not sure how to address this situation." After recounting the specifics of his encounter with Mrs. George, he concluded, "I think I need to support the teachers. They all seem to favor the policy and I don't want to go against the teachers in my first year, if at all possible, like you told me. Still, I don't know how to slow this down. The parent spoke in legalese."

The Superintendent's Response

"Jeff, I am not going to tell you how to run your school except to say that I do not want parents making accusations about the fairness of our policies, questioning competing policies, or engaging in legal action. What I will tell Mrs. George tomorrow, when I accept her call, is that you have the responsibility for making school decisions." The superintendent concluded, "Jeff, get your teacher leaders together and come up with a reasonable solution for this problem so it goes no further. Monday evening, I look forward to hearing how this was resolved and how everything is moving along.

Source: Karen Stansberry Beard
* Pseudonyms for the community, school, teachers, principal and superintendent are used throughout the case study.

LEARNING ACTIVITY 4.3

1. Is equity jeopardized in Mr. Reed's decision not to allow Gabe and the female student the incentive offered to their peers? Is fairness?

2. Juxtapose the principles of institutional care and the ethic of Justice in Mr. James decision-making process.

3. Is there a right decision? Mr. James wants to appease both his concerned parent(s) and his teachers. If Mr. James finds that pleasing both sides is not possible, where should his loyalty lie? (Please use one of the ethical frameworks to justify your decision.)

4. What could Mr. James have done immediately to show support for Mrs. George? For Mr. Reed?

5. How will you handle Mr. Reed if it is determined after further investigation that he is biased against students of color and female students?

SUMMARY OF KEY POINTS

- Increasing diversity in U.S. schools and society is inevitable.
- Disparities have persisted in schools and society as long as populations have been diverse.
- Students thrive in integrated, inclusive school environments.

- School leaders are positioned at the helm of possibility for change. They are further charged with promoting positive change in their schools and in the communities where their schools are located.
- Social justice leaders are committed to promoting positive change in schools and communities.
- Culturally responsive school leadership provides a framework that promotes an appropriate education for students of all backgrounds.

OTHER DIVERSITY AND INCLUSION CASES

Within UCEA's *Journal of Cases in Educational Leadership* (JCEL), there are appropriate cases that fit well with this chapter. Locate one or more of the following articles:

Castangno (2008). Improving Academic Achievement, but at What Cost?: The Demands of Diversity and Equity at Birch Middle School.

Daugird, Everett, Jones, & White (2015). Diversity and Inclusion in Social Media: A Case Study of Student Behavior.

Diem & Carpenter (2013). If I Don't Use the Word, I Shouldn't Have to Hear it: The Surfacing of Racial Tensions in a Leadership Preparation Classroom.

Fusarelli & Eaton (2011). Transgender Day of Remembrance and a Prospective Student Open House: How One Student Inspired a School to do Both.

Tooms (2004). Developing Leadership Strategies Inside the Politics of Language, Diversity, and Change.

OTHER LEARNING ACTIVITIES

LEARNING ACTIVITY 4.4

Suggested learning activities and assessments for this chapter include the following: View the film *New Immigrants Share their Stories: The Students of Newcomers High School*. Have students create their own mini-films that capture the experiences of at least three newcomers to their area. Newcomers can include parents or community members.

Students will be responsible for creating the curriculum for a social justice workshop/professional development for school workers. They should be given the guidelines below to follow as they develop their curriculum.

1. I must build my lesson plan around topics and concepts I hope to cover, then design or choose activities that can lead to an exploration of those topics or concepts. I must not build my lesson plan around which activities I most enjoy facilitating.

2. I must diversify the types of activities and exercises I use. Every group of participants will have a range of learning styles and comfort levels with different types and formations of activities. Some enjoy big group work, others prefer to work in pairs. Some like simulations and role plays, others prefer narrative and story-telling activities. I must try to pull from a range of approaches when designing my plan.

3. One key to social justice learning is deep dialogue. I must avoid filling so much of my class or workshop with activities and exercises that I fail to leave ample time for dialogue and processing.

4. Too often, multicultural or social justice program designs call for People of Color to teach White people about racism, women to teach men about sexism, and so on. I must avoid activities that call for oppressed groups to teach privileged groups about their oppression.

5. Whenever possible and appropriate, I must model a willingness to be vulnerable by participating in class exercises and activities. This can be particularly effective when activities call for story-sharing or personal narratives. In these cases, I can set the tone for the kinds of stories or narratives I hope others will share.

6. Many popular diversity activities simulate life through role plays or other experiences in which participants are asked to take on one or more predefined identities. These can be effective, interactive, and engaging, but I must balance them with activities or discussions that draw from the actual lived experiences of the participants.

7. Films can provide excellent illustrations of concepts, leading to fruitful dialogues. But I must avoid using long films that drain away dialogue time. (Many filmmakers produce two versions of their films—a full-length version and a shorter "training" version.) In addition, I must be thoughtful about how to transition from a film back to the personal experiences of the participants.

8. I must be creative. Too often, educators and facilitators become dependent on one or two activities or exercises. But only I know the context in which I am working—canned activities and exercises are not designed for every context. I have a sense for what will and will not work within that context. I must be willing to take the time to thoughtfully design new activities or modify existing ones.

LEARNING ACTIVITY 4.5

Students will write "Who I Am" poems. This activity increases self-awareness and encourages self-development. The "Who I Am" activity provides a non-threatening starting point for encouraging self-reflection and introspection. It is a safe way for participants to think about and share influences that have shaped their identity. In this activity students take 10–15 minutes to write a poem called "Who I Am." Each line should begin with the words "I am . . ." Statements are left to students, although they can include where they're from regionally, ethnically, religiously, and so on. Memories from different points in their lives, interests and hobbies, mottoes and credos, favorite phrases, family traditions and customs, and whatever they feel defines who they are. Students will then be asked to read their poems to the class. The instructor should first share their poem so that it is easier for the students to share. A sample can be found below.

Sample "Who I Am" Poem

I am basketball on a snowy driveway.
I am fish sticks, crinkle-cut frozen french fries and frozen mixed
    vegetables.
I am primarily white, upper-middle class neighborhoods and racially
    diverse schools.
I am Donkey Kong, Ms. Pac Man, Atari 2600 and sports video
    games.
I am football on Thanksgiving and New Year's Day.
I am "unity in diversity" and "speaking from your own experience."
I am triple-Wahoos, earning three degrees from the University of
    Virginia.
I am diversity, multicultural education, identity, introspection, self-
    reflection, and social action.
I am Daffy Duck, Mr. Magoo, Hong Kong Phooey, Foghorn Leghorn,
    and other cartoons.
I am Tae Kwon Do, basketball, the batting cages, a soccer family,
    and the gym.
I am a wonderful family, close and loving and incredibly supportive.
I am films based on true stories and documentaries
I am the History Channel, CNN, ESPN, BRAVO, and Home Team
    Sports.
I am a passion for educating and facilitating, personal development
    and making connections.

LEARNING ACTIVITY 4.6

Student fishbowl activity

This activity forces participants to listen actively to the experiences and perspectives of a specific group of people. A student fishbowl gives pre-service and in-service educators an opportunity to hear the experiences, ideas and feedback of current students while giving the students an opportunity to be active in the dialogue on educational equity.

Students and administrators should be reminded that they are the most important part in the success of this activity.

Directions for the activity are as follows:

1. 8–10 K-12 students are selected to sit in a circle in the middle of the room. Educators should sit around these students.
2. One of the students acts as facilitator.
3. Topics discussed should be relevant to your class topic. Fishbowl participants should have an opportunity to take the conversation wherever they want—or need—it to go.
4. Topics to push the conversation along might include:
   a. What are your favorite things about school?
   b. What aspects of your school do you feel should be improved?
   c. What can your teachers do to help you learn better?
   d. Share a story about when one of your teachers did something that made you feel especially included in the learning process.
   e. Who is your favorite teacher? Why?
   f. Who is your least favorite teacher? Why?
   g. What do you feel is the role of school in your life?
   h. What do you feel should be the major goals of school?
5. Make sure everyone in the fishbowl has an opportunity to talk.
6. Allow the fishbowl discussion to continue for at least 30 minutes. After the fishbowl discussion winds down, divide the participants and the students (audience) into small groups of 6–10. This will allow an opportunity for debriefing and clarification of points made during the fishbowl activity. They should use the small group discussions to learn more about the students who were in the fishbowl.
7. After the small groups, call the fishbowl back together. A variety of points can guide the next discussion, including:
   a. To the observers: Was it difficult not to respond to the fishbowl students?

    b. To the fishbowl students: How did it feel to share your feelings about school, knowing that these principals were listening closely?

    c. To the fishbowl students: Do you usually have opportunities to share your perspectives on school and your education?

    d. To the observers: Did you hear anything from the fishbowl that surprised you?

LEARNING ACTIVITY 4.7

Unequal resources. Have students create a poster about a specific topic. Let them know that there will be a "prize" such as snacks or some other prize that would motivate the groups to desire to win. Let students know that their posters will be judged upon content as well as how colorful they are, how creative they are, and how many designs they had. The theme could be related to the class topic, curricular, or an upcoming holiday.

Proceed as follows:

1. Distribute noticeably unequal resources to the groups and make sure that each group sees the resources all of the other groups are getting. Remind them that sharing between groups disqualifies them from the contest. Some groups should be given bare bones and few colors and decorations, while others groups should be given more.

2. Give the groups 30–35 minutes to create their posters.

3. Award the prize to the best poster, even though the parameters when compared to resources allotted were clearly unfair.

4. Have the following discussions:

    a. How did you feel when you noticed that some people clearly had more materials than you? Others?

    b. How did you feel when you noticed that some people had fewer resources than you?

    c. In what ways did resources affect your project?

    d. Did you feel the contest was fair?

    e. Can you relate this to standardized testing and other issues that arise in schooling? How do they relate?

5. After doing this activity, do you feel it is important to consider individual circumstances and opportunities before judging a person's capabilities? Why or why not?

6. Did this impact the way you feel about equality and equity? How so?

RESOURCES

Ed Exchange—Multicultural, Anti-bias, and Diversity Activities: www.edchange.org/multicultural/activities/model.html

More Diversity Activities for Youth and Adults—Penn State University: http://extension.psu.edu/publications/ui378

REFERENCES

Akiba, M., LeTendre, G. K., & Scribner, J. P. (2007). Teacher quality, opportunity gap, and national achievement in 46 countries. *Educational Researcher, 36*(7), 369–387.

Bass, L. (2009). Fostering an ethic of care in leadership: A conversation with five African American women. *Advances in Developing Human Resources, 11*(5), 619–632.

Beard, K. S. (2012). Making the case for the outlier: An African American female administrator who decided to close the achievement gap. *International Journal of Qualitative Studies in Education, 25*(1), 59–71.

Beard, K. S. (2016). Tracking in Schools. In K. Lomoty, P. Jackson, M. Adem, P. Ruf, V. Copeland, A. Huerta, N. Iglesias-Prieto, & D. Brown (Eds.), *People of color in the United States: Contemporary issues in education, work, communities, health, and immigration* (pp. 367–373). Santa Barbara, CA: Praeger.

Beard, K. S. (Forthcoming) Getting on track: Aligning the achievement and opportunity gap conversation with ethical educational practice. *International Journal of Leadership in Education.*

Beck, L. G. (1994). *Reclaiming educational administration as a caring profession.* New York: Teachers College Press.

Burris, C. C., & Welner, K. G. (2005). Closing the achievement gap by detracking. *Phi Delta Kappan,* 594–598.

Burris, C. C., Heubert, J. P., & Levin, H. M. (2004). Math acceleration for all. *Educational Leadership, 61*(5), 68–72.

Burris, C. C., Heubert, J. P., & Levin, H. M. (2006). Accelerating mathematics achievement using heterogeneous grouping. *American Educational Research Journal, 43*(1), 137–154.

Burris, C. C., Welner, K. G., Wiley, E. W., & Murphy, J. (2007). A world-class curriculum for all. *Educational Leadership, 64*(7), 53.

Capper, C. A., & Young, M. D. (2014). Ironies and limitations of educational leadership for social justice: A call to social justice educators. *Theory into practice, 53*(2), 158–164.

Coleman, M. (2012). Leadership and diversity. *Educational management administration & leadership, 40*(5), 592–609.

Cologon, K. (2013). Inclusion in education. *Issues Paper.*

Foster, W. (1986). *Paradigms and promises: New approaches to educational administration.* Buffalo, NY: Prometheus Books.

Frankerberg, E., Lee, C., & Orfield, G. (2003). *A multiracial society with segregated schools: Are we losing the dream?* The Civil Rights Project, Harvard University.

Fullan, M. (Ed.). (2003). *The moral imperative of school leadership.* Corwin Press.

Furman, G. C. (2003). Moral leadership and the ethic of community. *Values and Ethics in Educational Administration, 2*(1), 1–7.

Furman, G. C. (2004). The ethic of community. *Journal of Educational Administration, 42*(2), 215–235.

Furman, G. (2012). Social justice leadership as praxis developing capacities through preparation programs. *Educational Administration Quarterly*, *48*(2), 191–229.

Gay, G. (2101). *Culturally responsive teaching: Theory, research, and practice.* Teachers College Press.

Gerstl-Pepin, C., & Aiken, J. A. (Eds.). (2012). *Social justice leadership for a global world.* IAP.

Gilligan, C. (1982). *In a different voice.* Cambridge, MA: Harvard University Press.

Giroux, H. A. (1992). *Border crossings: Cultural workers and the politics of education.* New York: Psychology Press.

Gurin, P., Nagda, B. A., Lopez, G. (2003). The benefit of diversity in education for democratic citizenship. *Journal of Social Issues*, *60*(1), 17–34.

Haring-Smith, T. (2012). Broadening our definition of diversity. *Liberal Education*, *98*(2), 6–13.

Hoy, W. K. & Miskel, C. G. (2013). *Educational administration: Theory, research, and practice* (9th ed.). New York: McGraw-Hill

Johnson, K. M., & Lichter, D. T. (2010). Growing diversity among America's children and youth: Spatial and temporal dimensions. *Population and Development Review*, *36*(1), 151–176.

Johnson, K. M., Schaefer, A., Lichter, D. T., & Rogers, L. T. (2014). The Increasing Diversity of America's Youth. Durham, NC: Carsey Institute, University of New Hampshire.

Khalifa, M. A., Gooden, M. A., & Davis, J. E. (2016). Culturally responsive school leadership: A synthesis of the literature. *Review of Educational Research*, *86*(4), 1272–1311.

Kucsera, J., & Orfield, G. (2014). New York state's extreme school segregation: Inequality, inaction and a damaged future. Los Angeles, CA: The Civil Rights Project.

Ladson-Billings, G. (1995a). But that's just good teaching! The case for culturally relevant pedagogy. *Theory into Practice*, *34*(3), *Culturally Relevant Teaching* (Summer), pp. 159–165.

Ladson-Billings, G. (1995b). Toward a theory of culturally relevant pedagogy. *American Educational Research Journal*, *32*(3), 465–491.

Ladson-Billings, G. (2006). From the achievement gap to the education debt: Understanding achievement in US schools. *Educational researcher*, *35*(7), 3–12.

Lumby, J., & Coleman, M. (2010). *Leadership and diversity.* London: Sage.

Madsen, J., & Mabokela, R. (2014). Leadership challenges in addressing changing demographics in schools. *NASSP Bulletin*, *98*(1), 75–96.

Maxwell, L. (2014). US school enrollment hits majority-minority milestone. *Education Week*, *33*(37), 1.

Milner IV, H. R. (2012). Beyond a test score: Explaining opportunity gaps in educational practice. *Journal of Black Studies*, *43*(6), 693–718.

Milner, H. R. (2013). Rethinking achievement gap talk in urban education. *Urban Education*, *48*(1), 3–8.

Moody, J. (2001). Race, school integration, and friendship segregation in America. *American Journal of Sociology*, *107*(3), 679–716.

Noddings, N. (1988). An ethic of caring and its implications for instructional arrangements. *American Journal of Education*, *96*(2), 215–230.

Oakes, J. (2005). *Keeping track: How schools structure inequality* (2nd ed.). New Haven, CT: Yale University.

Orfield, G. (2001). *Schools more separate: Consequences of a decade of resegregation.* Cambridge, MA: Harvard University, Civil Rights Project.

Persell, C. H., Catsambis, S., & Cookson Jr, P. W. (1992). Differential asset conversion: Class and gendered pathways to selective colleges. *Sociology of Education*, 208–225.

Plyler v. *Doe*, 457 U.S. 202 (1982).

Reardon, S. F., & Owens, A. (2014). 60 Years after Brown: Trends and consequences of school segregation. *Annual Review of Sociology*, *40*, 199–218.

Saenz, V. B., & Ponjuan, L. (2008). The vanishing Latino male in higher education. *Journal of Hispanic Higher Education*.

Santamaría, L. J. (2014). Critical change for the greater good multicultural perceptions in educational leadership toward social justice and equity. *Educational Administration Quarterly*, *50*(3), 347–391.

Shapiro, J. P., & Stefkovich, J. A. (2016). *Ethical leadership and decision making in education: Applying theoretical perspectives to complex dilemmas*. Routledge.

Stefkovich, J., & Begley, P. T. (2007). Ethical school leadership defining the best interests of students. *Educational Management Administration & Leadership*, *35*(2), 205–224.

Stefkovich, J. A., & Michaele O'Brien, G. (2004). Best interests of the student: An ethical model. *Journal of Educational Administration*, *42*(2), 197–214.

Strike K. A., Haller E. J., & Soltis J. F. (2005). *The ethics of school administration* (3rd ed.). New York: Teachers College Press.

Tatum, B. D. (2003). *"Why are all the Black kids sitting together in the cafeteria?": And other conversations about race*. New York: Basic Books.

Taylor, R. W. (2010). The role of teacher education programs in creating culturally competent teachers: A moral imperative for ensuring the academic success of diverse student populations. *Multicultural Education*, *17*(3), 24.

Theoharis, G. (2007). Social justice educational leaders and resistance: Toward a theory of social justice leadership. *Educational administration quarterly*, *43*(2), 221–258.

US Census Bureau. 2008. "2008 national population projections". Retrieved April 2016 from: www.census.gov/population/www/projections/2008projections.html.

Welner, K., & Burris, C. C. (2006). Alternative approaches to the politics of detracking. *Theory into Practice*, *45*(1), 90–99.

Welner, K., Burris, C., Wiley, E., & Murphy, J. (2008). Accountability, rigor, and detracking: Achievement effects of embracing a challenging curriculum as a universal good for all students. *The Teachers College Record*, *110*(3), 571–607.

Whitla, D. K., Orfield, G., Silen, W., Teperow, C., Howard, C., & Reede, J. (2003). Educational benefits of diversity in medical school: a survey of students. *Academic Medicine*, *78*(5), 460–466.

CHAPTER 5

The Moral and Legal Dimensions of Decision Making

Susan Bon

CHAPTER OVERVIEW

This chapter will discuss the role of educational leaders as moral and ethical agents who are simultaneously bound by laws and legal doctrines. Given the significance of law and ethics as pertains to school leadership, this chapter instructs leaders to recognize ethical and legal principles as compatible sources of authority in education. There is a delicate balance between adhering to the doctrinal boundaries of law and preserving the moral imperative of educational opportunities. A consideration of National Educational Leadership Preparation (NELP) Standard 6 and its balance with Standard 2 directs the various topics and issues presented here.

INTRODUCTION

Educational leaders are moral and ethical agents who are simultaneously bound by laws and legal doctrines. From a historical perspective, the influence of law on education and educational opportunity has been profound, particularly in light of a number of judicial decisions interpreting students' constitutional and statutorily protected rights. High-profile decisions such as *Brown* v. *Board of Education* (1954) remind us of the powerful influence the law has had on local school systems and students' educational rights.

Education is not, however, primarily a legal enterprise; rather, education has a moral foundation that is grounded in teaching itself (Dewey, 1909). In other words, the goal of teaching is to provide an education that "is primarily focused on the process of enrichment and growth through the immersion in knowledge and its possibilities" (Bon, 2012, p. 290). Despite the increasing focus on preparing school leaders to be conscious of the law in today's litigious environment (Schimmel & Militello, 2008), school leaders continue also to serve as moral stewards bound by both legal and ethical principles.

Ethical standards and competencies are an emerging focus for school leaders who are expected to act according to moral and legal principles to protect the educational rights of all children (Begley, 2001; Fullan, 2001; Starratt, 2004). This moral purpose is heightened in the educational community where social complexity and wicked problems (Conklin, 2001) threaten to disrupt communication and defy resolution. Wicked problems are especially prevalent in settings where there are multiple "stakeholders [who] have different views about what the problem is and what constitutes an acceptable solution" (p. 7). Furthermore, there is likely not to be clear right or wrong solutions to the dilemmas that leaders encounter in education.

Even without the complexity of dilemmas or wicked problems, schools regularly make decisions that implicate the delicate balance between ethical and legal principles. Although education is an inherently moral enterprise (Noddings, 1998), complex laws increasingly pressure school leaders to over-emphasize legal compliance at the expense of ethical principles (Howe & Miramontes, 1991; Bon & Bigbee, 2011). In response to these challenges, this chapter instructs leaders to recognize ethical and legal principles as compatible sources of authority in education in an effort to preserve the moral imperative of educational opportunities.

The importance of school leaders finding the right balance between legal and ethical principles has been reinforced by the National Educational Leadership Preparation (NELP) Standards, specifically element 6.4 of Standard 6. Standard 6 focuses broadly on preparing educational leaders who focus on student, teacher, and leader success through the application of skills and knowledge regarding management operations, data and resources, communication, and legal principles. This chapter is focused primarily on element 6.4, but also addresses the necessary balance between law and ethics, which is the focus of element 2.2 of Standard 2. Element 6.4 asserts that educational leaders must understand the applicable laws, rights, policies, and regulations in order to promote student and adult success, while element 2.2 seeks to ensure that school leaders are prepared to make decisions that reflect awareness of both moral and legal principles.

In the following sections, this chapter will examine the moral, ethical, and legal principles that underpin the very foundation of education. Through closer examination of the intersecting, yet distinct nature of these principles, this chapter also seeks to promote school leaders' understanding of a common language to discuss and respond to ethical dilemmas. Finally, this chapter will provide school leaders with practical guidelines and application of a proposed ethical decision-making framework. The goal is for these guidelines to enhance efforts to bridge the perceived gap between ethical leadership theories and leadership practice in education (Beck & Murphy, 1994; Starratt, 1994; Strike, Haller, & Solstice, 1988).

MORAL AND ETHICAL DIMENSIONS OF EDUCATIONAL LEADERSHIP

Beck and Murphy (1994) focus on the school leader as an ethical actor who serves primarily as a moral agent with a direct and substantial impact on schooling. Noddings (1998) draws heavily from Dewey's extensive writings (see e.g. Dewey & Tufts, 1908) to support her critical assertion that education is an inherently moral enterprise. She identified Dewey's important contributions to the moral domain of education as follows: "there is a moral aspect of almost everything we do . . . the methods common to science could be used effectively in the moral domain" (p. 486). In other words, all aspects of education have moral implications and in order to resolve moral problems, individuals need to think through the consequences of their decisions.

Empirically demonstrating the moral aspects of educational leadership has been an elusive task despite Dewey's (1902/1990) contention that ethics is a science guiding decisions about right and wrong or good and bad (Shapiro & Gross, 2008). Frick and Gutierrez (2008) conducted phenomenological-like interviews with public school principals in response to this lack of empirical evidence. Their focus was on validating the notion that school leaders adhere to an essential professional ethic. According to the school leaders' responses, Frick and Gutierrez concluded that the commitment to value, educate, and adhere to laws, policies, and professional responsibilities on behalf of students evinces the unique moral aspects of educational leadership (2008, p. 54).

Fullan (2003) encouraged school leaders to accept their moral purpose and opportunity to lead as agents of change. His assertion is premised on the assumptions that schools must educate all students, reduce the achievement gap between students, and promote learning as a moral imperative. According to Fullan, the school leader's moral imperative emerges as an obligation to make a difference in the lives of students. Despite the "significant importance to school leaders, there is no clear nexus in how moral leadership is practiced in schools today" (Gregory, 2010, p. 2). Further, as Sergiovanni (1992) observes, school leaders exercise moral authority, but their actions are rarely recognized as leadership.

The perhaps unstated sense of concern to recognize the moral aspects of leadership is driven by the idea that school leaders have tremendous influence over school communities. Given their responsibilities and roles in education, school leaders are expected to function in ways that promote the best interests of children (Walker, 1998). Fiedler and Van Haren (2008) assert that individual beliefs are premised on the awareness of an ethical foundation that subsequently guides actions and decisions. Similarly, Starratt (2004) described ethical leadership as the effort to act in a manner consistent with essential beliefs, values and principles.

Adherence to a moral or ethical stance, however, may be in conflict with legal mandates or may simply be perceived to be in conflict given misperceptions about the law and ethics. Thus, school leaders need both legal and ethical awareness in order to make decisions that have greater likelihood of redressing the inequities and injustice in our schools and communities.

LEGAL COMPLIANCE IN SCHOOLS

The prominence of legal issues in schools is revealed quite publicly through legislative enactments, court decisions, and an array of rules and regulations at both the federal and state levels of governance. In response, legal knowledge is consistently framed as an essential component of school administration programs (Bon, 2012; Haller & Kleine, 2001). The complexity of the legal process on school policies places an increasing burden on school leaders (Cambron-McCabe, McCarthy, & Thomas, 2004). Although the law, through constitutions, statutes, and courts, may offer protection of rights and relief from abuse of students' rights, school leaders are encouraged to recognize that legal compliance should not come at the expense of moral stewardship.

While several researchers have recognized the delicate balance between legal and ethical awareness (Bon & Bigbee, 2011; Howe & Miramontes, 1991), legal literacy (Schimmel & Militello, 2008) continues to be championed as a critical skill for future school leaders. Legal literacy can also serve as a powerful mechanism for social justice because school leaders who are knowledgeable about the essential rights of disadvantaged students will be better prepared to advocate for the protection of their rights. Hess and Kelly (2007) reported that about 50% of principal preparation programs focus on education law as a core course topic. In addition, they observed that education law, which they categorized as a technical knowledge course, also has value given the focus on practical tasks.

The increasing number of federal regulations, policies, and statutes has the potential to lead to a surge of litigation given competing interests and the likely impact on the rights of multiple stakeholders. As such, school leaders must be adequately prepared to respond to potential legal issues that are often complex, implicate the rights of teachers, students, and communities, and have the potential to disrupt the learning environment and consume a school leader's time. Scholars and school law faculty often review Supreme Court rulings that visibly impact students' rights, such as the Fourteenth Amendment equal protection clause (*Brown* v. *Board of Education*, 1954), federally protected disability rights (*Board of Education of Hendrick Hudson* v. *Rowley*, 1982), or educational rights for undocumented students (*Plyler* v. *Doe*, 1982). These cases have "served as catalysts for significant reform in society and public school systems across America" (Bon, 2012, p. 288). These and other court decisions, along with the various state laws, federal laws, and regulations are glaring reminders to school leaders to be vigilant of the legal boundaries that impact their decisions.

Legal compliance issues are especially relevant in special education given the distinctive educational needs of students with disabilities. Amid concerns about legal compliance, overemphasis on special education laws, and fears of litigation, the ethical foundations of special education may be overlooked according to Howe and Miramontes (1991). Bon and Bigbee examined this concern in a qualitative focus group study of special education case managers and concluded that the "complex pressures of legal compliance and administrative directives" (2011, p. 342) made it difficult to reconcile competing ethical principles, such as the best interests of the child demands. Legal issues are prevalent, however, beyond the boundaries of special education given the expanding influence of federal laws and regulations on public school systems.

> The distinction between legal and ethical responsibilities must be consistently enforced given the potential for conflicts between law and ethics (Ozar, 1993).

Given the increasingly litigious nature of society and growing concerns about moral corruption of leaders in general (Manz, Anand, Joshi, & Manz, 2008), it is not surprising to observe a groundswell of interest in school leaders' abilities to make legally defensible decisions and to respond to competing concerns about moral stewardship (Sergiovanni, 1992). On the other hand, the distinction between legal and ethical responsibilities must be consistently entertained (consider, for example, the U.S. Immigration and Customs Enforcement's (ICE) deportation activity and school age children's rights) given the potential for conflicts between law and ethics (Ozar, 1993). As Ozar asserts:

> While the law may direct a person to do what is morally correct, the law is not a fundamental determinant of what is morally correct, which is why we look to morality to tell us what the law ought to be, rather than vice versa.
>
> (p. 161)

Providing future school leaders with this foundational understanding of the distinction between what is legally and ethically required is crucial to their development as ethical decision-makers. Law and ethics are undoubtedly related topics, but understanding the differences between these dimensions of administrative leadership is especially important. Bon and Bigbee (2011) discovered that the majority of special education leaders who participated in their focus group study struggled to distinguish between professional ethics and the laws, rules, and regulations pertinent to special education. In response, the authors asserted that there is a need for collective dialogue about ethics and for the development of a common language to discuss and respond to ethical dilemmas. In the following section, an ethical decision-making process is proposed as a source of guidance for future school leaders.

ETHICAL DECISION-MAKING FRAMEWORK

Several scholars have sought to identify a common and accessible language to decode ethics from an elusive concept to a tangible decision-making model for managing dilemmas (Campbell, 1997; Strike, 1995). Campbell (1997) emphasized the importance of engaging leaders in collaborative discussions about ethics in order to develop their intuitive awareness and ability to manage complex ethical dilemmas. In other words, simply having an ethical code is insufficient; school leaders must be intrinsically aware of how the key ideals and ethical principles inform the decision-making process (Campbell, 2001). Similarly, Johnson (2012) asserts that leaders should use an ethical decision-making model to enhance their abilities to make morally informed decisions.

Ethical decision-making models have been widely proposed across various professional fields, including education, global ethics, and public policy. Preston, Samford. & Connors (2002) presented a model for the public sector with five steps that an individual would follow to guide ethical decision-making. Their model is premised on public sector values (such as the common good) as sources of insight for resolving ethical dilemmas. The key elements of their model include individual values, organizational climate, alternative assessment, and making a final decision or judgment. Several of these elements also reflected factors to consider such as policy and practice, goals, and accountability. As can be seen, the model addresses concerns and issues that are relevant to the schooling sector as well.

Starratt (1991) also advocated for practical guidelines to inform daily decision-making, asserting that school leaders often lacked preparation or sufficient guidance. He introduced three ethical domains of justice, care, and critique as guides for leaders who serve as moral agents in education (Starratt, 1991, 1994). Several scholars have targeted their efforts to bridge the perceived gap between ethical leadership theories and leadership practice in education (see e.g. Starratt, 1994; Strike, Haller, & Solstice, 1988).

Beck & Murphy (1994) presented ethical leadership as a two-step process. First, leaders must recognize ethics as a set of fundamental principles that guide their decision-making process. Applying ethical principles to daily decision making affords the leader the opportunity to make decisions that are ethically sound (Furman, 2003). Second, leaders must embrace ethics as a necessary element reflecting their own personal values, beliefs, and character. Accordingly, "Ethics is less about making decisions using objective principles and more about living morally in specific situations" (Beck & Murphy, 1994, p.33). Furman (2003) proposed merging the two-step process in order to focus on the essential role of school leaders as ethical or moral actors who impact education.

Building upon this body of work, Shapiro and Stefkovich (2001, 2005, 2011) proposed a multiparadigm approach that included the ethic of the profession to the existing ethical viewpoints. If their premise is accepted, an additional domain of ethical leadership—justice, care, critique, *and* the profession—should be used to guide the decision-making processes of administrators. While there are numerous models to choose among, the Shapiro and Stefkovich conceptual model has been widely embraced as a sound framework for educational leaders. Their model was informed in part by their teaching and observations that many students had trouble separating personal and professional codes of ethics. This realization informed their focus on the best interests of the child standard (derived coincidently from the law) as a key component of the professional ethic paradigm because it encourages

Table 5.1 Ethical Decision-making Process

Sequence	Factors	Ethical Paradigms
Assess	Essential Values	Ethic of Critique
	Policy and Practice	Ethics of Justice and Profession
	Dispositional Goals	Ethic of Care
Analyze	Legal Parameters	Ethics of Justice and Profession
	Alternative Solutions	Ethics of Critique and Care
Act	Make Decision	Ethic of Justice and Profession
	Document and Reflect	Ethic of Care and Critique

educators to balance their professional and personal codes of ethics when faced with ethical decisions.

Kidder (1995) reminds us that leadership is by its very nature an ethical and moral endeavor, whether in business, education, or global sectors. He examines moral courage at length in an effort to demonstrate the inherent importance of ethics as abiding principles to guide our decisions. Gibson (2008) proposed a framework of analysis which includes three steps: 1) identify the ethical problem, 2) interpret the problem and isolate the facts, and 3) recommend a solution to the problem (pp. 302–303).

Drawing extensively from these existing frameworks, this chapter proposes a decision-making process in Table 5.1 for purposes of operationalizing ethical leadership. Table 5.1 reflects a modification of the structured approach proposed by Gibson (2008), the key factors that emerged from a combination of the ethical model developed by Preston, Samford, & Connors (2002) and the model adopted by Kidder (1995). Finally, the sequence and factors identified in Table 5.1 are complemented by consideration of the multiparadigm approach advocated by Shapiro and Stefkovich (2001, 2005, 2011).

The first column in Table 5.1 sets forth the specific action-oriented steps that school leaders should adopt in determining how to proceed when facing an ethical dilemma. The leader should then assess an array of factors and the ethical paradigms that further guide decision making that reflects the intersection of practical realities and ethical principles or ideals. Recognizing this intersection of practical realities, particularly legal and political facets of school leadership, with ethical principles, is an important first step to ensure legitimacy and integrity in decisions.

NELP STANDARD AND LEARNING ACTIVITIES

The proposed National Educational Leadership Preparation (NELP) Standards have replaced the previously adopted Interstate School Leaders Licensure Consortium (ISLLC) Standards. Similar to the ISLLC Standards, NELP Standards establish a framework to guide the preparation of educational leaders who are equipped to effectively respond to new challenges in schools as a result of changing population, enhanced focus on student learning, and dynamic school conditions. The subsequent focus of this chapter is on how future school leaders are prepared, evaluated, and provided with the ongoing development needed to ensure that they recognize "both the moral and legal consequences of decision making" (Council of Chief State School Officers, 2008).

School leaders are by definition decision-makers, and in any era their decisions impact and are impacted by legal and moral considerations. For the aspiring leader to be prepared, she/he needs to see the wider context of the challenges of decision-making. Specifically, education leaders need to see their role as more than a functionary in a bureaucratic machine and yet be able to remain a viable agent within their school and district. They need to understand the dynamic and evolving nature of our legal system and grasp the opportunities for social justice and social responsibility that this orientation to change promotes. Finally, they need to model moral literacy and promote the same awareness and sensibility to the children in their schools through the curriculum and school activities. Through these steps, school leaders will increase the chances for developing an educational community that understands the legal and moral consequences of decision-making.

Pedagogical approaches that incorporates student-centered activities based in part on Bloom's (1956) taxonomy of educational objectives are offered here. Bloom proposed a tiered approach to learning that begins with basic comprehension of knowledge and ends with mastery knowledge that promotes critical thinking and analysis. In order to provide future school leaders with opportunities to enhance their knowledge and skills as identified in NELP Standards, suggested learning activities and strategies include active engagement in role play, issue analysis, reenactment, networking and case study analysis, where scaffold learning occurs both emotionally and cognitively (Bandura, 1997; Vygotsky, 1978).

Strategies such as ethical dilemma scenarios are central to teaching ethical reasoning and could help reduce misperceptions about the role of ethics in education (Ehrich, Kimber, Millwater, & Cranston, 2011). Case studies are effective tools that enhance leadership practice by providing opportunities to engage in the practical application of knowledge. Given the increasing importance of ethics as a function of educational leadership, resolving ethical dilemmas through the case study approach is beneficial to practitioners who may otherwise be inexperienced and thus less likely to draw upon theories of ethical leadership to inform their practice as school leaders.

Underscoring Aristotle's observations on virtues, Kidder (1995) indicates that moral courage can be taught through repeated practice, and this would apply to one's active practice of ethical decision making. To ensure an optimal learning experience, the case study method of analysis should also follow a structured sequence of steps (Gibson, 2008). As explained earlier, the sequence in Table 5.1 is proposed as a structured ethical decision-making process for analyzing ethical dilemmas. The case study scenario presented in the following section is used to demonstrate the adoption and application of a proposed ethical decision-making process in order to resolve a typical ethical dilemma—*Changing Jamie's Teacher*—faced by leaders.[1]

ETHICAL DECISION-MAKING PROCESS

In an effort to maintain the critical connection between ethics and leadership, the dilemma outlined below is situated to present actual professional experiences that warrant consideration of the complex intersection of legal and ethical principles. Contextualizing the dilemma in this manner reflects the suggested practice of using issue and case study analyses to promote active engagement in the decision-making process and the application of ethical leadership theories to inform practice. The dilemma is then analyzed using the proposed ethical decision-making process in Table 5.1.

Table 5.1 presents a process that is deliberately succinct with respect to the sequence and factors proposed to guide a school leader's decision-making efforts. The ethical domains are significant parameters which should further guide the process to promote recognition of the intersection between law and ethics. Thus, as the discussion in the following section reveals, legal and ethical principles are critically important to examine throughout the Assess, Analyze, Act sequence of the proposed process. Parts of the process are applicable to a role-play scenario that can provide an even stronger experiential dimension of active engagement with the case.

CASE STUDY 5.1: CHANGING JAMIE'S TEACHER

Ms. Mary Richards is the new principal of Selter Elementary School, which is a large school serving a K-5 student population. She has enjoyed a reasonably smooth first week of school and is beginning the second week today. Her predecessor retired after a 30-year career in the district and has already moved out of the district. While reading through emails and correspondence, Principal Richards turns her attention to one specific email from the Parent Teacher Organization President, Mrs. Wright, who holds an apparently coveted role in the wider school community because of influential families vying for the position year to year. Principal Richards met Mrs. Wright briefly at the school open house. The email begins with a warm welcome to Selter Elementary School from Mrs. Wright—acting in her official capacity as PTO President—but soon turns to another subject. The final paragraph of the email states:

> On another note, I am not happy with my son Jamie's classroom assignment. You have put him in class with Miss Burkett, who has little experience as this is her first year of full-time teaching. Jamie is a gifted child and he has an IEP. Clearly, a young and inexperienced teacher will be unable to meet Jamie's needs. So, I request that you reassign Jamie to Dr. Norris's class. Dr. Norris is a "Master Teacher" and has significant experience teaching in this district. Thank you very much.

Principal Richards realizes that this is an email she must address soon; thus, she begins gathering information to help guide her identification of a reasonable resolution to this issue. Her initial effort to discover information includes a review of the school culture, policies, and past practices. Through this carefully conducted review process (talking to key personnel, reading school and district documents, placing inquiries to the school district, among other activites) she learns that Selter Elementary is characterized by a collaborative vision that focuses on meeting the needs of all children.

To guide her decision about the case study presented above, Principal Richards should consider the factors that are likely to impact decisions made at each stage of the suggested sequence while also considering ethical viewpoints proposed by Shapiro and Stefkovich (2001, 2005, 2011) to inform her plan to resolve the identified dilemma. The section below provides a cursory discussion of how Principal Richards could resolve the dilemma using the proposed ethical decision-making process in Table 5.1.

Ethical decision-making process
Assess essential values, policies, and goals.
Analyze the issues and solutions.

Assess. Principal Richards should first consider the essential values that guide her practice as a school leader and that should inform any decision that she makes that affects the school community. As guidance, she draws from Sergiovanni's (1992) virtuous school concept, to support her belief that all parents, teachers and students should be treated with respect and dignity. She should also rely on the ethic of critique to inform her consideration of the essential values that are at stake in this particular case.

The ethic of critique might lead Principal Richards to question the position of privilege that Mrs. Wright is invoking for the sole benefit of her own child. A critique framework may further problematize the issue by making the distinction between whether there is an underlying assumption about children in gifted education as privileged and/or have privileged parents as advocates. As such, making a clear determination about Mrs. Wright's request (demand) as a mother or as her role as PTO President will be very important. If the essential value—treating all parents, teachers and students with respect and dignity is truly embraced—Principal Richards is bound to critically asses a system that privileges power based on societal status and results in the perpetuation of educational disparities. Given the context of apparent undue influence, she should be critical and careful in determining the nature of the request and its motivating source(s). Permitting some parents to exert their power in order to give their children an unfair advantage over other students in the school should signal strong concern.

Another factor to consider during her assessment of the ethical dilemma is whether policy or past practice established expected norms or behaviors (such as the assignment of students to classes or to teachers, the grouping of students, or other technical scheduling issues). In other words, to reach a just resolution to this dilemma, Principal Richards needs to carefully examine the formal rights of students and parents, and the informal expectations of teachers in the school. During this phase of the process, the ethics of justice and of the profession are significant viewpoints to consider. Adherence to school policy and past practice may appear to align with an ethic of justice by not disrupting expected organizational patterns and operating procedures, but to assume such is flawed because what if past expectations and operating procedures are unfair? What if student placement with teachers were based on fiat or capriciousness? Even more problematic, a single teacher who bullies the others and makes the placements herself? Also, sensitivity to an ethic of the profession would compel a close examination of what is being done, and what are the various outcomes achieved, in light of students' best interests.

In this scenario, for example, students are commonly removed from a teacher's classroom if significant disciplinary problems are negatively impacting the instructional setting and other students; if the student's behavior is impairing the teacher's ability to provide meaningful instruction; or if the parent, teacher and principal determine that the student's best interests will be served by a classroom change. Given the parameters of school policy and practice, as well as her status as a new principal, Principal Richards must be cautious to ensure that she makes decisions that are both supportive and respectful of the school community, which include numerous parent, teacher, and student stakeholders.

Although she is bound to act in accordance with legal mandates, policies, rules or regulations established by federal, state, and local mandates, she also has a duty to the make a fair and just decision for the student, Jamie. Investigating the claim of Jamie's giftedness and his Individualized Education Plan (IEP) should be pursued in order to inform a fair and just decision. Principal Richards must also be astute given the significant role that Jamie's mother, Mrs. Wright, plays in the school as PTO President. Principal Richards wants to avoid creating a relationship with Mrs. Wright that could negatively affect the PTO's support of the school.

Finally, during the assessment phase of the sequence, Principal Richards should consistently access her dispositional goals—that is, what motivates her to act and how her conscience guides her decisions. Kidder (2005) infers that conscience is an individual's moral courage to face an ethical dilemma guided by her own sense of a moral purpose. Despite past evidence suggesting that parents perceived as powerful and privileged in the community are likely to have a greater voice than other parents, Principal Richards chooses to assess the essential school values and her own dispositional goals from an ethic of care viewpoint. Focusing deeply on her motivations, orientation, and commitment to the well-being, formation, and potential growth of both the individual child and all children collectively.

Analyze. After assessing the various factors, such as the essential values, policies, and her own dispositional goals, Principal Richards should then analyze the issue to determine if there are legal constraints that might influence her final decision. For example, recognizing the ethic of justice, Principal Richards should consider the associated rights of the individuals and the community as well as any enforceable or mandatory legal obligations (Horner, 2003) that may delineate existing rights and responsibilities. Finally, examining the issue through this lens of justice, she should also seek to determine how to resolve the issue in a fair manner and whether or not there are exceptions to the applicable laws or policies. She should next consider the influence of the ethic of the profession and how this relates to the legal parameters.

The ethic of the profession at its core focuses on promoting the best interests of students (Stefkovich, 2011). It is relatively undisputed that when children have qualified and effective teachers in their classrooms, this can greatly contribute to student achievement, which is essential to student well-being and success in school. Furthermore, as a student, Jamie has a legitimate expectation that decisions will be made in his best interest. After a full week in Miss Burkett's classroom, Jamie appears to be building a positive relationship with her and his classmates based on direct observation and formal inquiries. If Jamie is moved, there may be the possibility that he may have difficulty adjusting to a new environment, or he may be unjustly labeled as a discipline problem by other students or teachers if the customary process for student reassignment in the school is based on the problematic descriptions presented above. Thus, Principal Richards recognizes that the ethic of the profession appears to favor resolution of this issue according to Jamie's best interests by squarely focusing on his particular identified needs.

During the analysis phase, Mary Richards should also consider alternative solutions and how the ethic of the profession might guide her response. The unilateral removal of a student from a teacher's class has negative connotations and could be interpreted as an indication that Principal Richards lacks confidence in Miss Burkett's ability as an educator. In fact, Miss Burkett is a capable teacher, fully certified, with extensive field-placement experiences prior to her hiring. She has demonstrated her competence to work with students of varying ability levels as a result of her rigorous professional education at a nationally recognized college of education. Finally, Principal Richards is keenly aware that an ethic of care focuses on the "integrity of human relationships" (Starratt, 1991, p. 195). Successful resolution of the dilemma hinges on her ability to maintain three important and potentially competing relationships — that is, she must seek a solution that preserves her fidelity to parents, students, and teachers.

Act. After careful assessment and analysis of the various factors and ethical viewpoints pertinent to the ethical dilemma, changing Jamie's teacher, Principal Richards is charged with making a good decision (Maxwell, 2002). In essence, she must accept her role and leadership responsibility to tackle a wicked problem and propose a solution. Through her careful reflection on the ethical domains of justice, care, critique, and profession, Principal Richards determines that both the ethic of care and ethic of the profession are steering her towards a decision to maintain Jamie's current placement in Ms. Burkett's class. She views this decision as beneficial to Jamie because it is in his best interest to continue the positive learning environment that exists in Ms. Burkett's class and because she believes that this decision would, in the end, demonstrate her commitment to building strong relationships with all parents, teachers, and students.

As part of the final phase of her decision-making process, Principal Richards engages in documentation and reflection on her efforts to achieve a positive resolution of the ethical dilemma regarding Jamie's classroom assignment. She thoughtfully assembles the evidence she previously gathered supporting her final decision: school policy and practice, school vision statements, and other indicators that emphasize the core school values that privilege students' best interests over other competing demands.

At this point, Principal Richards might also review Burns's (1978) theory of transforming leadership as she reflects on her final decision. According to Burns's theory, serving as a transformational leader also involves accepting one's role as a moral leader who is concerned with values such as liberty, justice and equality. As Principal Richards reflects, she is confident and prepared for her discussion with Mrs. Wright because she has not compromised her dispositional or essential school values. She remains committed to the core leadership principles in school that promote individual empowerment and growth for all persons who are part of the school community.

Finally, Principal Richards recognizes that the ethic of critique and care again inform her to address the unfair distribution of power to those with privilege at the expense of others who lack voice due to their lack of position in communities. As part of her final decision and reflection, Principal Richards revisits all of the ethical domains to find the moral courage to share her decision with Jamie's mother, Mrs. Wright. She should be confident that her decision to maintain Jamie's current placement is centered on his best interests and also will move her and the school community to an advanced ethical level of leadership.

SUMMARY

Kidder (2005) shared a story of moral courage exercised by a school leader and his staff in Baltimore, Maryland. I close with this example to illustrate how powerful a lesson can be for a school community when difficult choices involving a great degree of sacrifice are made for the sake of preserving integrity and standing up for principle. The setting for Kidder's story is a religious-affiliated private school where a historically successful and popular lacrosse team became embroiled in controversy. The controversy arose when a 16-year-old player videotaped and then proceeded to play this video of his sexual encounter with a 15- year-old girl from another private school without her knowledge. His teammates had all gathered to watch game tapes and when the video began playing, not a single young man objected or asked to stop the tape.

As the story unfolds, the school leadership team's response evinced moral courage that became the defining moment of their character. The headmaster expelled the player who made the video, suspended 30 varsity players, who were also required to attend counseling, benched 8 junior varsity players, and terminated the entire varsity season. Despite raucous backlash by a few parents, community members, and lacrosse fans, the end of this story reveals an unexpected outcome. Soon after the leadership teams' decision, the school experienced an increase of applications and benefited from a number of new financial donors who specifically expressed their gratitude for the moral courage displayed by school leadership. The essence of this story, Kidder (2005) indicates, is the willingness of leaders to put values into practice. As this chapter's focus on the element 6.2 of NELP Standard 6 reveals, it is especially relevant and important for future school leaders to be prepared to put values into practice while being informed of the law.

The emphasis on aligning educational leadership preparation with the NELP standards is part of a wider educational reform strategy focused on improving leadership programs (Tucker, Young, & Koschereck, 2015). These program reform initiatives almost directly emerge from the "body of research suggesting that successful school leaders influence student achievement" (Tucker, Young, & Koscherck, 2015, p. 162). Acknowledgment of the connection between effective schools and effective leaders has sparked statewide focus on leadership program development and performance. Although the discussion frequently centers on student achievement in policy debates, school leaders are called to be ethically and morally responsive (Sergiovanni, 1992) in an environment that can make it "difficult to discern how ethical and legal principles are compatible sources of authority in education" (Bon, 2012, p. 289). Thus, it is important to prepare school leaders who recognize "both the moral and legal consequences of decision making" (Council of Chief State School Officers, 2008).

LEARNING ACTIVITY 5.1

Candidates could be engaged in the following types of activities:

- **Role play**. The instructor will present cases, such as the one illustrated above, and students will act out various scenarios as they demonstrate their decision- making abilities in complex dilemmas.
- **Issue analysis**. Identify a current issue with moral and legal implications for decision making (such as a current event captured in popular press or a problem that is discussed and/or analyzed in academic literature), define

the issues and analyze from a moral and legal stance, and share with a practicing leader for feedback.

- **Re-enactment**. Re-enact key legal decisions, such as *Board of Education of Hendrick Hudson* v. *Rowley* through simulations and engage in guided debriefing sessions that demonstrate the evolution of our thinking and legal precedents.
- **Network**. Develop a personal support network of school-based and external people and groups to help frame values issues in new ways and respond effectively to conflict.
- **Case study analysis**. Engage and discuss case study scenarios that are similar to actual professional experiences and participate in decision-making processes that draw upon theories of ethical leadership to inform leadership practice.

CASES

Additional case study scenarios can be found in a number of publications, including, for example, UCEA's *Journal of Cases in Educational Leadership* (JCEL). Case studies provide startling reminders of the types of ethical dilemmas that school leaders encounter. Furthermore, by wrestling through the issues and questions presented in case studies, future school leaders are engaged directly in the messy experience of making hard decisions. As such, case studies reveal how difficult it can be to make ethical decisions when conflicts between personal and professional codes arise in a public school setting.

In one case study from the JCEL titled "Leaders on the Front Line—Managing Emotion for Ethical Decision Making: A Teaching Case Study for Supervision of School Personnel," the authors present a scenario involving ethical decision making as it relates to personnel supervision (Tenuto, Gardiner, & Yamamoto, 2016). This case study reveals the potential conflicts between leaders and teachers when politics, confidentiality, and professional ethics compete in a laissez-faire school culture. Another possible case study, "The Adult Fantasy Center" (Shapiro & Stefkovich, 2001, pp. 33–37), presents future leaders with issues that derive from inherent tensions between the personal and professional lives of educators.

IMPORTANT RESOURCES

The School Superintendents Association (AASA): AASA's Statement of Ethics for Educational Leaders: www.aasa.org/ (retrieved from: www.aasa.org/content.aspx?id=1390)

National Association of Secondary School Principals (NASSP) Ethics for School Leaders: www.nassp.org/who-we-are/board-of-directors/position-statements/ethics-for-school-leaders?SSO=true

National Policy Board for Educational Administration (NPBEA): www.npbea.org/educational-administration-resources/

NOTE

1. Bon, S. C., Gerrick, W. G., Sullivan, D., & Shea, C. (2006). Ethical Leadership: A Case Study Framework. *Academic Exchange Quarterly, 10*(2), n.p.

REFERENCES

Bandura, A. (1997). *Self-efficacy: The exercise of control*. New York: W.H. Freeman.

Beck, L. G., & Murphy, J. (1994). *Ethics in educational leadership programs*. Thousand Oaks, CA: Corwin Press.

Begley, P. T. (2001). In pursuit of authentic school leadership practices. *International Journal of Leadership in Education, 4*(4), 353–366.

Bloom, B. S. (Ed.). (1956). *Taxonomy of educational objectives, the classification of educational goals—Handbook: Cognitive Domain*. New York: McKay.

Board of Education of Hendrick Hudson v. Rowley, 458 U.S. 176 (1982).

Bon, S. C. (2012). Examining the crossroads of law, ethics and education leadership. *Journal of School Leadership, 22*, 285–308.

Bon, S. C., & Bigbee, A. (2011). Special education leadership: Integrating professional and personal codes of ethics to serve the best interest of the child. *Journal of School Leadership, 21*(3), 324–359.

Brown v. Board of Education of Topeka, 347 U.S. 483 (1954).

Burns, J. M. (1978). *Leadership*. New York: Harper & Row.

Cambron-McCabe, N. H., McCarthy, M. M., & Thomas, S. B. (2004). *Public school law: Teachers' and students' rights* (5th ed.). Boston, MA: Pearson/Allyn & Bacon.

Campbell, E. (1997). Ethical school leadership: Problems of an elusive role. *Journal of School Leadership, 7*(3), 287–300.

Campbell, E. (2001). Let right be done: Trying to put ethical standards into practice. *Journal of Education Policy, 16*(5), 395–411.

Conklin, J. (2001). *Wicked problems and social complexity*. CogNexus Institute. Retrieved from: http://cognexus.org/wpf/wickedproblems.pdf

Council of Chief State School Officers (2008). *Educational leadership policy standards*. Retrieved from: www.google.com/webhp?sourceid=chrome-instant&ion=1&espv=2&ie=UTF-8#q=isllc%20standards%202008

Dewey, J. (1909). *Moral principles in education*. Cambridge, MA: Riverside Press.

Dewey, J. (1990). *The school and society and the child and the curriculum*. Chicago, IL: University of Chicago Press (original works published 1900, 1902).

Dewey, J., & Tufts, J. H. (1908). *Ethics*. New York: Holt & Co.

Ehrich, L. C., Kimber, M., Millwater, J., & Cranston, N. (2011). Ethical dilemmas: A model to understand teacher practice. *Teachers and Teaching: Theory and Practice, 17*(2), 173–185.

Fiedler, C. R., & Van Haren, B. (2009). A comparsion of sepcial education administrators' and teachers' knowledge and application of ethics and professional standards. *The Journal of Special Education, 43*(3), 160–173.

Frick, W. C., & Gutierrez, K. J. (2008). Those moral aspects unique to the profession: Principals' perspectives on their work and the implications for a professional ethic for educational leadership. *Journal of School Leadership, 18*, 32–61.

Fullan, M. (2001). *Leading in a culture of change.* San Francisco, CA: Jossey-Bass.

Fullan, M. (2003). *The moral imperative of school leadership.* Thousand Oaks, CA: Corwin Press.

Furman, G. C. (2003). Moral leadership and the ethic of community. *Values and Ethics in Educational Administration, 2*(1), 1–8.

Gibson, P. A. (2008). Evaluative criteria to create and assess case studies for use in ethical decision-making analysis. *Journal of Public Affairs Education, 14*(3), 297–309.

Gregory, R. (2010). Moral and ethical leadership in administrator preparation. *International Journal of Educational Leadership Preparation, 5*(3), 1–6.

Haller, E. J., & Kleine, P. F. (2001). *Using educational research: A school administrator's guide.* New York: Pearson.

Hess, F. M., & Kelly, A. P. (2007). Learning to lead: What gets taught in principal-preparation programs. *Teachers College Record, 109*(1), 244–274.

Horner, J. (2003). Morality, ethics and law: Introductory concepts. *Seminars in Speech and Language, 24*(4), 263–274.

Howe, K., & Miramontes, O. B. (1991). A framework for ethical deliberation in special education. *Journal of Special Education, 25*(l), 7–25.

Johnson, C. E. (2012). *Meeting the ethical challenges of leadership: Casting light or shadow* (4th ed.). Los Angeles, CA: SAGE.

Kidder, R. M. (1995). *How good people make tough choices.* New York: William Morrow.

Kidder, R. M. (2005). *Moral courage.* New York: HarperCollins.

Manz, C. C., Anand, V., Joshi, M., & Manz, K. P. (2008). Emerging paradoxes in executive leadership: A theoretical interpretation of the tensions between corruption and virtuous values. *The Leadership Quarterly, 19*(3), 385–392. doi:10.1016/j.leaqua.2008.03.009

Maxwell, J. C. (2002). *The 21 Irrefutable Laws of Leadership.* Nashville, TN: Thomas Nelson.

Noddings, N. (1998). Thoughts on John Dewey's "Ethical principles underlying education." *Elementary School Journal, 98*(5), 479–488.

Ozar, D. T. (1993). Building awareness of ethical standards and conduct. In L. Curry & J. Wergin (Eds.), *Educating professional: Responding to new expectations for competence and accountability.* San Francisco, CA: Jossey-Bass.

Plyler v. *Doe,* 457 U.S. 202 (1982).

Preston, N., Samford. C., & Connors, C. (2002). *Encouraging ethics and challenging corruption.* Sydney, NSW: The Federation Press.

Schimmel, D., & Militello, M. (2008). Legal literacy for teachers. *Principal Leadership, 9*(4), 54–58.

Sergiovanni, T. J. (1992). *Moral leadership: Getting to the heart of school improvement.* San Francisco, CA: Jossey-Bass.

Shapiro, J. P., & Gross, S. J. (2008). *Ethical educational leadership in turbulent times: (Re)solving moral dilemmas.* Mahwah, NJ: Lawrence Erlbaum.

Shapiro, J. P., & Stefkovich, J. A. (2001). *Ethical leadership and Decision making in Education.* Mahwah, NJ: Lawrence Erlbaum.

Shapiro, J. P., & Stefkovich, J. A. (2005). *Ethical leadership and decision making in education* (2nd ed.). Mahwah, NJ: Lawrence Erlbaum.

Shapiro, J. P., & Stefkovich, J. A. (2011). *Ethical leadership and decision making in education: Applying theoretical perspectives to complex dilemmas* (3rd ed.). Mahwah, NJ: Lawrence Erlbaum.

Starratt, R. J. (1991). Building an ethical school. *Educational Administration Quarterly, 27*(2), 185–202.

Starratt, R. J. (1994). *Building an ethical school*. London: Falmer Press.

Starratt, R. J. (2004). *Ethical leadership*. San Francisco, CA: Jossey-Bass.

Stefkovich, J. A. (2011). *Best interests of the student: Applying ethical constructs to legal cases in education*. Mahwah, NJ: Lawrence Erlbaum.

Strike, K. A. (1995). Professional ethics and the education of professionals. *Educational Horizons, 74*(1), 29–36.

Strike, K. A., Haller, E. J., & Solstice, J. F. (1988). *The ethics of school administration*. New York: Teachers College Press.

Tenuto, P. L., Gardiner, M. E., & Yamamoto, J. K. (2016). Leaders on the front line—managing emotion for ethical decision making: A teaching case study for supervision of school personnel. *Journal of Cases in Educational Leadership, 19*(3), 11–2.

Tucker, P. D., Young, M. D., & Koschereck, J. W. (2015). Leading research-based change in educational leadership preparation: An introduction. *Journal of Research on Leadership Education, 7*(2), 155–171. doi 10.1177/1942775112455267

Vygotsky, L. S. (1978). *Mind in society: The development of higher psychological processes*. Cambridge, MA: Harvard University Press.

Walker, K. (1998). Jurisprudential and ethical perspectives on "The Best Interest of Children." *Interchange, 29*(3), 287–308.

CHAPTER 6

Supporting Socially Just, Equitable, and Inclusive Schools

Barbara L. Pazey and Carl Lashley

CHAPTER OVERVIEW

This chapter focuses specifically on the special education process that must be implemented by law, and in doing so, provides a lens for examining the potential of an instructional program being socially just, equitable, and inclusive. We discuss concepts and approaches in graduate educational leadership preparation that teach students about the implementation of special education and related services so as to discern the balance between legal compliance and ethical strategies that aspiring leaders need.

INTRODUCTION

Special education, with its roots in *Brown v. the Board of Education* (1954) and the War on Poverty (Ryan, 1976), is at its essence a civil rights project (Martin, Martin, & Terman, 1996; O'Malley, 2015; Smith, 2016). The U.S. Department of Education (USDOE) formalized the federal role in the education of students with disabilities by reorganizing the Division of Handicapped Children and Youth into the Bureau of the Education of the Handicapped (BEH) in 1966 (Martin, Martin, & Terman, 1996; Pazey & Yates, 2012). Targeted research efforts funded, in part, by the BEH revealed that children with disabilities might also be classified as children from families in poverty and/or who are culturally and linguistically diverse (Allan, 1976; Ryan, 1976; Sussman, 1969). As representatives of other disenfranchised groups had previously done, persons with disabilities, their parents, and advocates came together to demand equal rights and opportunities for individuals with disabilities so they could participate fully in U.S. society (Martin, Martin, & Terman, 1996; Pazey & Yates, 2012; Weintraub & Abeson, 1972, 1974). These efforts in the late 1960s and early 1970s culminated in the passage of the Education for All Handicapped Children Act (EHA) in 1975.

The EHA—renamed the Individuals with Disabilities Education Act (IDEA) in 1990 and reauthorized in 2004—works in concert with Section 504 of the Vocational Rehabilitation Act of 1973 to ensure access to public education for all school-aged children with disabilities. IDEA and Section 504 provide this guarantee through a set of provisions that include identification and referral, individual evaluation and re-evaluation, eligibility criteria, the individual education program (IEP), least restrictive environment (LRE), parental involvement, and due process of law. The legal provisions of IDEA stipulate the processes and procedures that school personnel are expected to implement to assure parents and families that their child with a disability receives the free and appropriate public education (FAPE) to which they are entitled. Section 504 protects students from discrimination on the basis of disability, thus establishing these efforts as civil rights guaranteed under federal statute and the 14th Amendment of the U.S. Constitution (Yell, 2016). IDEA and Section 504 have extended the nation's expressed commitment to equal access and equal educational opportunity for all students that has been the hallmark of civil rights movements throughout the latter half of the 20th century.

For school leaders, the special education process specifies certain procedures and operations that must be implemented, and provides a lens for examining whether their school's instructional program is socially just, equitable, and inclusive. In this chapter, we discuss concepts and approaches in graduate educational leadership preparation that teach students about the implementation of special education and related services and foster a school culture that is socially just, equitable, and inclusive. We begin with a brief discussion of the aspects of the special education process. We then provide the context and backdrop for the learning we expect from students and suggest alignments of these law and policy constructs to the draft National Educational Leadership Preparation (NELP) Standards (Council for Chief State School Officers [CCSSO] & National Policy Board for Educational Administration [NPBEA], 2015).

THE SPECIAL EDUCATION PROCESS

When we say "the special education process," we are referring to the set of school and district processes and procedures derived from federal and state law and regulations governing the education of students with disabilities. The special education process is relatively similar across the U.S. Most of the steps are legally required, although districts and schools occasionally add their own wrinkles that complicate implementation. The steps in the process are supplemented by knowledge, skills, and dispositions that come from special education history, research, and practice. The descriptions that follow assist students and practitioners in understanding essential concepts and vocabulary from the process. The steps are as follows: A student is identified and referred for evaluation, the IEP team considers the case, the student is placed in the least restrictive environment for her case, they receive the appropriate instruction to address their disability, and they are periodically re-evaluated to ensure that the appropriate services are being received.

Figure 6.1 The Special Education Operations Tradition

THE SPECIAL EDUCATION OPERATIONS TRADITION

The conceptions that follow are legal provisions from IDEA, which are also closely tied to the knowledge traditions in the discipline of special education. Leading special education programs lies at the crossroads of special education knowledge and the knowledge skills and dispositions of educational leadership and administration (Lashley & Boscardin, 2003; Pazey & Cole, 2013; Pazey, Cole, & Garcia, 2012). For the most part, the authors' efforts to prepare school leaders in special education leadership have been aimed at candidates seeking initial licensure as principals. As a result, this analysis relies on the NELP Standards for Building Level Leaders (CCSSO & NPBEA, 2015).

THE NELP STANDARDS AND SPECIAL EDUCATION

In our analysis of the NELP Standards for Building Level Leaders (CCSSO & NPBEA, 2015), we acknowledge that they implicitly address the specific knowledge, skills, and dispositions emphasized in the practice of special education leadership. We have sorted the applicable Standards and emphasized elements into seven categories.

Before we start, however, we highlight a critical, overarching disposition that must be possessed and displayed by every building leader throughout their administrative practice in order to foster, promote, and support a socially just, equitable, and inclusive school. This disposition is articulated in Standard 2, Ethics and Professional Norms: "to model ethical behavior in their actions and relationships with others" (Element 2.4). We recognize the tensions inherent in the practice of social justice leadership in the context of special education (DeMatthews & Mawhinney, 2014; Frick, Faircloth, & Little, 2013; Lashley, 2007; Pazey & Cole, 2013; Pazey, Cole, & Garcia, 2013). Nevertheless, we maintain that without a solid and unmovable commitment to adhering to "ethical behavior" in one's "actions and relationships with others" (NELP Element 2.4) as a building administrator overseeing special education programs in his or her school, none of the other NELP standards or elements will ever suffice. Therefore, this NELP Element should be incorporated in every aspect of one's administrative practice and applied to each of the seven categories listed below.

The remaining emphasized elements within the seven categories follow.

NELP Elements to be Emphasized

- **Normative decision making that focuses on individual needs:** "Academic and social supports, discipline, services, extracurricular activities, and accommodations to meet the full range of needs of each student" (NELP Element 1.3) by enacting "the professional norms of integrity, fairness, transparency, trust, collaboration, perseverance, learning and continuous improvement in their actions, decision making and relationships with others" (NELP Element 2.1) through consideration of "the moral and legal consequences of decisions" (NELP Element 2.2).
- **Culture that values equity:** Articulating, advocating, modeling, and cultivating a "set core of values" to "define the school's culture" and the values of equity (NELP Elements 1.2, 2.3) and developing an equitable culture that values responsiveness to "student marginalization, deficit-based schooling, and low expectations" (NELP Elements 3.1, 3.2, 3.3, 3.4).
- **Culture that values diversity:** Modeling the values of diversity (NELP Element 2.4) and a culture that values the "race, culture and language, gender, disability, or special status" of students and families (NELP Element 3.4) as well as a "commitment to shared vision, goals, and objectives pertaining to the education of the whole child" (NELP Element 7.2).
- **Equitable systems of support:** Creating learning systems (NELP Element 4.1) and learning supports that "support equitable access to learning for all students" (NELP Element 4.4).
- **Parental engagement:** Ensuring "each student and parent is treated fairly, respectively" and "free from biases" such as "race, culture, language, gender, disability, or special status" (NELP Element 3.4) and communicating with parents (NELP Element 5.1) to engage them "in strengthening student learning in and out of school" (NELP Element 5.2).
- **Legal and ethical compliance:** Developing operations and management systems that comply with applicable state and federal law (NELP Elements 6.1 and 6.4) and take into account "the moral and legal consequences of decisions" (NELP Element 2.3).
- **Instructional leadership:** (NELP Elements 4.1, 4.2, 4.3, 4.4, and 7.4).

Our readers will note that we have included NELP Standard 4: Instructional Leadership as a stand-alone feature of our categories. We supplement NELP Standard 4 with Element 7.4 of NELP Standard 7, which underscores the prerequisite for instructional leaders to both "understand" and have the ability to "implement research-anchored systems of supervision and evaluation that provide actionable feedback about instruction and other professional practices."

Our position is that special education leadership that fully and energetically carries out the demands of special education programs *is* instructional leadership. Authentic instructional leaders translate, interpret, and enact special education law and policy through their day-to-day administrative practice. They scour the research literature and pursue professional development designed to strengthen their knowledge and skill sets so they can buttress and/or improve the teaching and learning process on behalf of every student. When principals and other building leaders carry out the requirements of IDEA (2004) and Section 504 (1973), they are implementing a responsive system of individual supports that meet the needs of each student with a disability (Bateman & Bateman, 2014); and, when they exercise instructional leadership, they are implementing support systems in a school culture that values equity and diversity, and attends to the needs of all children. The two efforts coincide. Leadership preparation efforts to develop instructional leadership in candidates should include knowledge, skills, and dispositions related to the education of students with disabilities by default. To emphasize the importance of instructional leadership as an aspect of special education leadership development, we comment on instructional leadership separately from our discussions of the other elements.

An Overview of the Special Education Process

Special education programs in the U.S. have been implemented to comply with the provisions of IDEA (2004), which stipulates that required procedures should be carried out so an appropriate IEP is developed that provides special education and related services in the LRE (Smith, 2016; Yell, 2016). When a student comes to the attention of school personnel or parents such that he or she is suspected of having a disability, the student is referred for an individual evaluation to gather the data necessary to determine the nature of the student's educational difficulties. If the data indicate that the student is eligible for services under IDEA, the IEP team, which includes the parent(s) or guardian(s), meets to consider what kinds(s) of special education and related services the student will need and how those services will be provided. Due-process procedures serve as a safeguard, to protect the student's rights and allow parents the right to object formally if they and the school system cannot agree on the nature of the student's IEP (Osborne & Russo, 2014; Yell, 2016).

An aspect of special education implementation that is troubling to many school administrators is the necessity for dispute resolution throughout the process. If a student has a disability or is suspected of having a disability, his or her parents must be involved in educational decisions made on the child's behalf (Osborne & Russo, 2014; Yell, 2016). By democratizing educational decision-making, this provision removes the school's unilateral power to determine what constitutes a student's education.

Parents have contested whether or not a student should be identified, the nature of the evaluation process, whether or not a student meets eligibility criteria, whether the IEP is appropriate, and what constitutes the LRE (Yell, 2016). There are additional issues like paying for private school placements and determining whether decisions pertaining to disciplinary actions have taken into account the interaction between a behavioral problem and the specific disability (Russo & Osborne; Yell, 2016). The opportunity for dispute can result in a less than amicable relationship between parents and schools. Complicating this further is the lack of preparation on the part of some school personnel and parents about the complexity of disability and approaches to educating students who do not respond successfully to typical school arrangements (Pazey & Cole, 2013).

In summary, then, we have chosen the elements and the language in our categories to delineate areas of emphasis that characterize special education and related services in 21st-century schools. Special education has a reputation for being legally driven and compliance oriented (NELP 6.4), sometimes to the detriment of students, teachers, and schools, and the moral sensibilities of administrators. Although compliance is an important factor in school operations and management (NELP 6.1), many compliance requirements represent important aspects of equitable, data-driven, participative, success-oriented schooling that the NELP Standards, in general, imply and the NELP Elements we identified for Instructional Leadership delineate (NELP 4.1, 4.2, 4.3, 4.4, 7.4). Building leader candidates enrolled in leadership preparation programs need to understand that they are responsible for making sure that educational decisions made about a student with a disability will adequately meet his or her individual needs (NELP 1.3, NELP 7.2). This responsibility stands out as an awesome moral and legal burden (NELP 2.2) and requires the articulation of professional norms (NELP 2.1). Those decisions and the implementation processes they require should occur in a school culture that values equity (NELP 1.2, 2.3, 3.1, 3.2, 3.3, 3.4) and diversity (NELP 3.4). Special education programs are part of an equitable system of learning supports intended to meet the needs of *all* students (NELP 4.1, 4.4). The development of such learning supports and programs requires members of the school community to (a) treat each student and his or her family with respect, free from potential bias or discrimination (3.4), and (b) create a culture that promotes extensive and intensive involvement, participation, and engagement with parents (NELP 5.1, 5.2).

Table 6.1 The Special Education Operations Tradition

Categories of Standards Emphasized in the Practice of Special Education Leadership	NELP Elements
Normative Decision Making that Focuses on Individual Needs	**Element 1.3 (SUPPORT SYSTEM)** Program completers understand and demonstrate the capability to build, maintain, and evaluate a coherent system of academic and social supports, discipline, services, extracurricular activities, and accommodations to meet the full range of needs of each student.
	Element 2.1 (PROFESSIONAL NORMS) Program completers understand and demonstrate the capability to enact the professional norms of integrity, fairness, transparency, trust, collaboration, perseverance, learning and continuous improvement in their actions, decision making and relationships with others.
	Element 2.2 (DECISION-MAKING) Program completers understand and demonstrate the capability to evaluate the moral and legal consequences of decisions.
	Element 2.4 (ETHICAL BEHAVIOR) Program completers understand and demonstrate the capability to model ethical behavior in their actions and relationships with others.
Culture that Values Equity	**Element 1.2 (VALUES)** Program completers understand and demonstrate the capability to articulate, advocate, model, and cultivate a set of core values that define the school's culture.
	Element 2.3 (VALUES) Program completers understand and demonstrate the capability to model essential educational values of democracy, community, individual freedom and responsibility, equity, social justice, and diversity.
	Element 2.4 (ETHICAL BEHAVIOR) Program completers understand and demonstrate the capability to model ethical behavior in their actions and relationships with others.
	Element 3.1 (EQUITABLE PROTOCOLS) Program completers understand and demonstrate the capability to develop, implement, and evaluate equitable guidelines, procedures and decisions that ensure each stakeholder is treated fairly, respectfully, and with an understanding of culture and context.
	Element 3.2 (EQUITABLE ACCESS) Program completers understand and demonstrate the capability to ensure that each student has equitable access to effective teachers, learning opportunities, academic, social and behavioral support, and other resources necessary for success.
	Element 3.3 (RESPONSIVE PRACTICE) Program completers understand and demonstrate the capability to support the development of responsive practices among teachers and staff so they are able to recognize, confront, and alter institutional biases that result in student marginalization, deficit-based schooling, and low expectations.

continued

Table 6.1 continued

Categories of Standards Emphasized in the Practice of Special Education Leadership	NELP Elements
	Element 3.4 (SUPPORTIVE SCHOOL COMMUNITY) Program completers understand and demonstrate the capability to build and maintain a school culture that ensures each student and family is treated fairly, respectfully, in a responsive manner and free from biases associated with characteristics such as race, culture and language, gender, disability, or special status.
Culture that Values Diversity	Element 2.3 (VALUES) Program completers understand and demonstrate the capability to model essential educational values of democracy, community, individual freedom and responsibility, equity, social justice, and diversity.
	Element 2.4 (ETHICAL BEHAVIOR) Program completers understand and demonstrate the capability to model ethical behavior in their actions and relationships with others.
	Element 3.4 (SUPPORTIVE SCHOOL COMMUNITY Program completers understand and demonstrate the capability to build and maintain a school culture that ensures each student and family is treated fairly, respectfully, in a responsive manner and free from biases associated with characteristics such as race, culture and language, gender, disability, or special status.
	Element 7.2 (PROFESSIONAL CULTURE) Program completers understand and have the capability to develop and sustain a professional culture of engagement and commitment to shared vision, goals, and objectives pertaining to the education of the whole child.
Equitable Systems of Support	Element 2.4 (ETHICAL BEHAVIOR) Program completers understand and demonstrate the capability to model ethical behavior in their actions and relationships with others.
	Element 4.1 (LEARNING SYSTEM) Program completers understand and demonstrate the capability to develop, align, and implement coherent systems of curriculum, instruction, and assessment that are responsive to student needs, embody high expectations for student learning, align with academic standards within and across grade levels, and promote academic success and social emotional well-being for each student.
	Element 4.4 (LEARNING SUPPORTS) Program completers understand and demonstrate the capability to employ effective and appropriate technologies, staffing, professional development, structures, and communication to support equitable access to learning for each student.
Parental Engagement	Element 2.4 (ETHICAL BEHAVIOR) Program completers understand and demonstrate the capability to model ethical behavior in their actions and relationships with others.
	Element 3.4 (SUPPORTIVE SCHOOL COMMUNITY) Program completers understand and demonstrate the capability to build and maintain a school culture that ensures each student and family is treated fairly, respectfully, in a responsive manner and free from biases associated with characteristics such as race, culture and language, gender, disability, or special status.

Table 6.1 continued

Categories of Standards Emphasized in the Practice of Special Education Leadership	NELP Elements
	Element 5.1 (COMMUNICATION) Program completers understand and demonstrate the capability to maintain effective two-way communication with families and the community. Element 5.2 (ENGAGEMENT) Program completers understand and demonstrate the capability to engage families, community, and school personnel in strengthening student learning in and out of school.
Legal and Ethical Compliance	Element 2.3 (VALUES) Program completers understand and demonstrate the capability to model essential educational values of democracy, community, individual freedom and responsibility, equity, social justice, and diversity. Element 2.4 (ETHICAL BEHAVIOR) Program completers understand and demonstrate the capability to model ethical behavior in their actions and relationships with others. Element 6.1 (MANAGEMENT AND OPERATION SYSTEMS) Program completers understand and demonstrate the capability to develop, monitor, and evaluate school management and operation systems to address and support each student's learning needs. Element 6.4 (LEGAL COMPLIANCE) Program completers understand and demonstrate the capability to comply with applicable laws, rights, policies, and regulations as appropriate so as to promote student and adult success.
Instructional Leadership	Element 2.4 (ETHICAL BEHAVIOR) Program completers understand and demonstrate the capability to model ethical behavior in their actions and relationships with others. Element 4.1 (LEARNING SYSTEM) Program completers understand and demonstrate the capability to develop, align, and implement coherent systems of curriculum, instruction, and assessment that are responsive to student needs, embody high expectations for student learning, align with academic standards within and across grade levels, and promote academic success and social emotional well-being for each student. Element 4.2 (INSTRUCTIONAL PRACTICE) Program completers understand and demonstrate the capability to promote challenging and engaging instructional practice consistent with knowledge of learning theory, child development, and effective pedagogy. Element 4.3 (ASSESSMENT SYSTEM) Program completers understand and demonstrate the capability to employ technically appropriate system of assessment and data collection, management, analysis, and use to monitor student progress and improve instruction. Element 4.4 (LEARNING SUPPORTS) Program completers understand and demonstrate the capability to employ effective and appropriate technologies, staffing, professional development, structures, and communication to support equitable access to learning for each student. Element 7.4 (SUPERVISION AND EVALUATION) Program completers understand and have the capability to implement research-anchored systems of supervision and evaluation that provide actionable feedback about instruction and other professional practices, promoting collective accountability.

THE SPECIAL EDUCATION PROCESS AND THE NELP STANDARDS

Addressing the inequities and injustices that arise from the administration of special education and related services requires legal and ethical considerations that school leaders must learn about both prior to beginning their practice and on the job. The practice of special education administration is driven by the legal requirements in federal and state statutes. All areas of law and policy provide direction and guidance about what school leaders must do, but there are many areas of interpretation and complexities to disentangle. Special education programs are governed by prescriptive policies and procedures about which the courts periodically rule. In addition, the use of a democratic decision-making model that includes parents adds political considerations to an already complicated landscape. Finally, increased concerns about accountability measuring students' academic performance raises the stakes for school personnel.

Understanding the following nine concepts is foundational to understanding and implementing the special education process. We have used our categorizations of the NELP Elements to discuss the definitions and implications of these concepts.

Child with a Disability (34 CFR §300.8)

Under IDEA (2004), special education and related services are to be provided to a child with a disability, aged 3 to 21 (34 CFR §300.101), who is identified in one or more of the 13 categories of disability,[1] whose educational performance—due to the effects of the identified disability—will be adversely affected if the specialized education and related services are not made available. Some states have extended the ages of eligibility to match state statutes.

Eligibility determination occurs after a team of professionals and parents analyze the data from a multi-factored evaluation and match the student's profile with the categories stipulated in IDEA (2004). If the student's profile meets the criteria as defined for one or more of the disability categories, the team decides whether the student needs special education and related services in order to successfully make educational progress. If the student meets eligibility criteria and needs special education and related services, he or she is eligible to receive services under IDEA. By targeting students from under-served categories of disability, Congress pointed out the inequities that existed when some children were prohibited from attending school on account of their disabilities. Parents have also been quite vocal about their children's ability to attend publicly supported schools, citing the Equal Protection Clause of the U.S. Constitution.

Understanding *child with a disability* requires application of the knowledge, skills, and dispositions from these NELP Elements:

- Normative decision making that focuses on individual needs (NELP 1.3, 2.1, 2.2, 2.4).
- Culture that values equity (NELP 1.2, 2.3, 2.4, 3.1, 3.2, 3.3, 3.4).

- Culture that values diversity (NELP 2.3, 2.4, 3.4, 7.2).
- Legal and Ethical Compliance (NELP 2.3, 2.4, 6.1, 6.4).

Disability is an aspect of diversity that is frequently left out of discussions highlighting the critical need to address all aspects of a child when his or her education is being considered. A culture that values equity and diversity will operate using the professional norms that are indicated in the NELP Standards. Leadership preparation candidates must become knowledgeable about disability (its implications for learning and a post-secondary life) and must be fully prepared to engage in equity efforts that are necessary to respond effectively to the needs of students with disabilities.

Free Appropriate Public Education (34 CFR §300.17)

Each student with a disability is entitled to FAPE, a free appropriate public education, the description and determination of which is detailed in the Individualized Education Program (IEP) of each student covered under IDEA (2004). Although each letter of FAPE has important historical and legal significance, the most critical is A (appropriate), which was defined by the U.S. Supreme Court in *Rowley* v. *Hendrick Hudson Board of Education* (1982). An *appropriate* education is delineated on the student's IEP—developed collaboratively with members of the student's IEP Team—in compliance with IDEA (2004), and is designed to provide educational benefit. Setting this standard for the education of a student with a disability underscores the intent of Congress and the Court that students be afforded equitable access to an educational program specifically designed to meet their individual needs.

Providing FAPE is the standard that school districts must meet in the Individual Education Plan for each child. It is the commitment that districts make to parents that the special education and related services being provided meets the child's needs. Teaching leadership preparation candidates about FAPE includes references to the following NELP Elements:

- Normative decision making that focuses on individual needs NELP 1.3, 2.1, 2.2.
- Culture that values equity NELP 1.2, 2.3, 3.1, 3.2, 3.3, 3.4.
- Culture that values diversity NELP 2.3, 3.4, 7.2.
- Equitable systems of support NELP 4.1, 4.4.
- Parental Engagement NELP 3.4, 5.1, 5.2.
- Legal and ethical compliance NELP 2.3, 6.1, 6.4.

IDENTIFICATION AND REFERRAL

Determining which students receive special education and related services under IDEA (2004) begins with identification and referral process. If a teacher or parent suspects that a student may have a disability, informal data may be collected to add more detail or refute that suspicion, so a more informed decision can be made about whether to provide additional instruction or interventions that target the student's identified challenge or move forward in the process and conduct a multi-factored individual evaluation. Most campuses have student assistance teams or other committees that discuss a student who may be experiencing difficulties in school, and these teams can recommend that data be collected about the student's school academic performance. As schools have begun to use multi-tiered systems of supports (MTSS) for learning and behavior (see www.rti4success.org/essential-components-rti/multi-level-prevention-system and www.pbis.org/school/mtss), referenced as Response to Intervention (RtI) (see www.rtinetwork.org/learn/what/whatisrti), for academic difficulties and Positive Behavior Interventions and Supports (PBIS) (see www.pbis.org/), and for behavior difficulties as a means for determining whether a student might have a disability, the importance of quality considerations by these teams and the collection of substantive data prior to referring a student for a formal special education evaluation (Bateman & Bateman, 2014; Smith, 2016; Yell, 2016).

Identification and referral processes have traditionally been fraught with the dominance of deficit thinking. In general, identification and referral processes have focused on determining certain perceived "flaws" in a student that may or may not be a factor in contributing to his or her academic and/or behavioral difficulties. Processes like RtI and PBIS are intended to shift or eliminate this type of thinking. By creating these and additional systems of support for students in the classroom and drawing upon additional data collected on the effects of these support *prior to* making a referral for a special education evaluation, MTSS helps to avoid erroneous assumptions about a student's ability. Learning about the identification and referral process prepares the candidate through the following NELP Elements:

- Culture that values equity NELP 3.1, 3.2, 3.3, 3.4.
- Culture that values diversity NELP 2.3, 3.4, 7.2.
- Equitable systems of support NELP 4.1, 4.2.

Individual Evaluation (and Re-evaluation) (34 CFR §§300.15, 300.304–311, 300.303)

If a student is referred, he or she receives an individual evaluation in all areas related to the suspected disability, conducted by a licensed professional. These processes involve psycho-educational, academic, and other assessments, and they yield normative data that compare the student's performance to his/her grade-level peers' performance on these tests. An individual evaluation can also include an observation in the student's natural setting. IDEA (2004) stipulates that a variety of evaluation data be collected and reviewed during this process (§300.306). Increasingly, schools are utilizing and examining data that has been collected during the RtI and PBIS process to assess a student's classroom performance and behavior, and make determinations about whether the child may be eligible for special education and related services. RtI and PBIS rely on teacher-collected data about the student's academic and social behavior in his/her natural context, which typically occurs in the student's classroom and/or other school contexts (lunch, playground, extracurricular activities, and so forth).

Periodically, and at least every three years, students who have been receiving special education and related services receive an individual re-evaluation, which may or may not replicate the original battery of assessments used with the student in earlier evaluations.

The procedures used for evaluation and re-evaluation serve as a safeguard against making inaccurate decisions about a student who is suspected of having a disability; therefore, the decision-making process to determine initial or continued eligibility for special education and related services requires a collection and analysis of multiple sources of data, derived from a variety of individualized assessments. This reliance on data is prominent in arguments for casting instructional leadership (NELP Standard Four, Elements 4.1, 4.2, 4.3, 4.4) as a primary responsibility of school leaders. Understanding evaluation and re-evaluation processes is also directly aligned to these NELP Elements:

- Culture that values equity NELP 3.1, 3.2, 3.3, 3.4.

Eligibility (34 CFR §300.306)

When assessment data have been collected about the student, school professionals and the parents meet to discuss whether the student is eligible for special education and related services. Using the criteria established in IDEA (2004), the IEP Team determines whether the data collected through individual assessments indicate that the student is eligible for special education and related services in one or more of the 13 categories stipulated in IDEA. If the student is not eligible under IDEA, s/he may still be eligible for protection from discrimination under Section 504 (1973). Section 504 has a different definition of disability and different eligibility requirements (34 CFR §104.3).

Eligibility determination might be construed as applying the data collected about a student to criteria supplied in special education regulations in a legally compliant manner. However, the process yields a life-changing and schooling-changing decision with implications for schooling, post-secondary opportunity, employment, and social standing. The labels that result from eligibility determination can have a stigmatizing effect (Arceneaux, 2013), resulting in negative consequences for the student and his or her family. Although the intention of labeling is to provide information about the child and to generate resources to support his/her education, this intention must be carried out in a culture that values professional norms and celebrates the range of human diversity that is exemplified in characterizations of disability. Learning about the eligibility determination process and its implications is connected to these NELP Elements:

- Normative decision making that focuses on individual needs NELP 1.3, 2.1, 2.2.

- Culture that values diversity NELP 2.3, 3.4, 7.2.
- Legal and ethical compliance NELP 2.3, 6.1, 6.4

Individualized Education Program (34 CFR §300.23, §§300.320–324)

If the child is eligible for services under IDEA (2004), an IEP specific to the individual student must be developed through a collective effort of educational professionals, the parent, and, when applicable, the student. We refer to this conglomerate as the IEP Team.[2] The IEP must describe, in writing, the following components: (a) the student's current levels of academic and functional performance, (b) his/her progress in the general education curriculum, (c) a set of measurable academic and functional goals that provides access to the general education curriculum and specifies how the student's progress will be measured, and (d) a statement of the special education and related services the student will need to accomplish the annual goals. In addition, the IEP Team addresses other goals resulting from the student's disability, the annual assessment system in which the student will participate, and when and how long the services will be provided.

The IEP is the document that guides the education of a student with a disability. It is an agreement between the parents and the school to deliver FAPE for the child. As such, developing the IEP is a process that calls for legal and ethical decision-making to occur in a culture of equity and diversity (Lashley, 2007; Pazey & Cole, 2013). The program that results from the IEP development process must include the involvement of parents, teachers, and other service providers who work directly with the student and will be expected to provide various systems of support for the student. As such, understanding all aspects of the IEP and development process both (a) underscores our assertion regarding Element 2.4, supporting the imperative that school leaders must "model ethical behavior in their actions and relationships with others", and (b) entails aspects of all of the NELP Elements for each of our seven identified categories:

- Normative decision making that focuses on individual needs NELP 1.3, 2.1, 2.2.
- Culture that values equity NELP 1.2, 2.3, 3.1, 3.2, 3.3, 3.4.
- Culture that values diversity NELP 2.3, 3.4, 3.4, 7.2.
- Equitable systems of support NELP 4.1, 4.4.
- Parental engagement NELP 3.4, 5.1, 5.2.
- Legal and ethical compliance NELP 2.3, 6.1, 6.4.
- Instructional leadership NELP 4.1, 4.2, 4.3, 4.4, 7.4.

Least Restrictive Environment (34 CFR §§300.114–118)

Least restrictive environment (LRE) pertains to the determination made by the IEP Team to locate the physical learning environment in which a student with a disability will receive his or her instruction and/or supplementary aids and related services, as required by his or her IEP. Considerations applicable to the LRE concept include participation in extracurricular activities and other school programs or events. IDEA (2004) clearly stipulates that a student with a disability should spend as much time as possible with peers who do not receive special education. Consequently, the default placement for a student with a disability is the general education classroom or program: "to the maximum extent appropriate, children with disabilities . . . are educated with children who are non-disabled" [34 CFR §300.14, (a)(2)(i)]. In addition, "Special classes, separate schooling, or other removal of children with disabilities from the regular educational environment occurs only if the nature or severity of the disability is such that education in regular classes with the use of supplementary aids and services cannot be achieved satisfactorily" [34 CFR §300.14, (a)(2)(ii)].

The IEP Team makes a placement decision using the continuum of alternative placements (34 CFR §300.115) as its guide. The alternatives (34 CFR §300.38) range from the very least restrictive placement in the general education classroom to the most restrictive placements at home, in hospitals, and in residential facilities. The needs of the student drive the placement decision. The LRE expectation that students with disabilities are educated with his or her nondisabled peers is highly valued in IDEA (2004); therefore, the IEP Team must indicate in the IEP the degree to which the student is to be educated in the general education classroom and, if applicable, must explain why a student may be receiving his or her education within a placement other than the general education classroom.

Two terms have been used to describe the concept of the least restrictive environment. *Mainstreaming* refers to a model in which the academic instruction for a student with a disability may be provided in a classroom other than the general education classroom—a more restrictive educational environment. The student's education becomes the responsibility of the special education teacher(s), and he or she spends a greater portion of the school day in a special education "resource" or "self-contained" classroom. The student may spend *some* time with his or her nondisabled peers, with an intended goal to increase the percentage of time the student receives his or her education in the general education classroom. This model places a greater burden on the student, requiring him or her to be fully prepared to master the general education curriculum and meet the expectations the teacher sets for the general education classroom. On the other hand, *inclusion* is a model in which the special education and related services and supports a student with a disability needs to be successful are provided in the general education classroom. The student who *remains* in the general education classroom is able to gain access to the general education curriculum, and receives the same academic instruction and social benefits as his or her nondisabled peers. Since the enactment of the No Child Left Behind Act in 2002, the impetus for inclusion has become much more powerful due to the requirements for states to develop and implement a unified curriculum and an assessment and accountability system to measure a student's academic progress and performance on standardized tests.

LRE is an often-contested decision in schools. While early efforts at IDEA (2004) implementation resulted in the separation of students from their peers, current thinking about LRE emphasizes the importance of educating students with disabilities in the general education classroom where they can more easily access and receive instruction in the general curriculum. Elements in these categories are particularly important in learning about LRE:

- Culture that values equity NELP 1.2, 2.3, 3.1, 3.2, 3.3, 3.4.
- Equitable systems of support NELP 4.1, 4.4.
- Legal and ethical compliance NELP 6.1, 6.4.

The LRE principle offers the opportunity to teach the elements of Instructional Leadership in Standard Four (4.1, 4.2, 4.3, 4.4), since advocating for high expectations, instructional quality, and in-classroom supports are often required in order to make instructional arrangements in the general classroom successful. Implementing LRE also calls for personnel arrangements and working conditions that require instructional leadership in the form of instructional supervision and evaluation to promote teacher accountability, both individually and collectively, in meeting the needs of all students (Element 7.4).

Parental Involvement

Throughout IDEA (2004), the importance of school personnel working closely with parents is emphasized. Parents are required to be included as integral members of the IEP Team, and they must be given full access to information about their child. Written parental consent must be obtained prior to conducting the initial assessment to determine eligibility for special education as well as any other decision regarding special education and related services (Bateman & Bateman, 2014; Osborne & Russo, 2014; Yell, 2016). Requiring parent involvement and full consideration of their perspectives has been an important factor in improving the education of students with disabilities, although it has necessitated some shifts in perspective and procedures for school personnel. Some might say a more critical concern has been the establishment of complaint and due process procedures that give parents the right to challenge campus- or district-level decisions before the State Education Agency (SEA), impartial hearing officers, and ultimately, in court (Osborne & Russo, 2014; Yell, 2016).

The inclusion of parents in educational decision making and giving them the authority to formally complain and contest certain decisions occurred in an effort to democratize schools. While this aspect of IDEA (2004) has not proved to be as successful as was hoped, involving parents in their child's education as both instructional partners and collaborative decision makers expands the regularities of schooling to greater possibilities parents to be meaningfully involved in the overall education of their child and to engage in advocacy efforts on their child's behalf. Becoming proficient at involving parents requires school leaders to apply and carry out their professional norms and develop a culture and system of supports that include parents as required by the provisions in IDEA. These NELP Elements are implicated in parental involvement:

- Normative decision making that focuses on individual needs NELP 1.3, 2.1, 2.2.
- Culture that values equity NELP 1.2, 2.3, 3.1, 3.2, 3.3, 3.4.
- Culture that values diversity NELP 3.4, 7.2.
- Equitable systems of support NELP 4.1, 4.2.
- Parental engagement NELP 3.4, 5.1, 5.2.
- Legal and ethical compliance NELP 6.1, 6.4.

Due Process of Law (34 CFR §§300.500–537)

As previously stated, IDEA (2004) requires schools to obtain written consent from parents when making any decision about their child regarding special education and related services. This begins with written consent to evaluate the student and proceeds to identification, development of the IEP and review of the IEP goals, and ends with decisions about the student's educational placement. If parents and the school district disagree about any aspect or provision of the student's educational program, dispute resolution approaches and options have been made available in the law to make sure that parent and children rights are protected. Parents can file complaints to the SEA and/or the federal Office of Civil Rights. In addition, mediation, due process hearings, and hearing appeals procedures are included in IDEA.

Providing due process of law is fundamental to implementing the provisions of IDEA (2004). Due process is foundational to the legal entitlements children with disabilities have under the law, and forms the basis for the operational rules and regulations that drive IDEA implementation. Due process connects parents and schools in their efforts to educate students with disabilities. While many school leaders and educational practitioners tend to place more of a focus on due process protections as paperwork and procedural mandates, understanding the purposes *behind* due process becomes a critical component of special education leadership within the context of a socially just, equitable, and inclusive school. These elements include aspects of due process of law:

- Parental engagement NELP 3.4, 5.1, 5.2.
- Legal and ethical compliance NELP 6.1, 6.4.

As we can see, the knowledge, skills, and dispositions necessary for effective special education leadership at the building level can be merged with the Elements of the draft NELP Standards to form a program of preparation that merges general education and special education leadership. Bringing the knowledge traditions in general education, special education, and educational leadership together can result in preparation programs that prepare students to champion the education of all students (Burrello, Lashley, & Beatty, 2001; Pazey & Cole, 2013; Pazey, Cole, & Garcia, 2012).

PROFESSIONAL NORMS, ETHICS, AND DECISION MAKING: PREPARING LEADERS FOR SOCIAL JUSTICE

Leadership preparation students and administrators engaged in professional learning need frameworks and questions to guide them as they utilize professional norms and ethical deliberation to pursue justice, equity, and inclusion in their educational leadership practice. We utilize the frameworks offered by Shapiro and Stefkovich (2016); Furman (2003, 2004, 2012); Theoharis (2007), and Capper, Theoharis, and Sebastian (2006) to enhance students' understandings of their responsibilities for the education of all students, including those with disabilities. We turn now to a short discussion of each of the frameworks.

Socially Just Educational Leaders and Resistance

Theoharis (2007) argues that leadership for social justice is present when:

> principals make issues of race, class, gender, disability, sexual orientation, and other historically and currently marginalizing conditions in the United States central to their advocacy, leadership practice, and vision. This definition centers on addressing and eliminating marginalization in schools. Thus, inclusive schooling practices for students with disabilities, English language learners (ELLs), and other students traditionally segregated in schools are also necessitated by this definition.
>
> (p. 223)

Theoharis' definition of social justice leadership brings the inclusion of students with disabilities into the social justice discourse, which aligns with the NELP Elements included in two categories:

- Culture that values equity NELP 1.2, 2.3, 2.4, 3.1, 3.2, 3.3, 3.4.
- Culture that values diversity NELP 2.3, 2.4, 3.4 and 7.2).

In a study seeking to identify the ways in which seven school principals executed social justice in their schools, Theoharis (2007) found each principal committed to "equity and justice" and "enacted their own resistance by (a) raising student achievement, (b) improving school structures, (c) recentering and enhancing staff capacity, and (d) strengthening school culture and community" (p. 231), all of which are outcomes designated as highly valued by those who study school leadership. Yet, Theoharis (2007) maintains that these characteristics are not enough by stating: "Leadership that is not focused on and successful at creating more just and equitable schools for marginalized students is indeed not good leadership" (p. 253). Hence, leaders who advocate for social justice must intentionally attend to the needs of all students, especially those who have been historically marginalized.

A Framework for Preparing Leaders for Social Justice

Capper, Theoharis, and Sebastian (2006) reviewed the literature to determine the common themes that occurred in the discourse on preparing social justice leaders in education. When they noticed that the literature was devoid of recommendations for arming prospective school leaders with the knowledge, skills, and dispositions necessary to educate students with disabilities, they turned to the literature concerning special education leadership. Although they found research related to preparing leadership students to work with differences in student learning, they failed to "offer ideas for examining the intersection of disabilities with other areas of difference" (p. 210), further supporting the argument that preparing future school leaders to address the needs of students with disabilities and the operational aspects of special education programs has been lacking among leadership preparation programs (Capper & Young, 2014; Pazey & Cole, 2013).

Capper, Theoharis, and Sebastian (2006) offer a two-dimensional framework for constructing leadership programs, courses, and learning activities designed to prepare future building principals as social justice leaders. Along the horizontal dimension, they place "critical consciousness, knowledge, and practical skills focused on social justice" (p. 212). This dimension describes the knowledge, skills, and dispositions (critical consciousness) to which students must be committed to both understand social justice leadership and put it into practice. On the vertical dimension, they place curriculum ("content areas ... that can influence the consciousness, deepen the knowledge, and build skills" p. 213), pedagogy ("how content is delivered" p.213), and assessment ("how the consciousness, knowledge, and skills of future leaders are assessed" p. 214). They go on to discuss how the content on the horizontal and vertical dimensions interact to form a conceptual framework for leadership preparation programs that integrate social justice, and maintain this type of preparation must occur within a structure and culture that emphasize "emotional safety risk taking" (p. 212).

Ethical Leadership and Decision Making in Education

According to Shapiro and Stefkovich (2016), school leaders need to understand their own ethical positions before they can become authentic leaders for social justice in their schools and communities. They must interrogate the thoughts and actions that lead to the good life and ask these kinds of questions of their practice and the practice of others:

- What thoughts and actions lead to the greatest good?
- What is the right thing to think and do in this situation?
- How do I determine what the right thing to do is?

To bring about the habits of mind necessary to address such questions and issues, Shapiro and Stefkovich (2016) developed a framework for ethical leadership and decision-making, grounded in three traditional ethical paradigms: the ethic of justice, the ethic of care, and the ethic of critique.

Deliberating about the nature of justice and whether justice has been done is fundamentally a process of determining whether or not those affected by or engaged in a situation have received their due. From this point of view, justice theorists focus on rights, laws, and the interplay between individual rights and community values and stability. The good life results from a stable, reasoned understanding of the needs of both the individual and the community.

Proponents of the ethic of care value a society in which all people are nurtured, empowered, and treated fairly. Caring theorists focus on care, concern, and connection. Outcomes of caring consideration are empowerment, collaboration, and a concern about long-term consequences. The greatest good arises when all individuals are nurtured and feel their affiliation to the others in their communities and networks.

The ethic of critique has arisen out of concerns about the status of race, gender, ethnicity, socioeconomic status, and disability in American society, grounded in ethic of justice deliberation that has led to social inequity. Critical theorists strive to create a discourse that raises questions of power, privilege, resistance, and positionality. The distribution of power has obvious and subtle influences on what we consider to be the greatest good. We cannot envision the good life unless we ask difficult questions about the role of power in determining what the good life is and how its exercise affects the opportunity to access the good life.

Shapiro and Stefkovich (2016) argue that educational leaders use all three of the dominant perspectives in their decision-making; yet, they maintain that an additional ethic, the ethic of the profession, arises out of the merger of these dominant perspectives and their application to practice. An ethic of the profession is an amalgam of an individual's personal ethical principles and the ethical principles from the profession that guide practitioners in their work. While we recognize that an individual's personal principles and professional principles may be in conflict, we believe that both principles, in many cases, tend to be underdeveloped. Ultimately, practitioners must focus on the best interests of the student (Shapiro & Stefkovich, 2016). The greatest good arises when students have an equitable opportunity to access the resources, outcomes, and values necessary for their success and sense of belonging, regardless of the circumstances under which they have lived.

The ethic of the profession focuses on the needs of the individual student, which is particularly important in the practice of special education. When school personnel pursue the greatest good, they must also attend to the best interest of the individual student, considering the student's wants, needs, experiences, and aspirations.

The Ethic of Community

Furman (2003) contends that the ethics of justice, care, critique, and profession highlight the individual leader as the key decision-maker and "moral agent" (p. 3). To complement the other ethics, Furman (2003, 2004, 2012) adds a fifth ethic, the ethic of community, which focuses more on the decision-making process that is used or followed rather than the end product. This ethic places a higher priority on the community serving as the moral agent as opposed to any one individual.

A model of shared leadership that utilizes interpersonal and group processing skills and values input from others replaces the heroic model of leadership. Full participation is encouraged as individuals engage in dialogue and work together as a team to understand and fully value the input and insights of others, create a space where every voice can be heard, and work to achieve what is best for the overall community (Furman, 2003, 2004, 2012).

Special Education and Decision Making for Social Justice

Leadership personnel require language and frameworks to be able "to enact the professional norms of integrity, fairness, transparency, trust, collaboration, perseverance, learning and continuous improvement in their actions, decision making and relationships with others" (NELP Element 2.1) and "to model essential educational values of democracy, community, individual freedom and responsibility, equity, social justice, and diversity" (NELP Element 2.3). We have found the Shapiro and Stefkovich (2016) model with Furman's (2003, 2004, 2012) addition of an ethic of community to be helpful for developing the vocabulary, language, and frameworks useful for preparing future school administrators and practitioners to lead socially just, equitable, and inclusive schools. The model encourages practitioners and students to try out alternative perspectives with the ultimate goal of integrating multiple points of view when making critical decisions. The vocabulary, language, and frameworks also give these future school leaders and practitioners a background in many issues of the day, particularly when they are used to interrogate real-life cases and address school and district level issues.

Since its inception, the overall intent of IDEA (2004) has been expressed in the NELP Standards with each function providing the moral and ethical foundation for education leaders in action. Education leaders must be familiar with their students' vast continuum of needs as well as the types of services they can make available, especially for students with disabilities (Voltz & Collins, 2010). Promoting the success of *every* student requires administrators to provide the full array of benefits and services articulated in a student's IEP, so he or she can receive the academic, social, emotional, behavioral, and functional life supports necessary to achieve a quality of life. Within the context of special education, familiarity with legislation as it applies to students with disabilities and their families is an imperative for every educational leader (Bertrand & Bratberg, 2007; Bon, 2012; Conderman & Pederson, 2005; Finn, Rotherham, & Hokanson, 2001). Yet, beyond knowledge of special education law, an effective leader can no longer operate under the assumption that he or she will be capable of separating "fact from value" (Foster, 1984, p. 105). Hence, the Theoharis (2007) and Capper, Theoharis, and Sebastian (2006) frameworks add depth to the student's vision, values, and beliefs about marginalized students in general and students with disabilities in particular.

Many of the legislative mandates that dictate the delivery of special education and related services are linked to ethical principles implanted in our society, the individuals who introduced them, and the judicial authorities who, through the courts and their decision-making processes, have defined their meaning and intent.

Serving students with disabilities however, involves more than maintaining compliance with special education legislation. Howe & Miramontes (1992) highlight this contradiction by stating, "the law cannot take into account all the intricacies that characterize concrete ethical judgments" (p. 8). According to Bon (2012), protecting the equal opportunity right of every student to access a quality education is "deeply rooted in ethical principles, values, beliefs, and moral obligations" (p. 286). Without question, every decision having to do with special education is informed by some ethical perspective and must interact with the educational leader's personal or moral philosophy that guides his or her practice.

While most leaders strive to focus their decision-making efforts and actions on what is in the best interest of the student (Frick & Faircloth, 2007; Frick, Faircloth, & Little, 2013; Stefkovich, 2014), problematic situations can arise in special education that may require administrators to make decisions that can have a profound and lasting effect on students and their families (Black & Burrello, 2010; Kleinhemmer-Tramill, Burrello, & Sailor, 2013; Skrtic, 2012; Zaretsky, 2004). Several scholars acknowledge that this may be due, in part, to the reality that educational leaders encounter professional dilemmas that (a) put them at odds when trying to balance the needs of general education students and students with disabilities (Ewing, 2001; Frick, Faircloth, & Little, 2013; Seltzer, 2011), or (b) conflict with their own ethical beliefs (Williams, 2001) which may or may not correspond with the policies and procedural requirements of special education law (Fiedler & van Haren, 2009; Howe & Miramontes, 1992). Such dilemmas force them to choose from what they believe to be "the lesser of two evils" (Kauffman, 1992, p. xiii). Tomlinson (2014) argues:

> There is conflict in a variety of situations in special education, not least within professions, between professionals, between parents and professionals in special schools, and between mainstream and special schooling; and power and coercion play a large part in resolving conflicts.
>
> (p. 23)

If we are willing to examine our leadership practices in special education, we will immediately be exposed to the "inconsistencies and contradictions" (Skrtic, 1995, p. 52) that have been justified within the traditional aspects of both special education and educational administration.

To realize the tenets of administrative behavior and practice embedded in the NELP Standards, a curricula or conversation that encompasses the diverse needs of student learners from special population groups and/or individuals with disabilities is needed. Yet, in their analysis of leadership preparation curriculum and areas for future consideration, Osterman and Hafner (2009) identified special education as an area that has been largely omitted from preparation programs, strengthening the argument previously advanced by Capper, Theoharis, and Sebastian (2006). In addition, Osterman and Hafner (2009) cited a lack of attention or learning opportunities related to social justice issues, special education and special education administration issues, and ethics and moral issues. McCarthy and Forsythe (2009) illuminated the dearth in supply of resources pertaining to how leaders can facilitate educational programs for students with disabilities and how preparation programs can address the following areas related to individuals with disabilities: (a) identification of needs, (b) provision of appropriate instruction/programs, and (c) adherence to procedural protections for placement and discipline.

LEARNING ACTIVITY 6.1

- How does the ethic of community serve to guide a principals' decisions with respect to special education?
- Interview a principal with at least three years' experience and ask about an ethical dilemma faced with respect to a special needs student.

CASES PERTAINING TO SPECIAL EDUCATION LEADERSHIP

In our search for resources well aligned with the leadership roles and responsibilities inherent in meeting the variable needs of students with disabilities, we identified several cases in the *Journal of Cases in Educational Leadership* (JCEL). Both cases can be used to integrate the principles of special education leadership, special education law, and social justice leadership. Each case incorporates a reflective and experiential activity, requiring future and current leaders to grapple with similarities and differences inherent in their personal and professional code of ethics by exposing them to potential problems they may face in their administrative practice (Bowen, Besette, & Chan, 2006; Howe & Miramontes, 1992; Murdick, Gartin, & Fowler, 2014; Strike, 1998; Strike & Soltis, 1998; Strike & Ternasky, 1993). In doing so, they must be willing to reflect on how they "recognize and weigh" the details and considerations they incorporate into their "ethical deliberation" (Howe & Miramontes, 1992, p. 2), a process and activity that adheres to the need to draw upon an ethical leadership and decision-making framework (Furman, 2003, 2004, 2012; Shapiro & Stefkovich, 2016) to solve the dilemmas represented within each case. Engaging students in these reality-based cases and activities will invoke them to both acquire a knowledge base grounded in special education law (Pazey, Cole, & Garcia, 2012; Pazey & Cole, 2013) and correlate their administrative practice to the ethical frames as they relate to special education administration (Lashley, 2007). We follow here with two case examples taken from the *Journal of Cases in Educational Leadership*.

CASE STUDY 6.1: ANY IDEA WHAT TO DO WITH BILLY?

In *Any IDEA What to Do with Billy?*, Leech and Miller (2004) provide a thorough description of Cash High School's efforts to educate 160 students who have been identified as having serious emotional disturbances (SED) as defined in IDEA (2004). The case also describes the school's administrative history and the leadership philosophy and style of the principal. The essential question in the case has to do with what the school should do to address the significant behavioral problems presented by Billy, a 16-year-old sophomore who, since the age of two years, has been coming to the attention of school authorities for behavior that is both disruptive and destructive (NELP 2.1 and 2.2). Interventions by the schools, mental health professionals, and the courts have been unsuccessful (NELP 4.1 and 4.4).

The district in which Cash High School is located houses the only secondary school SED program at Cash to address Billy's problems and those of students like him. The program has not been successful with Billy, and it uses suspensions and "sent home" or early dismissal days to remove Billy from the school when his behavior is especially difficult (NELP 1.3, 2.1, 2.2). The case is written such that Billy's attendance at Cash encompasses a September-through-January period. He has been "sent home" for at least 18 days during that time, and his IEP is out of date. In addition, no Functional Behavior Assessment (FBA) has been conducted, and no Behavior Improvement Plan (BIP) has been written (NELP 2.3, 6.1, and 6.4). Billy's parents have contacted an advocacy group in their search for solutions (NELP, 3.4, 5.1, 5.2).

To facilitate and enrich the discussion of this case, Leech and Miller (2004) provide an annotated listing of resources that school leaders could explore as well as a set of discussion questions around issues of discipline, school culture, and working with parents and advocacy groups. They preface their teaching notes with comments about the necessity of establishing a safe and orderly school climate that is conducive to learning. By providing both teaching notes and case details, the authors problematize school practices related to educating students who present significant, disruptive behaviors that are resistant to intervention.

Any IDEA What to Do with Billy? provides school leaders and practitioners the opportunity to learn (a) the basic premises of due process of law, which are grounded in legal and ethical fairness, and (b) the implementation of IDEA (2004), which is grounded in providing access to an appropriate education for all students with disabilities, including those students whose behavior may disrupt the school leader's responsibility to provide a safe school climate that is conducive to learning for all students. Experiencing this case using the lenses of justice, caring, critique, the profession (Shapiro and Stefkovich, 2016), and community (Furman, 2003, 2004, 2012) generates multiple perspectives about school administrators' legal responsibilities to protect the rights of students under IDEA when the exercise of those rights presents a potential harm to the safety of the student body (NELP Standard 2).

Considering justice raises questions of the interaction of individual rights with concerns for the good of a community. Billy's disruptive behavior is a safety threat to other students, and it distracts from teaching and learning. Caring raises questions about the school's responsibility to nurture students and prepare them for the life ahead of them. The school has a responsibility to prepare Billy to be an educated, responsible adult; it cannot exercise that responsibility if Billy has to be regularly suspended or "sent home" so the staff and students can go about the business of teaching and learning. Critique asks how power plays into decision-making and who benefits from decisions that are being considered. The IEP process brings together administrators, teachers, and parents to make decision about students with disabilities. Whether power is exercised hierarchically or democratically in those meetings has a strong influence on the decisions that are made about an appropriate education for Billy.

Synthesizing all of these perspectives and inserting considerations from the practices of schooling and leadership gives students alternatives they can mull over as they consider approaches that are in the best interests of the student—in this case Billy, whose behavior will be a deterrent to his own success in life as well as a disrupter to the education of other students in the school. This case encourages students to think about the purposes of schooling and their responsibility for the education of all students while they must also take into account the educational, political, and personal consequences of their practice and the decisions they make, invoking the profession and overall school community. Articulating their understanding of the ethic of the profession prepares students for the challenges of leadership by developing a well-interrogated ethical code that is grounded in theory and thoughtfulness.

LEARNING ACTIVITY 6.2

- Read case *Any IDEA What to Do with Billy?*, and articulate your understanding in what is the best interest of the child, juxtaposed with an ethic of community.

CASE STUDY 6.2: INCLUSIVITY IN THE CLASSROOM: UNDERSTANDING AND EMBRACING STUDENTS WITH "INVISIBLE DISABILITIES"

In *Inclusivity in the Classroom: Understanding and Embracing Students with "Invisible Disabilities"*, Maxam and Henderson (2013) present the challenges faced by Mr. Lopez, the high school principal at Bryant High School, due to the district's failure to meet adequate yearly progress (AYP) and the danger of facing sanctions leveled against the school in accord with the No Child Left Behind Act (NCLB, 2002). While we recognize that AYP requirements no longer exist under the Every Student Succeeds Act (2015), building principals continue to face the pressure of making sure that their schools adhere to state expectations of academic performance and achievement which are determined by a school's overall performance on state-level assessments.

Further conflict abounds as Mr. Lopez attempts to reconcile the increasing number of students with disabilities comprising his school population and the faculty's negative mindset toward the presence of these students in their classrooms (NELP 2.3, 3.4, and 7.2). Referenced as "invisible disabilities" by Mr. Lopez, this case cameos the classroom contexts and struggles of several teachers who are in a quandary of how to maintain the standards and teaching style they have embraced as their own, muddled by the manifested behaviors and perceived disruption the presence of students with varying invisible disabilities impose due to their inclusion (NELP Standard 4).

Additional complications involve the lack of training in instructional strategies that honor and support an inclusive classroom environment. Yet, when Mr. Lopez takes steps to provide his school staff with a variety of low-cost professional development training opportunities necessary so the school can adopt a positive mindset toward students with disabilities and teachers can more effectively offer the instructional supports that will honor the learning profiles of each student in their classrooms, his plans are vetoed by his superiors (NELP 4.1 and 4.4). His highest priority must be focused on increasing test scores so the district can maintain its funding source.

Maxam and Henderson's (2013) case epitomizes the myriad pressures and stakeholders to whom school administrators are accountable, couched in a framework of stakeholder beliefs and attitudes toward students with disabilities that relates directly to the ethical framework for decision-making posed by Shapiro and Stefkovich (2016) and Furman (2003, 2004, 2012). Leaders must grapple with the principles of IDEA (2004) that stipulate that a student with a disability should be granted access to the general education curriculum and, to the maximum extent appropriate, be educated in the general education classroom with his or her nondisabled peers (NELP 2.3, 6.1, and 6.4). Furthermore, the nondiscriminatory protections of Section 504 (1973) extend to the rights of students with disabilities to have the opportunity to learn and receive the same benefits and treatment offered to their nondisabled peers (NELP Standard 4). By integrating the ethic of justice, care, critique, the profession, and community into the details of this case, school leaders must move beyond the procedural requirements encased within special education law and policy.

Initially, this case brings to the surface the three questions we proposed as necessary for school leaders to consider and act upon when they encounter a situation that forces them to choose between the good of the order and what is in the best interest of the student (NELP Standard 2). Considering the ethic of justice, the school leader must confront issues of fairness, equity, the potential of making exceptions to what s/he has been tasked to do, and determine, in this case, whether to follow his directives or take specific action to foster a more inclusive culture within his school. The ethic of care invokes school leaders to recognize the multiplicity of voices and examine the long-term effects of his decision on the students, teachers, and larger community. The ethic of critique fosters an intentional inner dialogue for each school leader to acknowledge and scrutinize, particularly in the realm of his/her interpretation of disability: through a medical or social model lens. The ethic of community latches onto the ethic of care while placing a greater premium on the community rather than the individual. The larger issue, in this case, is linked with determining which community determines the outcome of one's decision? Finally, the ethic of the profession invokes the school leader to consciously consider how s/he would act if in Mr. Lopez's shoes—in this case—settle the conflict arising from his personal ethical principles and the ethical principles of the profession that guide his practice. Maxam and Henderson (2013) provide the perfect context for this type of discussion by omitting these questions from the case.

LEARNING ACTIVITY 6.3

- Read the above case *Inclusivity in the Classroom: Understanding and Embracing Students with "Invisible Disabilities"*. Which ethical framework would you use to help you decide how to decide a course of action as a school leader? How would you decide this case? Why did you select this course of action?

SUMMARY

Considering the practice of maintaining separate educational programs and the theory that undergirds such practice, Frattura and Topinka (2006) challenge us, as educational leaders, to question the motives behind our administrative practice. From a larger perspective of social justice leadership and special education, we utilize the same question they asked, which applies to the administrative imperative to support socially just, inclusive, and equitable schools: "We have the knowledge. The question is, do we have the courage to assist in the development of social justice?" (p. 342). To effectively serve as ethical leaders of special education, we must engage in an ongoing and critical examination of each aspect of what we do within the organization and be willing to reevaluate or challenge current practice when the best interest of the students we are charged to serve are at stake (Foster, 1989).

Many school leaders and practitioners have become accustomed to the "two-box system" of general and special education that arose with IDEA (2004) implementation. In this system, special education, its students, its teachers, and its parents were maintained in a second subsystem of the educational system. Administration and leadership for the program were left to special education administrators whose offices were typically located at the district level. These special education administrators were often seen as the district's *principal(s) of special education.* As special education programs have grown and accountability for the education of all students has been invested at the school level, principals and other district leadership personnel have begun to recognize their need to develop knowledge and skills about these programs, and they have encountered many of the ethical issues that arise when schools strive to become more equitable. Learning about special education leadership serves the dual purposes of expanding practitioners' administrative and instructional repertoire and challenging them to engage in the ethical deliberations necessary to articulate the school's interests in addressing the just, caring, critical, community, and professional perspectives as they make decisions on behalf of all students.

NOTES

1. The 13 disability categories under IDEA (2004) are autism, deaf-blindness, deafness, developmental delay, emotional disturbance, hearing impairment, intellectual disability, multiple disabilities, orthopedic impairment, other health impairment, special learning disability, speech or language impairment, traumatic brain injury, and visual impairment, including blindness.
2. Members of the IEP team typically include the following individuals: the student, parents or guardians, a general education teacher who works directly with the student, the special education teacher serving as the student's case manager who is responsible for implanting the IEP, a local education agency representative or administrator who understands what resources are available and can commit those resources to meet the student's IEP goals, and a person who is qualified to interpret the evaluation results. Additional individuals who serve as related service providers may be included on an "as needed" basis (Bateman & Bateman, 2014; Yell, 2016).

REFERENCES

Allan, K. H. (1976). First findings of the 1972 survey of the disabled: General characteristics. *Social Security Bulletin, 10,* 18–37.

Arceneaux, M. C. (2013). Impact of the special education system on the Black–White achievement gap: Signs of hope for a unified system of education. *Loyola Law Review, 59,* 381–398.

Bateman, D. F., & Bateman, C. F. (2014). *A principal's guide to special education.* Alexandria, VA: Council for Exceptional Children.

Bertrand, L., & Bratberg, W. D. (2007). Promoting the success of all students: The principal's role in providing quality special education services. *Academic Leadership: The Online Journal, 5*(3), 14. Retrieved from: www.academicleadership.org/emprical_research/Promoting_the_Success_of_All_Students.shtml

Black, W. R., & Burrello, L. C. (2010). Towards the cultivation of full membership in schools. *Values and Ethics in Educational Administration, 9*(1), 1–8.

Bon, S. C. (2012). Examining the crossroads of law, ethics, and education leadership. *Journal of School Leadership, 22,* 285–308.

Bowen, C., Bessette, H., & Chan, T. C. (2006). Including ethics in the study of educational leadership. *Journal of College and Character*, 7(7), 1–8.

Brown v. *Board of Education*, 347 U.S. 483 (1954).

Burrello, L., Lashley, C., & Beatty, E. (2001). *Educating all students together: How school leaders create unified systems*. Thousand Oaks, CA: Corwin Press.

Capper, C., & Young, M. D. (2014). Ironies and limitations of educational leadership for social justice: A call to social justice educators. *Theory into Practice*, *53*, 158–164. doi: 10.1080/00405841.2014.885814

Capper, C., Theoharis, G., & Sebastian, J. (2006). Toward a framework for preparing leaders for social justice. *Journal of Educational Administration*, *44*(3), 209–224.

Conderman, G., & Pederson, T. (2005). Promoting positive special education practices. *NASSP Bulletin*, *89*(644), 90–98.

Council for Chief State School Officers & National Policy Board for Educational Administration (CCSSO & NPBEA) (2015). Draft national educational leadership preparation (NELP) standards *for* building level leaders. Retrieved from: www.ucea.org/2016/05/01/comment-on-the-new-nelp-standards-for-leadership-preparation-today/

DeMatthews, D., & Mawhinney, H. (2014). Social justice leadership and inclusion: Exploring challenges in an urban district struggling to address inequities. *Educational Administration Quarterly*, *50*(5), 844–881. doi: 10.1177/0013161X13514440

Ewing, N. J. (2001). Teacher education: Ethics, power, and privilege. *Teacher Education and Special Education*, *24*(1), 13–24.

Fiedler, C. R., & van Haren, B. (2009). A comparison of special education administrators' and teachers' knowledge and application of ethics and professional standards. *The Journal of Special Education*, *43*(3), 160–173. doi: 10.1077/0022466908319395

Finn, C. E., Rotherham, A. J., & Hokanson, C. R. (Eds.). (2001). *Rethinking special education for a new century*. Washington, DC: Thomas B. Fordham Foundation and the Progressive Policy Institute.

Foster, W. (1984). The changing administrator: Developing managerial praxis. In P. A. Sola (Ed.), *Ethics, education and administrative decisions: A book of readings* (pp. 103–121). New York: Peter Lang.

Foster, W. (1989). Toward a critical practice of leadership. In J. Smyth (Ed.), *Critical perspectives on educational leadership* (pp. 39–62). New York: Falmer.

Frattura, E. M., & Topinka, C. (2006). Theoretical underpinnings of separate educational programs: The social justice challenge continues. *Education and Urban Society*, *38*(3), 327–344. doi: 10.1177/0013124506287032

Frick, W. C., & Faircloth, S. C. (2007). Acting in the collective and individual "best interest of students": When ethical imperatives clash with administrative demands. *Journal of School Leadership*, *20*(1), 21–32.

Frick, W. C., Faircloth, S. C., & Little, K. (2013). Responding to the collective and individual "best interests of students": Revisiting the tension between administrative practice and ethical imperatives in special education leadership. *Educational Administration Quarterly*, *49*(2), pp. 207–242. doi: 10.1177/0013161X12463230

Furman, G. C. (2003). Moral leadership and the ethic of community. *Values and Ethics in Educational Administration*, *2*(1), 1–8. Retrieved from: http://rockethics.psu.edu

Furman, G. C. (2004). The ethic of community. *Journal of Educational Administration*, *42*(2), 215–235. doi: 10.1108/09578230410525612

Furman, G. C. (2012). Social justice leadership as praxis: Developing capacities through preparation programs. *Educational Administration Quarterly*, *48*(2), 191–229.

Howe, K. R., & Miramontes, O. B. (1992). *The ethics of special education*. New York and London: Teachers College Press.

Individuals with Disabilities Education Act (IDEA) (2004). 20 U.S.C. § 1400 *et seq.*

Kauffman, J. M. (1992). Foreword. In K. R. Howe & O. B. Miramontes, *The ethics of special education* (pp. xi–xviii). New York: Teachers College Press.

Lashley, C. (2007). Principal leadership for special education: An ethical framework. *Exceptionality, 15*(3), 177–187.

Lashley, C., & Boscardin, M. L. (2003). Special education administration at a crossroads: Availability, licensure, and preparation of special education administrators [COPSSE Document No. IB-8]. Gainesville, FL: University of Florida Center on Personnel Studies in Special Education. Retrieved from: www.coe.ufl.edu/copsse/pubfiles/IB-8.pdf

Leech, D. W., & Miller, L. (2004). Any IDEA what to do with Billy? *Journal of Cases in Educational Leadership, 7*(1). doi: 10.11778/155545890400700101

Martin, E. W., Martin, R., & Terman, D. L. (1996). The legislative and litigation history of special education. Retrieved from: www.futureofchildren.org/publications/docs/06_01_01.pdf

Maxam, S., & Henderson, J. E. (2013). Inclusivity in the classroom: Understanding and embracing students with "invisible disabilities". *Journal of Cases in Educational Leadership, 16*(2), 71–81. doi: 10.1177/1555458913487037

McCarthy, M. M. & Forsythe, P. (2009). An historical review of research and development activities pertaining to the preparation of school leaders. In M. D. Young, G. M. Crow, J. Murphy, & R. T. Ogawa (Eds.), *The handbook of research on the education of school leaders* (pp. 86–128). New York: Routledge.

Murdick, N. L., Gartin, B. L., & Fowler, G. A. (2014). *Special education law* (3rd ed.). Upper Saddle River, NJ: Pearson.

O' Malley, K. (2015). From mainstreaming to marginalization? IDEA's de facto segregation consequences and prospects for restoring equity in special education. *University of Richmond Law Review, 50*, 951–1075.

Osborne, A. G., & Russo, C. J. (2014). *Special education and the law: A guide for practitioners* (3rd ed.). Thousand Oaks, CA: Corwin.

Osterman, K. F. & Hafner, M. M. (2009). Curriculum in leadership preparation: Understanding where we have been in order to know where we might go. In M. D. Young, G. M. Crow, J. Murphy, & R. T. Ogawa (Eds.), *The handbook of research on the education of school leaders* (pp. 269–318). New York: Routledge.

Pazey, B. L., & Cole, H. (2013). The role of special education training in the development of socially just leaders: Building an equity consciousness in educational leadership programs. *Educational Administration Quarterly, 49*(2), 243–271. doi: 10.1177/0013161X12463934

Pazey, B. L., & Yates, J. R. (2012). Conceptual and historical foundations of special education administration. In J. Crockett, B. Billingsley, & M. L. Boscardin (Eds.), *Handbook of leadership in special education* (pp. 17–36). London: Routledge.

Pazey, B. L., Cole, H., & Garcia, S. B. (2012). A framework for an inclusive model of social justice leadership preparation: Equity-oriented leadership for students with disabilities. In C. Boske & S. Diem (Eds.), *Global leadership for social justice: Taking it from the field to practice* (pp. 193–216). Cambridge, MA: Emerald.

Ryan, W. (1976). *Blaming the victim* (rev. ed.). New York: Vintage Books.

Seltzer, M. (2011). The "roundabout" of special education leadership. *International Journal of Humanities and Social Science, 1*(15), 120–139.

Shapiro, J. & Stefkovich, J. (2016). *Ethical leadership and decision making in education: Applying theoretical perspective to complex dilemmas* (4th ed.). New York: Routledge.

Skrtic, T. M. (1995). *Disability and democracy: Reconstructing (special) education for postmodernity.* New York: Teachers College Press.

Skrtic, T. M. (2012). Disability, difference, and justice: Strong democratic leadership for undemocratic times. In J. Crockett, B. Billingsley, M. L. Boscardin (Eds.), *Handbook of leadership in special education* (pp. 129–150). London: Routledge.

Smith, T. E. C. (2016). *Serving students with special needs: A practical guide for administrators.* New York: Routledge.

Stefkovich, J. (2014). *Best interests of the student: Applying ethical constructs to legal cases in education* (2nd ed.). New York: Routledge.

Strike, K. A. (1998). *The ethics of school administration* (2nd ed.). New York: Teachers College Press.

Strike, K. A., & Soltis, J. F. (1998). *The ethics of teaching* (3rd ed.). New York: Teachers College Press.

Strike, K. A., & Ternasky, P. L. (Eds.). (1993). *Ethics for professionals in education: Perspectives for preparation and practice.* New York: Teachers College Press.

Sussman, M. B. (1969). Dependent disabled and dependent poor: Similarity of conceptual and research needs. *The Social Service Review, 43*(4), 383–395.

Theoharis, G. (2007). Social justice educational leaders and resistance: Toward a theory of social justice leadership. *Educational Administration Quarterly, 43*(2), 221–258.

Tomlinson, S. (2014). A sociology of special education. In S. Tomlinson. *The politics of race, class and special education: The selected works of Sally Tomlinson* (pp. 15–31). New York: Routledge. (Reprinted from 'Why a sociology of special education' in *A sociology of special education,* pp. 5–25, 1982, London: Routledge.)

Vocational Rehabilitation Act of 1973, Section 504 Regulations, 34 C.F.R. § 104.1 *et seq.*

Voltz, D. L., & Collins, L. (2010). Preparing special education administrators for inclusion in diverse, standards-based contexts: Beyond the Council for Exceptional Children and the Interstate School Leaders Licensure Consortium. *Teacher Education and Special Education, 33*(1), 70–82.

Weintraub, F. J., & Abeson, A. R. (1972). Appropriate education for all children: A growing issue. *Syracuse Law Review, 23*, 1037–1058.

Weintraub, F. J., & Abeson, A. R. (1974). New education policies for the handicapped: The quiet revolution. *Phi Delta Kappan, 55*(8), 526–529.

Williams, B. T. (2001). Ethical leadership in schools servicing African American children and youth. *Teacher Education and Special Education, 24*(1), 38–47. doi: 10.1177/088840640102 400106

Yell, M. L. (2016). *The law and special education* (4th ed.). Upper Saddle River, NJ: Pearson.

Zaretsky, L. (2004). Responding ethically to complex school-based issued in special education. *International Studies in Educational Administration, 32*(2), 63–77.

Future Directions in the Development of Ethical Leadership

Lisa Bass, William C. Frick, and Michelle D. Young

The text of this book was developed with the goal of impacting the field of educational leadership by aiding the teaching of Standard 2 of the Professional Standards for Educational Leaders (PSEL) and Standard 2 of the National Educational Leadership Preparation (NELP) Standards, both of which focus on professional norms and ethics for educational leaders. Just as Joan Shapiro declares her belief in the relevance of ethics in the Foreword to this text, all the editors and contributors believe that ethics matter more today than ever before.

Ethics are essential to the practice of educational leadership. Not only must leaders model ethical behavior in their decision making and interactions with others, they must be able to weigh the moral, ethical and legal consequences of their decisions. Developing a strong understanding of ethical standards is necessary to guide decision making by educational leaders through ethical dilemmas as well as through the turbulent times witnessed in contemporary school settings. Ethical standards can serve as a compass for school leaders as they negotiate the various challenges inherent in school leadership. In the following three subsections we share insight into some of the key challenges that educational leaders face which require solid grounding in ethics, some of the empirical literature supporting the standards, and the implications of the standards for developing educational leaders. Developing ethical educational leaders, however, does not take place within a vacuum. It is but one element, albeit an important element, of a coherent educational leadership development system. The final section of the chapter moves from the specific ethics standards to the larger role that the PSEL and NELP standards play within such a coherent educational leadership development system.

ETHICAL CHALLENGES FOR LEADERS

Educational leaders face multiple challenges in their work, many of which have ethical facets. Two such challenges include resource allocation and disciplinary decisions. The PSEL and NELP standards provide guidance concerning these and other such dilemmas.

School leaders are charged with the allocation of resources for their students. As such, they may be pressured by parents, teachers, and, in some cases, the greater community to use resources in ways that can undermine equity in schools. For example, some may believe that resources should be divided evenly among students rather than equitably, while others may believe that resources should be devoted toward the interests they champion. Ethical leaders understand that resource allocation is not this simple. Diverse schools have students with diverse and varying needs, which requires school leaders to make decisions in the best interest of all children. According to the principles outlined in PSEL 2 a., effective leaders should 'act ethically and professionally in their personal conduct, relationships with others, decision making, stewardship of the school's resources, and all aspects of school leadership' (NPBEA, 2016). Additional justification for equitable resource allocation is provided in PSEL 2 c., which states that effective leaders should 'place children at the center of education and accept responsibility for each student's academic success and well-being.' Adherence to the ethical standards included in PSEL and NELP will support educational leaders at all levels to allocate resources in ways that benefit all children, rather than giving in to parental, community or other societal pressures. Familiarity with these standards also provides principals with a justification for their decision making when the equitable distribution of resources is not popular.

Principals can benefit by applying standards based ethical decision making to their daily leadership practices. For example, discipline is an issue that all school leaders grapple with to some extent. In schools that have higher incidences of disciplinary infractions, principals are pressured to be tougher in disciplining students. Principals who are not perceived as being tough enough on students may unintentionally erode trust and goodwill on behalf of the teachers. Teachers may complain of not feeling supported if principals do not practice tough discipline practices and uphold zero tolerance policies. Principals guided by an ethic of care, on the other hand, may want to investigate situations thoroughly before punishing students. They may even seek alternative methods of disciplining students, such as restorative practices in student discipline (Buckmaster, 2016). Such ethical leaders understand that discipline is often applied unevenly and unfairly, and will seek to create fair and democratic buildings. Standard 2 d. provides justification for principals who seek fairness in applying discipline to students (NPBEA, 2015). This standard states that effective principals 'safeguard and promote the values of democracy, individual freedom and responsibility, equity, social justice, community and diversity.'

RESEARCH AND THE STANDARDS

Both the PSEL and NELP standards stress the importance of professional ethical norms, educational values, ethical decision making and ethical behavior. In addition to broad agreement about the importance of these areas of leadership practice, there is significant empirical evidence to support these standards. Below we share research concerning the importance of operating from a professional code of ethics, formulating ethical solutions to dilemmas, engaging in ethical decision making, and understanding the moral and legal implications of their work.

Research confirms that leaders require knowledge and skills that enable them to enact professional ethics as well as other important professional norms, including integrity, fairness and trust (Chouhoud & Zirkel, 2008; Gross & Shapiro, 2004; Mawhinney, 2003; Scanlan, 2013; Stefkovich, 2006). As such, it is also asserted that leaders should understand and work from a personal or professional code of ethics (Bush, 2013; Kowalski, 2006) as they model ethical behavior in their work and their interactions (Chouhoud & Zirkel, 2008; Khalifa, 2010; Theoharis & Haddix, 2011).

Research also highlights the importance of leaders' ability to formulate ethically sound solutions to educational dilemmas across a range of issues (Duke & Salmonowicz, 2010; Gross & Shapiro, 2004; Kaplan & Owings, 2001; Militello, Schimmel, & Eberwein, 2009). Similarly, there is evidence that in order to engage in ethical decision making leaders must have knowledge about current ethical and moral issues (Militello et al., 2009; Theoharis, 2008) as well as training that involves the use of multiple sources of data to weigh the potential consequences of various decisions (Bush, 2013; Cooper, 2009; Duke & Salmonowicz, 2010; Frick, Faircloth & Little, 2013; Gross & Shapiro, 2004; Militello et al., 2009; Theoharis & Haddix, 2011.

Perhaps the largest body of research in this area concerns legal issues, among which special education is of key concern (e.g., Van Horn, Burrello & DeClue, 1992; Zirkel & D'Angelo, 2002; Zirkel & Gischlar, 2008). Yet, Gross and Shapiro (2004) emphasize that leaders should not merely adhere to laws and regulations; they argue that all leadership decisions should rest on the moral principles of care, justice, and fairness.

IMPLICATIONS FOR EDUCATIONAL LEADERSHIP PREPARATION

The new PSEL and NELP standards offer what Osterman and Hafner (2009) describe as a recommended curriculum for the preparation, evaluation and development of educational leaders. They offer a path for thinking about the career-long development of educational leaders, starting with preparation. Educational leadership preparation programs are charged with enacting this recommended curriculum and preparing beginning-level school and district leaders.

The challenges that leaders will face are varied and unpredictable; however, when leaders are grounded in the ethics standards provided by PSEL and other related standards like NELP, they are much more likely to face ethical dilemmas with the skills and knowledge they need to be successful. Building such knowledge and skills can be accomplished through a variety of methods, the most powerful of which engage leaders in authentic leadership situations, either real or simulated. Such methods can include case study, role-play activities, simulated ethical dilemmas, as well as investigations and discussions. Regardless of the pedagogical method used, leaders should be equipped to make ethically sound decisions. It can be said that the strength of a leader is often measured by their ability to make wise decisions. This book seeks to empower school leaders by providing them with an ethical toolbox from which to draw to do just that. The current state of Educational Leadership policy was considered in the development of this seminal text.

Key Components of Coherent Leadership Policy Systems: Acknowledging our Current Policy Context

- Leadership Policy Standards in the form of PSEL Standards serve as national models for state leadership standards. States typically adopt or adapt the national policy standards so that they reflect their own state context and inform the development of content, preparation/program, and performance standards. Policy standards consist of a framework describing what school leaders need to know and be able to do to be effective in improving instruction and student learning. The related functions inform and support the practice of the particular school leaders by sharing how the standards can be attained.

- Content Standards provide states and districts with a model of what a school leader in a particular role (e.g., principal, superintendent, principal supervisor, etc.) needs to know and be able to do. The related functions inform and support the practice of the particular school leader by sharing how the standards can be attained.

- UCEA Routledge Series on the Professional Standards that includes The New Instructional Leadership, Political Contexts of Educational Leadership, and now Developing Ethical Leaders for Our Schools.

- Leadership Preparation Program Standards provide guidance concerning the knowledge and skills associated with quality school and district leadership, and thus serve as the foundation for the preparation of education leaders. In addition, these standards also can be used to guide accreditation of administrator preparation programs and are used in some states for professional development programs toward certification. Program standards are exemplified by the Council for the Accreditation of Educator Preparation (CAEP), administrator preparation Program Standards (ELCC/

NCATE, 2012), developed by the Education Leaders Constituent Council (ELCC). The newly developed PSEL Standards will be aligned to National Leadership Preparation Standards and an Accreditation Review Process through the ELCC Specialty Program Area coordinated by CAEP.

- Performance standards serve as a guide for implementing the PSEL policy standards for education leaders by helping to measure how well a leader performs under each standard. Performance standards help make policy standards operational by presenting them as they might be observed in practice in different leadership positions and at different points of a career, often with related rubrics. The performance standards use observable and measurable language that describes current responsibilities of leaders. They provide an important component of coherent state and local policy systems. The purpose of the performance standards and rubrics is to provide a bridge from the content standards to observable indicators that help districts measure how well a particular education leader's behavior embodies each standard. The development of performance standards will be an ongoing process.

- Leader Assessments and Evaluation Tools provide data and diagnostic information about education leader performance and development across the career continuum. The development of leader assessments and evaluation tools will be one of the next steps for education leaders. These tools must incorporate ways to measure important, but elusive, dimensions of Standard 2.

STANDARDS IN THE CONTEXT OF A COHERENT LEADERSHIP POLICY SYSTEM

There is a significant difference between merely *adopting* a set of standards and *using* or putting them to work. Standards have the potential to set expectations, guide improvements, and influence practice. However, if the processes designed to achieve these goals are not well conceived and effective, the potential impact of standards will fall short. In fact, one could go as far as saying that a set of standards is only as good as the processes through which the standards are applied and the fidelity with which the standards are implemented by each preparation program (Young, Mawhinney, & Reed, 2016, p. 11).

It is important to understand how the PSEL and NELP Standards work together within the larger leadership preparation, accreditation and policy systems. First, the PSEL Standards are professional standards that consist of a framework of descriptions of what a school leader needs to know and be able to do to be effective in improving instruction, increasing student learning, and achieving the holistic aims of education.

The Standards serve as a national model of standards for states to adapt or adopt. As is noted, the Standards are designed for all education leaders in all different leadership positions, career phases, and school contexts. The broadness of these standards allow them to be used by states in discussing the important role education leaders play in supporting effective instruction and improving student achievement. This common understanding and agreement then can be translated into state-level policy (laws, regulations, and other guidance) from which a coherent leadership support system can be developed. However, the generality of policy standards means that much more detail is required to operationalize the Standards at different career stages, at varied points of influence, and in different contexts—that is, the Standards are written broadly and incorporate aspirational language. Each function in the Standards requires more explicit detail to be brought to life in the varied contexts in which they are used (e.g., in preparation programs, in evaluation systems for principals and superintendents, in professional development systems, etc.).

The NELP Standards, in contrast, were developed from the PSEL standards specifically for the preparation of building and district-level leaders. Once adopted, the NELP standards will replace the ELCC standards and will be used by educational leadership preparation programs across the country to shape the content and experiences provided to aspiring school and district leaders. According to Young, Mawhinney and Reed (2016), there are two primary policy drivers associated with this work: state program approval and national accreditation. Nationally, the standards are used by CAEP to review leadership preparation programs. Many states partner with CAEP to review preparation programs; others use their own systems to determine the quality of leadership preparation (Anderson and Reynolds, 2015).

By aligning policy, content, preparation, and performance standards, a state is able to create a coherent leadership policy system. In a coherent leadership policy system, key policies and programs are aligned to support coherent and mutually reinforcing systems for recruitment, training, certification, induction, mentoring, assessment, evaluation, support, succession, and professional development of leaders. Newly enacted federal legislation through ESSA recognizes the importance of this coordinated system of leadership support in schools. When aligned with each other, this book, various standards resources, and the PSEL policy guidance ultimately support quality leadership, effective teaching, student learning, and the broad aims and purposes of schooling for our collective and individual good.

REFERENCES

Anderson, E., & Reynolds, A. (2015). A policymaker's guide: Research-based policy for principal preparation program approval and licensure.

Buckmaster, D. (2016). From the eradication of tolerance to the restoration of school community: Exploring restorative practices as a reform framework for ethical school discipline. *Values and Ethics in Educational Administration*, *12*(3), 1–8.

Bush, T. (2013). Leadership development for school principals: Specialised preparation or post-hoc repair? *Educational Management Administration & Leadership*, *41*(3), 253–255. doi: 10.1177/1741143213477065

Cooper, C. W. (2009). Performing cultural work in demographically changing schools: Implications for expanding transformative leadership frameworks. *Educational Administration Quarterly*, *45*(5), 694–724. doi: 10.1177/0013161x09341639

Chouhoud, Y., & Zirkel, P. (2008). The Goss progeny: An empirical analysis. *San Diego Law Review*, *45*(2), 353–82. Retrieved from: www.sandiego.edu/law/academics/journals/sdlr/

Duke, D., & Salmonowicz, M. (2010). Key decisions of a first-year 'turnaround' principal. *Educational Management Administration & Leadership*, *38*(1), 33–58. doi: 10.1177/174114 3209345450

ELCC/NCATE (2012). *Educational leadership program recognition standards*. Retrieved from www.ncate.org/LinkClick.aspx?fileticket=tFmaPVlwMMo%3D&tabid=676

Frick, W. C., Faircloth, S. C., & Little, K. S. (2013). Responding to the collective and individual "Best Interests of Students": Revisiting the tension between administrative practice and ethical imperatives in special education leadership. *Educational Administration Quarterly*, *49*(2), 207–242. doi: 10.1177/0013161x12463230

Gross, S., & Shapiro, J. (2004). Using multiple ethical paradigms and turbulence theory in response to administrative dilemmas. *International Studies in Educational Administration*, *32*(2), 47–62. Retrieved from: www.cceam.org/index.php?id=6

Kaplan, L. S., & Owings, W. A. (2001). Findings with national implications how principals can help teachers with high-stakes testing. *NASSP Bulletin*, *85*(15). doi: 10.1177/ 019263650108562203

Khalifa, M. (2010). Validating social and cultural capital of hyperghettoized at-risk students. *Education and Urban Society*, *42*(5), 620–646. doi: 10.1177/0013124510366225

Kowalski, T. J. (2006). *The school superintendent: Theory, practice and cases*. Thousand Oaks, CA: Sage Publications.

Mawhinney, H. B. (2003). Resolving the dilemma of rigor or relevance in preparing educational leaders: What counts as evidence of their knowledge and ability to act ethically? In F. Lunenberg & Carr, C. (Eds.), *Shaping the future: Policy, partnerships, and emerging perspectives* (pp. 146–184), *National Council for Professors of Educational Administration Annual Yearbook*. Lanham, MD: Scarecrow Press.

Militello, M., Schimmel, D., & Eberwein, H. J. (2009). If they knew, they would change: How legal knowledge impacts principals' practice. *NASSP Bulletin*, *93*(1), 27–52. doi: 10.1177/0192636509332691

Osterman, K., & Hafner, M. (2009). Curriculum in leadership preparation. In M. D. Young, G. M. Crow, R. T. Ogawa, & J. Murphy (Eds.), *Handbook of Research on the Education of School Leaders* (pp. 269–317). doi: 10.4324/9780203878866

Scanlan, M. (2013). A learning architecture: How school leaders can design for learning social justice. *Educational Administration Quarterly*, *49*(2), 348–391. doi:10.1177/0013161x12456699

Stefkovich, J. A. (2006). *Best interests of the student: Applying ethical constructs to legal cases in education*. Mahwah, NJ: Lawrence Erlbaum Associates.

Theoharis, G. (2008). "At every turn": The resistance public school principals face in their pursuit of equity and justice. *Journal of School Leadership*, *18*, 303–343. Retrieved from: https://rowman.com/page/JSL

Theoharis, G., & Haddix, M. (2011). Undermining racism and a whiteness ideology: White principals living a commitment to equitable and excellent schools. *Urban Education*, *46*(6), 1332–1351. doi: 10.1177/0042085911416012

Van Horn, G., Burrello, L., & DeClue, L. (1992). An instructional leadership framework: The principal's leadership role in special education. *Special Education Leadership Review*, *1*(1), 41–54.

Young, M. D., Mawhinney, H., & Reed, C. (2016). Leveraging standards to promote program quality. *Journal of Research on Leadership Education, 11*(1).

Zirkel, P. & D'Angelo, A. (2002). Special education case law: An empirical trends analysis. *West's Education Law Reporter, 161*(2), 731–753. Retrieved from: http://legalsolutions.thomson reuters.com/law-products/Case-Law/Wests-Education-Law-Reporter/p/100001793

Zirkel, P. & Gischlar, K. (2008). Due process hearings under the IDEA: A longitudinal frequency analysis. *Journal of Special Education Leadership, 21*(1), 22–31. doi: 10.1177/ 1044207310366522

Notes on Contributors

Lisa Bass, Ph.D., is an assistant professor of education at North Carolina State University. Dr. Bass received her Ph.D. in Educational Leadership and Policy Studies and Comparative and International Education from the Pennsylvania State University. Her work focuses on education reform through the ethics of caring and equitable education for all students. The goal for her work is to motivate others to become passionate about caring for *all students*, meeting their needs, and providing them with a high quality education. Her most recent studies include a study on the ethics of caring from diverse middle- and high-school student perspectives, and on the preparation of exemplary principals. Dr. Bass has published her work in books and education journals, and continues to work toward this endeavor. She co-authored a book, entitled, *Building Bridges from High Poverty Communities, to Schools, to Productive Citizenship: A Holistic Approach to Addressing Poverty through Exceptional Educational Leadership*. More recently, she also edited a book entitled *Black Mask-culinity: A Framework for Black Masculine Caring*, both with Peter Lang Publishing. Dr. Bass is currently co-editing an ethics textbook for the University Council of Education Administration (UCEA) sponsored series, which is currently under review by Routledge Publishing.

Susan Bon, Ph.D., J.D., is the Higher Education Program Coordinator and Professor in the Department of Educational Leadership and Policies at the University of South Carolina. Her scholarship focuses on the impact of law and ethics on leadership and special education leadership in K-12 schools and higher education programs. She has authored and co-authored over 50 articles and book chapters addressing the legal and ethical principles that inform administrative practice and impact leadership. Dr. Bon is an active leader in national law-related organizations focusing on education law and special education law. Prior to her university faculty service, she worked as the Ombudsman in the State Superintendent's Division of the Ohio Department of Education. Dr. Bon received her J.D. (law degree) and Ph.D. from The Ohio State University.

Susan C. Faircloth, Ph.D. (an enrolled member of the Coharie Tribe of North Carolina) is a Professor in the Educational Leadership Department at the University of North Carolina Wilmington. Prior to joining UNCW, Dr. Faircloth was an Associate Professor in the Department of Leadership, Policy, and Adult and Higher Education at North Carolina State University. She has also served as an Associate Professor and Director of the American Indian Leadership Program at the Pennsylvania State University. Dr. Faircloth's research interests include: Indigenous education, the education of culturally and linguistically diverse students with special educational needs, and the moral and ethical dimensions of school leadership. She has published in such journals as *Educational Administration Quarterly*, *Harvard Educational Review*, *The Journal of Special Education Leadership, International Studies in Educational Administration*, *Values and Ethics in Educational Administration*, *Tribal College Journal of American Indian Higher Education*, *Rural Special Education Quarterly*, and *Journal of Disability Policy Studies.*

Dr. Faircloth is a former Fulbright Senior Scholar to New Zealand, Ford Foundation Postdoctoral scholar with the Civil Rights Project/Proyecto Derechos Civiles at the University of California Los Angeles, and a Fellow with the American Indian/Alaska Native Head Start Research Center at the University of Colorado Denver. She is also a William C. Friday Fellow for Human Relations.

Dr. Faircloth is a senior associate editor of the *American Journal of Education* and recently completed a two-year term as associate editor of the *American Educational Research Journal—Social and Institutional Analysis.* She is also a member of the editorial boards of the *Journal of American Indian Education* and *American Secondary Education.*

Dr. Faircloth currently chairs the technical review panel for the National Indian Education Study and is a member of the North Carolina State Advisory Council for Indian Education, the Bureau of Indian Education's Special Education Advisory Board, and the Technical Working Group for the Study of Title III Native American/Alaska Native Children (NAM) Program.

William C. Frick, Ph.D., is the Rainbolt Family Endowed Presidential Professor of Educational Leadership and Policy Studies in the Jeannine Rainbolt College of Education at the University of Oklahoma. He is the founding director of the Center for Leadership Ethics and Change, an affiliate body of the international Consortium for the Study of Leadership and Ethics in Education (CSLEE) of the University Council for Educational Administration (UCEA). He serves on the editorial board of the *Journal of School Leadership* and the IAFOR *Journal of Education* and is currently the editor of *Values and Ethics in Educational Administration.* He is widely published in selective registers and is a former Core Fulbright U.S. Scholar to the Republic of Georgia. His tripartite scholarly research agenda includes: 1) ethics in educational administration, 2) linkages between school system reform and broader community revitalization efforts, and 3) cultural studies in education addressing the intersection of identity and schooling.

Steven J. Gross, Ph.D., is Professor of Educational Leadership at Temple University and Founding Director of the New DEEL (Democratic Ethical Educational Leadership). His work focuses on initiating and sustaining democratic reform and Turbulence Theory. His books include: *Democratic Ethical Educational Leadership* (2016) (co-authored with Joan Poliner Shapiro), *The Handbook on Ethical Educational Leadership* (2014) (co-edited with Christopher Branson), *and Ethical Educational Leadership in Turbulent Times* (with Joan Poliner Shapiro) (2013 2nd ed). Gross has been a Distinguished Visiting Research Scholar (Australian Catholic University). He received the Willower Award for Excellence (Consortium for the Study of Leadership and Ethics in Education), the University Council for Educational Administration's Master Professor Award, and was named an honorary member of the Golden Key International Honour Society.

Carl Lashley, Ph.D., is Associate Professor in the Department of Educational Leadership and Cultural Foundations at the University of North Carolina at Greensboro. He holds the Bachelor of Arts in Political Science and the Master's in Education in Special Education from West Virginia University and the Ed.D. in Educational Leadership from Indiana University. He has been a general and special education teacher, an elementary school principal, Director of Special Education, and Director of Curriculum and Instruction in public schools in West Virginia. Dr. Lashley's primary intellectual and advocacy interests in equity, justice, and community come from his career-long concerns about poverty, equitable opportunity for all children, and the power of schooling as a mode of social change. His research interests are in special education law, policy, and practice; education law and policy; social justice leadership; technology; and school leadership preparation.

Barbara L. Pazey, Ph.D., is an Associate Professor in Educational Leadership within the Department of Teacher Education and Administration at the University of North Texas. She received her Ph.D. in Educational Administration at The University of Texas at Austin, a Master of Arts degree from The Ohio State University, and a Bachelor's degree in Music from Muskingum University. Her research interests focus on the development of equity-oriented leadership preparation programs; ethical leadership and decision-making processes; education and dis/ability policy and reform; and the analysis of P-12 education programs within urban and/or turnaround school settings. Throughout her research and teaching, she seeks to honor student voice; recognize and foster the growth of students' 21st-century skills; and provide them with the prerequisite knowledge, skills, and dispositions necessary to graduate high school, able to pursue a postsecondary education and/or enter the workforce. Pazey has served as an educational administrator and educator in both K-12 education and higher education.

Joan Poliner Shapiro, Ed.D., is Professor of Higher Education at Temple University's College of Education. Previously, she served as Associate Dean for Research and Development, and as Chair of the Educational Leadership and Policy

Studies Department at Temple. She has also been Co-Director of the Women's Studies Program at the University of Pennsylvania, taught middle school and high school in the United States and United Kingdom, and supervised intern teachers. Most recently, she was the President of Temple University's Faculty Senate and currently, she is the Co-Director of an educational community network, called the New DEEL (Democratic Ethical Educational Leadership). She holds a doctorate in educational administration from the University of Pennsylvania; in addition, she completed a post-doctoral year at the University of London's Institute of Education. Among her most recent honors are the Lindback Distinguished Teaching Award, the University Council for Educational Administration's Master Professor Award and Temple University's Great Teacher Award. In the area of scholarship, along with the 4th edition of *Ethical Leadership and Decision Making in Education*, she has co-authored the following books: *Reframing Diversity in Education* with Trevor E. Sewell and Joseph P. DuCette (Rowman & Littlefield, 2001); *Gender in Urban Education* with Alice E.Ginsberg and Shirley P. Brown (Heinemann, 2004); *Educational Ethical Leadership in Turbulent Times* (2nd ed.) with Steven Jay Gross (Routledge, 2013); and *Democratic Ethical Educational Leadership* with Steven Jay Gross (Routledge, 2016). She has also written over sixty journal articles and book chapters focusing on accountability and gender issues in education and on ethical leadership.

Karen Stansberry Beard, Ph.D., is an assistant professor of Educational Administration at The Ohio State University where she teaches Ethics, School and Community relations, Policy, and the Social and Political Context of Education. Her research focuses on Educational Administration and preparing leadership to work successfully in diverse contexts. Through the intentional exploration of positive psychology and related constructs (Flow, Academic optimism, PERMA(H) and Grit), she pursues best practices, organizational dynamics, and policies that reduce gaps in achievement and support creating conditions for cross-cultural understanding, student engagement, and well-being.

Marla Susman Israel, Ed.D., is the Director of Student Learning Programs at Stevenson High School in Lincolnshire, IL, where she is responsible for leading the school-wide RtI process and the Equity, Race and Diversity professional learning community. Before joining the Stevenson leadership team, she was an Associate Professor and Department Chair of Administration and Supervision at Loyola University Chicago. Her research interests are guided by her experience as an educational leader for over 30 years in the Chicagoland area. She has authored multiple articles and book chapters focusing on school leadership, ethics, and the needs of minority and refugee students.

Alison S. Wilson is a Ph.D. candidate, and full-time graduate research assistant in Educational Administration, Curriculum, and Supervision at the University of Oklahoma. Her research interests include opportunity to learn, equity, and ethical leadership. For two years, she worked under an AERA research grant sponsored by

NSF titled "How do school leaders support student opportunity to learn." Alison is a Graduate Student Representative and Newsletter Managing Editor for the Leadership for School Improvement (LSI) SIG. She also serves as the Editorial Assistant for the *Values and Ethics in Educational Administration* (VEEA) journal. Alison served as Communications Co-Chair for the Division A Graduate Student Committee for the 2016–2017 term. In 2015, she received the University Council of Educational Administration (UCEA) Graduate Student Summer Fellowship, which funded her work with the OU center affiliate to the Consortium for the Study of Leadership and Ethics in Education (CSLEE). Alison has five years of experience as a secondary language arts teacher and three years as department head in a large public school district in Oklahoma. She received her B.A. in English from the University of Central Arkansas and completed her M.Ed. in Educational Administration, Curriculum, and Supervision at the University of Oklahoma.

Michelle D. Young, Ph.D., is the Executive Director of the University Council for Educational Administration (UCEA) and a Professor of Educational Leadership and Policy at the University of Virginia.

Dr. Young's scholarship focuses on how university programs, educational policies and school leaders can support equitable and quality experiences for all students and adults who learn and work in schools. She is the recipient of the William J. Davis award for the most outstanding article published in a volume of the *Educational Administration Quarterly*. Her work has also been published in the *Review of Educational Research*, the *Educational Researcher*, the *American Educational Research Journal*, the *Journal of School Leadership*, the *International Journal of Qualitative Studies in Education*, and the *Journal of Educational Administration and Leadership and Policy in Schools*, among other publications. She recently edited, with Joseph Murphy, Gary Crow and Rod Ogawa, the first *Handbook of Research on the Education of School Leader*.

Index

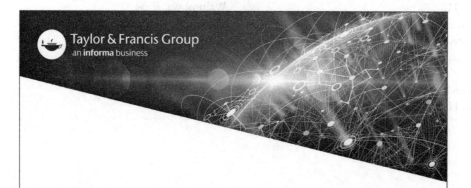